Embedded, Everywhere

A Research Agenda for
Networked Systems of Embedded Computers

Committee on Networked Systems of Embedded Computers

Computer Science and Telecommunications Board

Division on Engineering and Physical Sciences

National Research Council

NATIONAL ACADEMY PRESS
Washington, D.C.

NOTICE: The project that is the subject of this report was approved by the Governing Board of the National Research Council, whose members are drawn from the councils of the National Academy of Sciences, the National Academy of Engineering, and the Institute of Medicine. The members of the committee responsible for the report were chosen for their special competences and with regard for appropriate balance.

Support for this project was provided by the Defense Advanced Research Projects Agency and the National Institute of Standards and Technology. Any opinions, findings, conclusions, or recommendations expressed in this material are those of the authors and do not necessarily reflect the views of the sponsor. Moreover, the views, opinions, and findings contained in this report should not be construed as an official Department of Defense position, policy, or decision, unless so designated by other official documentation.

Library of Congress Control Number: 2001093511
International Standard Book Number 0-309-07568-8

Additional copies of this report are available from:

National Academy Press
2101 Constitution Avenue, N.W.
Box 285
Washington, DC 20055
800/624-6242
202/334-3313 (in the Washington metropolitan area)
http://www.nap.edu

Printed in the United States of America

THE NATIONAL ACADEMIES

National Academy of Sciences
National Academy of Engineering
Institute of Medicine
National Research Council

The **National Academy of Sciences** is a private, nonprofit, self-perpetuating society of distinguished scholars engaged in scientific and engineering research, dedicated to the furtherance of science and technology and to their use for the general welfare. Upon the authority of the charter granted to it by the Congress in 1863, the Academy has a mandate that requires it to advise the federal government on scientific and technical matters. Dr. Bruce M. Alberts is president of the National Academy of Sciences.

The **National Academy of Engineering** was established in 1964, under the charter of the National Academy of Sciences, as a parallel organization of outstanding engineers. It is autonomous in its administration and in the selection of its members, sharing with the National Academy of Sciences the responsibility for advising the federal government. The National Academy of Engineering also sponsors engineering programs aimed at meeting national needs, encourages education and research, and recognizes the superior achievements of engineers. Dr. Wm. A. Wulf is president of the National Academy of Engineering.

The **Institute of Medicine** was established in 1970 by the National Academy of Sciences to secure the services of eminent members of appropriate professions in the examination of policy matters pertaining to the health of the public. The Institute acts under the responsibility given to the National Academy of Sciences by its congressional charter to be an adviser to the federal government and, upon its own initiative, to identify issues of medical care, research, and education. Dr. Kenneth I. Shine is president of the Institute of Medicine.

The **National Research Council** was organized by the National Academy of Sciences in 1916 to associate the broad community of science and technology with the Academy's purposes of furthering knowledge and advising the federal government. Functioning in accordance with general policies determined by the Academy, the Council has become the principal operating agency of both the National Academy of Sciences and the National Academy of Engineering in providing services to the government, the public, and the scientific and engineering communities. The Council is administered jointly by both Academies and the Institute of Medicine. Dr. Bruce M. Alberts and Dr. Wm. A. Wulf are chairman and vice chairman, respectively, of the National Research Council.

Preface

C ontinued advances in information technologies are enabling a growing number of physical devices to be imbued with computing and communications capabilities. Aircraft, cars, household appliances, cellular telephones, and health monitoring devices all contain microprocessors that are being linked with other information processing devices. Such examples represent only the very beginning of what is possible. As microprocessors continue to shrink, wireless radios are also becoming more powerful and compact. As the cost of these and related technologies continues to decrease, computing and communications technologies will be embedded into everyday objects of all kinds to allow objects to sense and react to their changing environments. Networks comprising thousands or millions of sensors could monitor the environment, the battlefield, or the factory floor; smart spaces containing hundreds of smart surfaces and intelligent appliances could provide access to computational resources.

Getting to this point will not be easy. Networks of embedded computers pose a host of challenges qualitatively different from those faced by more traditional computers or stand-alone embedded computers because they will be more tightly integrated with their physical environments, more autonomous, and more constrained in terms of space, power, and other resources. They will also need to operate, communicate, and adapt in real time, often unattended. Enabling such innovation will require that a number of research challenges be overcome. How can large numbers of embedded computing devices assemble themselves seamlessly into an integrated network? How can their performance be guaranteed? How can social issues raised by the advent of more pervasive information collection and processing—for example, concerns about privacy, robustness, and usability—be addressed?

CHARGE TO THE COMMITTEE

To improve understanding of these issues and help guide future research endeavors, the Defense Advanced Research Projects Agency (DARPA) and the National Institute of Standards and Technology (NIST) asked the Computer Science and Telecommunications Board (CSTB) of the National Research Council (NRC) to conduct a study of networked systems of embedded computers (EmNets) that would examine the kinds of systems that might be developed and deployed in the future and identify areas in need of greater investigation. This report identifies opportunities for the use of EmNets, examines the ways EmNets differ from more traditional systems, and delineates the research topics that need to be addressed. The objective is to develop a research agenda that could guide federal programs related to computing research and inform the research community (in industry, universities, and government) about the challenging needs of this emerging research area. This report examines both issues related to components of embedded computers—such as hardware needs, operating systems, programming capabilities, and human interfaces—and systems-level issues resulting from the interconnection of multiple embedded computers—system architectures, coordination, adaptation, reliability, security, safety, interoperability, stability, and guaranteed performance. To that end, the committee attempted to answer questions such as the following:

• What are networked systems of embedded computing systems? How do networks of embedded computers differ from more traditional computer networks? How do these differences affect research needs?
• What types of applications could arise from greater networking of embedded systems? What are the general characteristics of different applications? What would be the benefits and capabilities of such systems?
• How can systems of interconnected embedded processors be more easily designed, developed, and maintained? How can system reliability, safety, operability, and maintainability be ensured in networked systems? How do such considerations differ for embedded and more traditional forms of computing?
• What kinds of advances are needed in enabling component technologies, such as hardware devices, operating systems, and communications networks, to make EmNets possible and more capable?

- What types of user interfaces are needed to allow users to interact with and to program systems composed of large numbers of inter-connected embedded systems? How do these requirements differ for different kinds of users (experts, novices, system integrators)? What types of "programming" will consumers be expected to perform?

- How can the stability and effectiveness of interconnected systems of embedded computers be assured if individual components come from a wide variety of developers and use a variety of hardware and software platforms, some of which may run the latest versions of the software, and others of which may be several generations behind?

COMMITTEE COMPOSITION AND PROCESS

To conduct the study, CSTB assembled a committee of 15 members from industry and academia with expertise in areas of apparent importance to EmNets, such as computing devices, very-large-scale integrated circuit technology, networking, wireless communications, embedded operating systems, software safety, distributed computing, programming languages, human-computer interfaces and usability, and computer system security.[1] Several committee members brought with them a familiarity with federal research programs related to EmNet technologies and provided invaluable insight into the challenges of organizing research programs in this area. Several committee members changed their organizational affiliation during the course of the study, attesting to the dynamic nature of this field. Indeed, because of growing commercial interest in ubiquitous or pervasive computing technology, two of the original committee members, Walter Davis from Motorola and Ajei Gopal from IBM, were unable to continue their participation in the project.

The committee met six times between December 1999 and March 2001 to plan its course of action, solicit testimony from relevant experts, deliberate its findings, and draft its final report. It continued its work by electronic communications into the spring of 2001. During the course of the project, the committee heard from information technology researchers in industry and universities and from directors of government agencies involved in funding computing research (including research related to EmNets).[2] It also met with people involved in developing and deploying EmNets to serve a range of missions, from controlling lighting and heating systems in office buildings and automating manufacturing lines, to

---

[1]See Appendix A for biographies of committee members.
[2]See Appendix B for a list of briefers to the committee.

monitoring the health of astronauts in space and of patients in emergency rooms. The committee also gathered information on major initiatives to pursue research on ubiquitous and pervasive computing, and it collected data on microprocessors, microcontrollers, wireless communications nodes, and their applications in order to track the emergence of an EmNet environment.

ACKNOWLEDGMENTS

As with any project of this magnitude, thanks are due to the many individuals who contributed to the work of the committee. First, thanks are due to the members of the committee itself, who volunteered considerable time during the course of the study to attend meetings, engage in e-mail and telephone discussions, draft sections of the report, and respond to comments from external reviewers.

Beyond the committee, numerous persons provided valuable information through briefings to committee meetings: Andrew Berlin, Xerox Palo Alto Research Center; Stephen P. Boyd, Stanford University; Janusz Bryzek, Maxim Integrated Products, Inc.; David D. Clark, Massachusetts Institute of Technology; Alan Davidson, Center for Democracy and Technology; Robert Dolin, Echelon Corporation; John Hines, National Aeronautics and Space Administration; Rodger Lea, Sony Distributed Systems Laboratory; K. Venkatesh Prasad, Ford Research Laboratory; Jonathan Smith, University of Pennsylvania; Karen Sollins, National Science Foundation; and Keith Uncapher, Corporation for National Research Initiatives.

Thanks are also due to those who sponsored the study. David Tennenhouse, formerly the director of the Defense Advanced Research Project Agency's (DARPA) Information Technology Office (ITO) and now vice president of research at Intel Corporation, provided the original impetus for the study, identifying networked systems of embedded computers as a potentially revolutionary set of technologies and laying out a vision for the field. Shankar Sastry and Janos Sztipanovits ensured continued DARPA support for the project as they expanded ITO's research efforts in EmNets of different kinds. Sri Kumar, also of DARPA's ITO, provided considerable guidance and input related to sensor networks. Jerry Linn, formerly of the Information Technology Lab at NIST, generated interest and financial support from several laboratories within NIST. Other members of the Technology Policy Working Group also supported the concept of the study, even if they did not provide financial support.

Many others also provided valuable input or services to the committee that should not go unnoted. Martin Herman and Alden Dima of NIST provided relevant information about NIST programs near the end of the study process. As she has done so many times in the past, Laura Ost, a free-lance editor, provided invaluable assistance in preparing the manuscript for review. Jim Igoe, with the National Academies library, was helpful with background research. Craig Kaplan of the University of Washington assisted with cover design. Jeffrey Risberg of TIBCO Software, Inc.; Maja Mataric of the University of Southern California; Gaurav Sukhatme of the University of Southern California; Scott Stadler of the Massachusetts Institute of Technology's Lincoln Laboratory; Gregory J. Pottie of the University of California at Los Angeles; and Steven T. Sonka of the University of Illinois at Urbana-Champaign also provided background information to the committee.

Finally, the committee would like to acknowledge the work of the NRC staff. During the first 12 months of our study, Jerry Sheehan shaped the content and process of the report. He contributed vision, guidance, feedback, and discipline. Moreover, he continued to act as a key consultant after his official departure. We were all quite anxious about Jerry's departure midway through our process; frankly, I was not sure we could carry it off without him. However, we were tremendously pleased to find that his replacement, Lynette Millett, was able to come in and march us to completion without missing a beat. She ferreted out our inconsistencies, turned our bullets into prose, implemented innumerable reorganizations and rewrites, and last but not least, came up with the title for the report! Lynette's contributions are certainly embedded everywhere in this report. Alan Inouye worked with Lynette behind the scenes during the final phases of the project, providing advice and feedback and helping shepherd the project to completion. Liz Fikre made significant editorial contributions to the final manuscript. Claudette Baylor-Fleming, Carmela Chamberlain, and David Padgham assisted with final report preparation. Suzanne Ossa provided the committee with excellent support during meetings and assisted with background research and editorial work. Finally, we thank Marjory Blumenthal, whose vision and commitment directly and indirectly shaped the report through her hiring and mentoring of excellent staff and her detailed comments on many versions of the report.

Deborah L. Estrin, *Chair*
Committee on Networked Systems
of Embedded Computers

Acknowledgment of Reviewers

This report has been reviewed in draft form by individuals chosen for their diverse perspectives and technical expertise, in accordance with procedures approved by the NRC's Report Review Committee. The purpose of this independent review is to provide candid and critical comments that will assist the institution in making its published report as sound as possible and to ensure that the report meets institutional standards for objectivity, evidence, and responsiveness to the study charge. The review comments and draft manuscript remain confidential to protect the integrity of the deliberative process. We wish to thank the following individuals for their review of this report:

Michael DeWalt, Certification Services,
Batya Friedman, University of Washington,
Matthew S. Jaffe, Emory Riddle Aeronautical University,
Randy H. Katz, University of California at Berkeley,
Alan Kay, Walt Disney Imagineering,
Edward A. Lee, University of California at Berkeley,
John McHugh, CERT, Software Engineering Institute, Carnegie Mellon University,
Kristofer S.J. Pister, University of California at Berkeley,
Rush D. Robinett, Sandia National Laboratories,
Daniel P. Siewiorek, Carnegie Mellon University, and
Andrew J. Viterbi, Viterbi Group, LLC.

Although the reviewers listed above have provided many constructive comments and suggestions, they were not asked to endorse the conclusions or recommendations, nor did they see the final draft of the report before its release. The review of this report was overseen by Robert J. Spinrad, Xerox PARC (retired), appointed by the Division on Engineering and Physical Sciences, who was responsible for making certain that an independent examination of this report was carried out in accordance with institutional procedures and that all review comments were carefully considered. Responsibility for the final content of this report rests entirely with the authoring committee and the institution.

Contents

Embedded, Everywhere

A Research Agenda for
Networked Systems of Embedded Computers

Executive Summary

Information technology (IT) is on the verge of another revolution. Driven by the increasing capabilities and ever declining costs of computing and communications devices, IT is being embedded into a growing range of physical devices linked together through networks and will become ever more pervasive as the component technologies become smaller, faster, and cheaper. These changes are sometimes obvious—in pagers and Internet-enabled cell phones, for example—but often IT is buried inside larger (or smaller) systems in ways that are not easily visible to end users. These networked systems of embedded computers, referred to as EmNets throughout this report, have the potential to change radically the way people interact with their environment by linking together a range of devices and sensors that will allow information to be collected, shared, and processed in unprecedented ways. The range of applications continues to expand with continued research and development. Examples of ways in which EmNets will be applied include the following: EmNets will be implemented as a kind of digital nervous system to enable instrumentation of all sorts of spaces, ranging from in situ environmental monitoring to surveillance of battlespace conditions; EmNets will be employed in personal monitoring strategies (both defense related and civilian), combining information from sensors on and within a person with information from laboratory tests and other sources; and EmNets will dramatically affect scientific data collection capabilities, ranging from new techniques for precision agriculture and biotechnological research to detailed environmental and pollution monitoring.

The use of EmNets throughout society could well dwarf previous milestones in the information revolution. The effects of Moore's law[1] and related trends in computing and communications are making all of this possible. Ongoing work in microelectromechanical systems (MEMS) will enable sensing and actuation on the scale of a nanometer. The possibilities for miniaturization extend into all aspects of life, and the potential for embedding computing and communications technology quite literally everywhere is becoming a reality. IT will eventually become an invisible component of almost everything in everyone's surroundings.

WHAT IS DIFFERENT ABOUT EMNETS?

EmNets are more than simply the next step in the evolution of the personal computer or the Internet. Building on developments in both areas, EmNets will also be operating under a set of constraints that will demand more than merely incremental improvements to more traditional networking and information technology. EmNets will tend to be tightly coupled to the physical world. Unlike a desktop computer, which is itself a piece of office furniture, EmNets will be integrated into furniture and other objects in the environment. Individuals will interact with the objects and devices of which EmNets are a part, but it is unlikely that they will think of it as interacting with a computer system. A complex, networked, computational system will often be invisible when things are working properly.

EmNet components will also be highly resource constrained. In contrast to the Internet, which still consists primarily of tethered devices, EmNet components are likely to be small, untethered devices operating under physical constraints such as limited energy and the need for adequate heat dissipation. EmNets will also be constrained by bandwidth and memory limitations.

In addition to the physically coupled, resource-constrained nature of these systems, another constraint on EmNets is the fact that often they will be integrated into objects or systems that are likely to last for long periods of time. EmNets in buildings, bridges, vehicles, and so on will be expected to last as long as the objects in which they are embedded. This expectation of longevity will need to be taken into account when designing, deploying, and managing these systems. A further constraint is the

---

[1]Moore's law refers to the observation by Gordon Moore in 1965 that each new microprocessor contains roughly twice as much capacity as its predecessor, and each chip is usually released within 18 to 24 months of the previous chip. As this trend has continued, computing power has risen exponentially.

likely heterogeneity and large number of interacting elements that will make up an EmNet; this makes interoperability a key concern. Finally, EmNets will often be used and interacted with by people who are not experts in EmNet-related technology. Managing all of these constraints and creating a system that functions properly for the application domain while remaining understandable and manageable by human operators, users, and—in many cases—casual passersby, is a large challenge for EmNet designers.

As an example, consider a transportation information system based on EmNet technology. Such a system will certainly be large in size and scale, possibly encompassing the entire highway system of the United States. Components of it would probably be embedded in long-lived physical structures (such as bridges, traffic lights, individual cars, and perhaps even the paint on the roads). Some components will be tethered, but many would be resource constrained while computing data and communicating it wirelessly when necessary. The many pieces of such a system will of necessity be heterogeneous, not only in form but also in function. There may be subsystems that communicate to consumers in private vehicles, others that relay information from emergency vehicles to synchronize traffic lights, still others that provide traffic data and analysis to highway engineers, and perhaps some that communicate to law enforcement. Issues of how information will be communicated to those interacting with the system are of great importance in such an environment. Safety is a critical concern; issues of privacy and security arise as well, along with concerns about reliability.

The rest of this report identifies areas in which research is needed to enable such EmNets and to make them a successful reality. Below are highlights of some of these areas as well as particular recommendations to federal funding agencies.

KEY AREAS OF INQUIRY

Realizing the great promise of EmNets requires more than the mere advance of individual technologies—it will rely on numerous subsystems working together in an efficient, unattended, comprehensible, and trustworthy manner. Many aspects of the needed research are highly interdisciplinary because of the intricate ways in which EmNet systems interact with the physical world. In the absence of programs aimed at solving some of the basic research problems, it is likely that many of the benefits of EmNets will simply not be realized.

As with any technology there are risks. In the case of EmNets, the potential benefits come with associated risks that may be exacerbated by the EmNets' very pervasiveness. Pervasive information creates security, safety, and privacy protection issues. As EmNets become increasingly critical to our communication, transportation, power distribution, and health-care infrastructures, the consequences of failures and security breaches will become increasingly severe. By the time EmNets are broadly deployed, it may not be feasible to give them technological fixes because their components are so widely dispersed.

This report by the Committee on Networked Systems of Embedded Computing, convened by the Computer Science and Telecommunications Board of the National Research Council, identifies and explores the many research questions that must be answered before there can be implementation and use of widespread networked embedded computing devices. It examines the enabling technologies that will facilitate the development and broad deployment of EmNets, and it explores three key areas in which a great deal of new research will be required for EmNets to achieve their full potential: (1) self-configuration and adaptive coordination, (2) building trustworthy EmNets (including issues of privacy, security, reliability, safety, and usability), and (3) models of computation. Enabling technologies and these key areas of research, explored in depth in Chapters 2, 3, 4, and 5, are briefly described below.

Self-configuration and Adaptive Coordination

Given the expected pervasive and ubiquitous nature of EmNets, it will be necessary for these systems to be able to configure themselves and adapt to their environments automatically. *Self-configuration* and *adaptive coordination* comprise a spectrum of changes that a system makes to itself in response to occurrences both internal to it and external. EmNets will be relatively long lived, which greatly increases their chances of being upgraded, extended, and otherwise modified. Moreover, EmNets will be exposed to both continual environmental and component dynamics. In effect, the original EmNet must be designed with automatic reconfiguration and adaptation in mind, especially when the specifics of that reconfiguration cannot be known at design time. Current work in distributed systems has not solved the problem of systems operating under the constraints that networked systems of embedded computers will experience, particularly with respect to computational resources, communication limitations, and energy restrictions.

Self-configuration is the process of interconnecting available elements into an ensemble that will perform the required functions at the desired performance level. Self-configuration in existing systems is evidenced by the notions of service discovery, interfaces, and interoperability. In this report, the research challenges related to self-configuration focus on mobile code and discovery. EmNets present a number of constraints: They will appear in hybrid environments of mobile and static networks; their nodes will be diverse in capability, energy availability, and quality of connectivity; the wireless layer is both diverse and limited by energy constraints, making low power discovery a challenge. Some of the issues that will need to be investigated and resolved for configuration and adaptation to succeed in EmNets include stable localized control, abstraction, and memory use. Research issues related to service discovery include the scaling of discovery protocols, security, and the development of adequate failure models for automatically configured networks.

Adaptive coordination involves changes in the behavior of a system as it responds to changes in the environment or system resources. Coordination will not be mediated by humans because EmNets are so large and the time scale over which the adaptation will need to take place is too short for a human to be able to intervene. Achieving adaptive coordination in EmNets will not only require drawing on the lessons learned from adaptive coordination in existing distributed systems, but it will also require meeting the radical new challenges of EmNets that are due to the physically embedded nature of the collaborative control tasks and the massive numbers of elements, all combined with the relatively constrained capabilities of individual elements. Adaptive coordination is a fairly new area of investigation, particularly as it applies to EmNets. To obtain necessary adaptability in EmNets, research is needed in three areas: exploiting massive redundancy to achieve system robustness and longevity, decentralized control, and collaborative processing.

Building Trustworthy EmNets

EmNets will be deployed in large numbers and will become an essential part of the fabric of everyday life. In the same way that people often assume that electric power and telephone service will be available (recent events in California notwithstanding), they will assume the availability and proper functioning of EmNets. But in contrast to those utility services, EmNets will be deployed in situ, often without the dedicated expert service and maintenance associated with utilities, making the trustworthiness of EmNets triply difficult: EmNets are real-world systems, often directly affected by wind, weather, and interference; they must embody the redundancy needed for dependability without compromising the basic economics, and they must adequately and safely convey to a nonexpert user how much of that redundancy is available (thereby determining the system's safety margins) so that users can make reasonable decisions concerning their use. This report discusses five features that must be addressed in the design of EmNets from the outset: reliability, safety, security, privacy, and usability.

Reliability is the quality of a system that is satisfying its behavioral specifications under a given set of conditions and within defined time periods. Current verification techniques are not readily applicable to EmNets because of the large number of elements, highly distributed nature, and environmental dynamics. Simply testing individual components is insufficient. Moreover, it is not clear that the community has the vocabulary to fully characterize what will be required of EmNets. Research is needed on fault models and recovery techniques for EmNets, monitoring and performance-checking facilities, and verification tools and techniques.

Safety refers to the ability of a system to operate without causing an accident or unacceptable loss. It is distinct from reliability and poses another set of research problems for EmNets. EmNets increase the number of possible behaviors and the complexity of the possible interactions within the system. Further, they operate in real time and with limited human intervention and are likely to exhibit emergent or unintended behaviors. Analyzing and designing such systems with regard for safety considerations is a challenge. Several safety topics deserve further research effort, including hazard analysis for EmNets, validating requirements, designing for and verifying safety, and ensuring safety in upgraded hardware.

Security is difficult to achieve in virtually all information systems, but EmNets again present particular challenges. The networking of embedded devices will greatly increase the number of possible points of failure, making security analysis even more difficult. Defining and then protecting system boundaries where physical boundaries are likely to be nonexistent and where nodes can automatically move in and out of the system will be a serious challenge. Further, managing the scale and complexity of EmNets while at the same time handling the security challenges of mobile code and the vulnerability to denial-of-service attacks will require significant attention from the research community.

Related to but separate from the issue of security is the issue of personal privacy. EmNets of the future will be able to gather more information than current systems and will do so in a much more passive manner. Achieving consensus on privacy and confidentiality policies will be exacerbated by the pervasiveness and interconnectedness of EmNet systems. Notifying users that they are being monitored, especially in the case of wide-ranging sensor networks, is a challenge, and acquiring consent in a meaningful fashion is an even greater challenge. Determining how to handle the vast amounts of personal information that will be collected and implementing privacy policies once they are decided on is a large area ripe for research.

Finally, and related to all of the above, EmNets will need to be usable by persons with little or no formal training. Unfortunately, usability and safety often conflict, and decisions on trade-offs will need to be made. Understanding the way people create mental models of the systems they use and interact with is a good way for designers to begin to address the issues of usability and manageability. In particular, more research is needed in designing for a range of persons—including system administrators, users who are explicitly operating the EmNet, and persons who are interacting with objects in their environment without explicit knowledge of the system behind them—and in enhancing mental models and user training.

Models of Computation

While there is always some divide, the gulf between theory and practice in EmNets seems to be extremely wide and continuing to grow. In addition to the systems research proposed, more theoretical work is also required. In particular, new models of computation are needed to describe, understand, construct, and reason about EmNets effectively. A critical question is, How should large aggregates of nodes be programmed to carry out their tasks in a distributed and adaptive manner?

Current distributed computing models such as distributed objects and distributed shared memory do not fully address all of the new requirements of EmNets. EmNets' tight coupling to the physical world, the heterogeneity of their systems, the multitude of elements, and timing and resource constraints, among other things, demonstrate the need for a much richer computing model. Computational models for EmNets will need to incorporate resource constraints, failures (individual components may fail by shutting down to conserve energy, for example), new data models, trust, concurrency, and location.

Developing these computational models for EmNets will require a new approach. As experience is gained with applications and implementations of the technology, designers and implementers will discover which of the new abstractions are useful. Research in this arena will thus require a balance between system implementation and experimentation and the development of the model itself. Run-time environments will also be required that support the models being developed, allowing for faster construction of the experimental systems. This cycle of concurrent development—whereby the computational model feeds into the implementation, experimental results from which feed back into the computational model—will facilitate more accurate and effective models for EmNets.

Enabling Technologies

The evolution leading to EmNets derives from the revolutionary advances in information technology during the last several decades, with silicon scaling as the driving force. Exponentially increasing processor performance has contributed to a world in which sophisticated chips can be manufactured and embedded easily and cheaply. Continued improvements (in line with Moore's law) in the price and performance of chip technology are expected throughout the decade. Even though the creation of EmNets will be supported in general by advances in the enabling information technologies, research is needed on specific aspects of communications, geolocation, software and operating systems, and MEMS.

As silicon scaling has drastically reduced the cost of computation, it has also driven down the cost of communication for both wireline and wireless systems. As wireless technology continues to become less expensive and more sophisticated, the vision of connecting embedded processors everywhere becomes increasingly feasible. However, most of the progress to date in wireless technology has focused on medium- to long-range communications (as in cellular phones and pagers) and is not sufficient for the widespread deployment of EmNets. Work is needed to understand how to create network architectures and designs for low-power, short-range wireless systems.

Related to wireless are the issues surrounding geolocation technology. Unlike conventional computer networks, which are more dependent on the relative positioning of elements in a network topology, EmNets are often inextricably tied to the physical world (a primary purpose often being to measure and control physical-world attributes or objects), so location in physical space is more important. Many EmNets will therefore require ready access to absolute or relative geographic information.

Work should continue in MEMS technology in order to achieve real-world physical sensing and actuation. Experimental progress in EmNets will be enabled by the availability of a wider range of MEMS-based sensor components. While this technology has advanced tremendously in the past decade, attention must be given to the effective integration of MEMS devices into EmNets.

Continuing research into operating systems for networks of embedded computers and into the development of software that has the required characteristics will also be necessary. EmNets software will need to be tailorable to physical constraints and application requirements in deployment, be upgradable, have high availability, and be able to work with new hardware. EmNets will be embedded in long-lived structures but will also have to evolve, depending on changing external conditions and advances in technology as time passes. Software (operating systems and applications) that can cope with this type of evolution will be critical. Further, EmNets will often impose real-time and performance-critical constraints on software. New methods of software development may be needed in order to ensure that complex EmNet software is up to coping with the constraints placed on it.

RECOMMENDATIONS AND RESEARCH THEMES DISTILLED

Research Themes

Networked systems of embedded computers will be implemented and deployed even if there is no additional research. Some of them may succeed, and others may appear to have succeeded at least for a time. But any such attempts will somehow have to overcome the fundamental gaps in knowledge that are described throughout this report. To realize functionally powerful, flexible, scalable, long-lived, and trustable systems, a spectrum of research is essential. Moreover, the committee (composed of people from both academia and industry) believes that while some of the questions raised in this report may be answered without a concerted, publicly funded research agenda, leaving this work solely to the private sector raises a number of troubling possibilities. Of great concern is that individual commercial incentives will fail to bring about work on problems that have a larger scope and that are subject to externalities: interoperability, safety, upgradability, and so on. Moreover, a lack of government funding will slow down the sharing of the research, since the commercial concerns doing the research tend to keep the research private to retain their competitive advantage. The creation of an open research community within which results and progress are shared is vital to making significant progress in this arena.

The committee generated eight overarching themes that intersect the three key areas for research described above (self-configuration and adaptive coordination, trustworthiness, and computational models). Research into all of the themes is required before EmNets can fulfill their potential. Research in broadly relevant areas such as *networking* and *usability* that pervade many of the themes described below is also essential:

- *Predictability and manageability.* Methodologies and mechanisms for designing predictable, safe, reliable, manageable EmNets;
- *Adaptive self-configuration.* Techniques to allow adaptive self-configuration of EmNets to respond to volatile environmental conditions and system resources in an ongoing dynamic balance;
- *Monitoring and system health.* A complete conceptual framework to

help achieve robust operation through self-monitoring, continuous self-testing, and reporting of system health in the face of extreme constraints on nodes and elements of the system;

- *Computational models.* New abstractions and computational models for designing, analyzing, and describing the collective behavior and information organization of massive EmNets;
- *Network geometry.* Ways to support and incorporate network geometry (as opposed to just network topology) into EmNets;
- *Interoperability.* Techniques and design methods for constructing long-lived, heterogeneous systems that evolve over time and space while remaining interoperable;
- *Integration of technical, social, ethical, and public policy issues.* Fundamental research into the nontechnical issues of EmNets, especially those having to do with the ethical and public policy issues surrounding privacy, security, reliability, usability, and safety; and
- *Enabling technologies.* Ongoing research into the various component and enabling technologies of EmNets.

The committee also recognizes that to ensure that the right kinds of research are conducted to advance EmNets, the structure and conduct of the research enterprise need to be adapted. Achieving these adaptations may not be easy, but the committee identifies them as goals: Effective collaboration between industry and academia, with support from federal funding agencies, is a necessity. Further, inter- and multidisciplinary endeavors will be crucial to the success of this field. Balancing the roles of industry and university, balancing applications with fundamental research, and incorporating multidisciplinary perspectives are all requirements for the EmNet research endeavor that will require a fresh perspective from the community.

Recommendations to Federal Agencies

The Defense Advanced Research Projects Agency (DARPA), the National Institute of Standards and Technology (NIST), the National Science Foundation (NSF), and other federal agencies all have significant roles to play in the development of robust EmNets and EmNet-related research.

Defense Advanced Research Project Agency

DARPA has an ongoing investment in EmNet technologies. Indeed, EmNets will be incredibly important and have tremendous implications for almost all aspects of defense activities, from battlespace monitoring and coordination to asset monitoring to logistics. EmNets will support defense activities from the seafloor to space. It is now time for DARPA to build on past programs in this area; to expand research in information technology, networking, and the particular areas described above; and to move forward to meet the challenges posed by networked systems of embedded computers. Without DARPA-guided investment in this area, systems issues will not get the critical attention that they need, resulting in more expensive and much less robust systems. The effort requires immediate and sustained attention. A single program will not meet the challenges presented by EmNets. Several programs could be set up, including the following:

- Designing for predictability, reliability, and safety;
- Collaborative signal processing;
- Multiscale location-aware systems; and
- Interoperability over time and space.

While the committee considers that work in these programs is necessary, this list is by no means comprehensive. Instead, it is intended to serve as a starting point for ideas for future programs.

The research agenda for EmNets (outlined in depth in this report) is broad and deep, requiring long-term attention. Follow-on programs even beyond the ones described above will be critical. DARPA should aggressively pursue programs that build upon and interact with one another's intellectual contributions and with some of the seed programs that have already begun explorations in related areas. To better meet the needs of EmNet-related research, the committee also makes two specific recommendations to DARPA:

Recommendation 1. The Information Technology Office of the Defense Advanced Research Projects Agency should revise both the substance and process of its EmNet-related programs to better address the research needs identified in this report. DARPA has several ongoing programs that could be revised or expanded to better meet the needs outlined here.

Recommendation 2. The Defense Advanced Research Projects Agency should encourage greater collaboration between its Information Technology Office and its Microelectronics Technology Office to enable greater experimentation. Greater collaboration between these offices would facilitate rich and significant experimentation in EmNet-related areas.

National Institute of Standards and Technology

NIST has worked in a variety of areas to help make information technology more secure, more reliable, more usable, and more interoperable. All of these characteristics are crucial to current and future EmNet-related technologies. Specifically, the committee recommends as follows:

Recommendation 3. The National Institute of Standards and Technology should develop and provide reference implementations in order to promote open standards for interconnectivity architectures. It will be important to promote open standards in the area and promote system development using commercial components by making public domain device drivers available.

Recommendation 4. The National Institute of Standards and Technology should develop methodologies for testing and simulating EmNets in light of the diverse and dynamic conditions of deployment. Comprehensive simulation models and testing methodologies for EmNets will be necessary to ensure interoperable, reliable, and predictable systems. In particular, the development of methodologies for testing specification and interoperability conformance will be useful.

National Science Foundation

NSF's multidisciplinary efforts, its work to integrate research and education, and its coordinated systems efforts will be of great importance in the support of EmNet-related research projects. NSF should continue these efforts and include cross-divisional efforts where appropriate. Specifically, the committee recommends as follows:

Recommendation 5. The National Science Foundation should continue to expand mechanisms for encouraging systems-oriented multi-investigator, collaborative, multidisciplinary research on EmNets. NSF can facilitate collaborative multidisciplinary research both through the programs it supports and through the use of a flexible process that encourages the incorporation of perspectives from a broad range of disciplines.

Recommendation 6. The National Science Foundation should develop programs that support graduate and undergraduate multidisciplinary educational programs. It could take the lead in tackling institutional barriers to interdisciplinary and broad systems-based work. NSF has a history of encouraging interdisciplinary programs and could provide venues for such work to be explored as well as foster and fund joint graduate programs or joint curriculum endeavors.

Other Agencies

Other agencies such as the Department of Energy (DOE) and the National Aeronautics and Space Administration (NASA) can play an important role by sharing their specialized knowledge in this area with others working in less specialized areas in the broader community. These and other federal agencies should coordinate their EmNet-related development efforts with the programs at DARPA, NSF, and NIST to ensure that open-platform systems of various scales, low-power components and their software drivers, debugging techniques and software, and traffic generators can all be shared among research programs when applicable, avoiding redundancy in those parts of the system where there is more certainty. It is expected that this sharing and associated coordination needs can be supported by the various organizations and groups associated with federal information technology research and development.

LOOKING FORWARD

EmNets will radically transform the way in which people interact with and control their physical environment. They have tremendous implications for all aspects of society, from national defense and government applications to wide-ranging commercial concerns to systems that private individuals will use in everyday life. As it moves forward in the research areas described above, the research community, including academia, industry, and funding agencies, must remain cognizant of one basic message: New approaches to the study of *systems* (not just individual components) must be developed in order to harness the emergent properties of the many networked, physically embedded computing elements that will make up EmNets. Attention must be paid to designing systems in a way that incorporates strategies from a range of disciplines and to designing systems that can address a range of problem domains. Without concerted effort on the part of the research community to address the questions outlined in this report, the potential inherent in networked systems of embedded computers will not be realized. With significant inter- and multidisciplinary research efforts that focus on the systems issues that EmNets bring to the fore, the promise of this technology can be realized.

1

Introduction and Overview

Information technology (IT) is on the verge of another revolution. Fueled by the increasing capabilities and ever-declining costs of computing and communications devices, IT is being embedded into a growing range of physical devices linked together through networks. These changes are sometimes obvious—pagers and Internet-enabled cell phones, for example—but often IT is buried inside larger (or smaller) systems in ways that are not easily visible to end-users. Audiovisual equipment, home or office appliances, automobiles, aircraft, and buildings themselves all contain growing numbers of microprocessors that are networked together. The range of applications continues to expand with continued research and development. Aircraft manufacturers are already examining the possibility of incorporating processing devices into the wings of aircraft to allow fine-grained control of airflow and, hence, lift and drag; health researchers are investigating microscopic sensors that could traverse the bloodstream, monitoring health conditions and reporting them wirelessly; consumer electronics and information technology companies envision homes filled with intelligent devices that can interact with each other, homeowners, and appliance manufacturers to improve the quality of daily life. The Internet, wireless networking, inexpensive cameras, and automotive telematics can be combined to pass information to millions of commuters in large cities so as to reduce delays, frustration, energy use, and air pollution. Sensor networks can be deployed in large agricultural areas to monitor and report on crop quality and the environment, adjusting irrigation and fertilization as necessary.

To some extent, the emergence of networked systems of embedded computers (EmNets) is simply a natural evolution of the historical trend in computing and communications technologies toward smaller, more powerful information technology devices that have become more ubiquitous (see Box 1.1). As computing has migrated from mainframe computers to minicomputers, personal computers, laptops, and, most recently, palmtop computers and information appliances, it has become more widespread and more a part of everyday life for millions. Meanwhile, embedded computers have been used in automobiles, aerospace engineering, and military applications for quite some time. Advances in networking technologies, including the expansion of the Internet and wireless communications networks, have amplified these trends by making information easier to share and increasing the amount of information that is shared.

At the same time, the shift to EmNets represents a radical departure from this lineage. While most traditional computers tend to interact directly with human operators—typically accepting input through a keyboard and providing output on a visual display—EmNets will interact more directly with the physical world. They will sense their environ-

---

BOX 1.1
Toward Ubiquitous, Networked Computing

The vision of a world filled with large numbers of computing elements, many of which are hidden inside other objects and networked together, is not new. Trends in the miniaturization of computing and communications elements have been manifested for decades, leading to numerous predictions of computing power being integrated imperceptibly into daily life. One of the leading visionaries, the late Mark Weiser, formerly the chief technologist at the Xerox Palo Alto Research Center (PARC), described in the early 1990s a concept of ubiquitous computing in which computation would blend invisibly into the environment, much as written communication has become so common a part of the physical world that little thought is given to the technology of writing (Weiser, 1991; 1993). Others have elaborated on related themes, coining terms such as pervasive computing (NIST, 1999) and invisible computing (Norman, 1998) to describe the proliferation of information technology into myriad devices and applications. Although differing somewhat in their details, these visions of the future of computing derive from a common set of observations about the rapid pace of innovation in information technology: namely, advances in very-large-scale integrated circuits (VLSI), the increasing bandwidth of wireless and wireline communications media, improvements in wireless communications technologies, and significant efforts in architecture and infrastructure. (See Chapter 2 for a more detailed discussion of enabling technologies.)

ments directly, compute necessary responses, and execute them directly. EmNets will also need to operate in a highly resource-constrained environment. There may be limited power, limited communications bandwidth, limited time, and limited memory. EmNets' heterogeneous components will often be embedded in long-lived structures, thereby making interoperability over time an important issue. All of the above will require new ways of thinking, not just at the input and output ends, but about the very fundamentals of computing and communications. Ways will be needed to ensure that such systems operate reliably, safely, and predictably; that they provide their users with necessary information about their current operating state; and that they can accommodate changes in the overall system configuration or in their operating environment. In addition, EmNets present new opportunities for pervasive, transparent monitoring and information aggregation while at the same time generating a host of privacy and other ethical concerns.[1]

This report identifies and examines research challenges posed by EmNets and provides guidance for addressing them. It addresses fundamental research issues, primarily at the system level, with some attention given to components. The report recognizes that if current technology is applied naively to EmNets, the results could be disastrous. Failures that are all too common today in information technology systems (e.g., security lapses, system outages, safety problems, unanticipated performance) could have even more serious consequences. As such, this report builds on previous work by the Computer Science and Telecommunications Board (CSTB) in the areas of large-scale systems and applications and trustworthy networked information systems (CSTB, 1999; 2000), but in the context of EmNets. It offers recommendations for organizing research and education programs to better ensure that the challenges are being adequately addressed.

EXAMPLES

Characterizing EmNets precisely and uniquely is a challenge. To facilitate this task, the committee decided to introduce three examples, which help to show the variety of systems this report is addressing. Many examples could have been chosen to illustrate EmNets, so those selected

---

[1]Bill Joy's wide-ranging discussion of robotics, nanotechnology, and genetic engineering and their ethical and social concerns (Joy, 2000) attracted attention because of the author's reputation as a technologist. But only a little imagination is required to link EmNets to scenarios that would call for considering ethical and social issues while the technologies are under development.

should not be seen as canonical in any sense. Moreover, it is virtually a certainty that EmNets will be used in ways that are currently unforeseeable. These examples, which are very distinct applications, should be viewed as representing the potential of EmNet technology. All three combine a number of separable subsystems that would normally be developed independently, preferably with an eye toward interoperation and integration over time. They all offer significant functional and economic incentives for deployment and proliferation. In addition, they exemplify tensions between often opposing forces: complexity and comprehensibility, information aggregation and privacy, and safety and autonomous power.

Notwithstanding all of the above, these examples can be seen as demonstrating, in broad strokes, the potential of EmNets at several different scales. The first example discusses automotive telematics, where the main locus of interaction is a vehicle. The second describes precision agriculture, where the EmNet is distributed over a wide area. The final example incorporates individuals, vehicles, and the surrounding environment into a comprehensive defense systems scenario. A further complication arises that increases the already formidable challenges presented by EmNets when one imagines the experiences of an individual who "joins" and subsequently "leaves" various EmNets while moving through space and time. Whether location- or domain-specific, EmNets will be connected to each other for certain functions, adding yet another level of complexity.

Example 1: Automotive Telematics

It should come as no surprise that the modern automobile is already a rolling network of embedded computers. In model year 2001, cars have between 20 and 80 microprocessors controlling everything from the running of the engine to the brake system to the deployment of the airbags. These numbers are expected to grow dramatically over the next several years as automobile manufacturers look for ways to transition electro-mechanical control systems into electronic control systems. Microprocessors also control the windshield wipers and the door locks and are increasingly used in the entertainment systems. These microprocessors are rarely self-contained; almost all interact with other microprocessors in the automobile through a network, which can be one of half a dozen proprietary or industry-specific designs.

Currently, these networks are highly engineered systems in which each microprocessor and the overall network are carefully designed as a whole. In fact, there are generally two distinct networks in today's cars. The first is the network of safety-critical components, such as those that control the engine and the braking system. The second, often called the telematics system, controls non-safety-critical functions such as the entertainment systems, door locks, and trunk release. These two networks are completely separate, ensuring that the safety-critical portions of the car cannot be compromised by the telematics components.

However, as the complexity of the network and the functionality of the networked elements grows, the ability to approach the networks as single, fully engineered, closed systems is being strained. In particular, a number of forces work against the fully engineered, closed systems approach, including the following:

• *The disparity between the design cycle of the car and the design cycle of the embedded components.* A car takes approximately 5 years to design, and the embedded components are among the first things designed into the car. This has meant that cars contain embedded systems that are significantly less functional than the systems available at the time of the car's manufacture.

• *The desire to allow easy upgrade, either by the manufacturer (in the case of safety-critical components) or third parties (in the case of telematics), over the lifetime of the car.* Such flexibility generates cost savings, as the recall of a part can be tremendously expensive, and also reflects the reality that the lifetime of a car is now 8 to 10 years rather than 3 to 5, so building a post-purchase income flow has become important.

• *The desire to allow owners to integrate their own devices into the auto.* Such devices include personal digital assistants (PDAs) and cellular phones, which can be made more useful (by, for instance, integrating the address book in a PDA with the navigation system in the car) or safer (by, for instance, integrating the cell phone with the speaker system of the car, making the phone hands-free) if such integration is possible.

There is also pressure to break down, to some degree, the strong division between the safety-critical network in the car and the telematics network. Many automobile manufacturers want to move away from the current model of diagnostics to a model of prognostics, which allows them to monitor their products for upcoming faults and allow those faults to be corrected before they happen. For this to be possible, there needs to be a way for the information gathered by the safety-critical parts of the automobile to be sent to the automobile manufacturer. One obvious way of doing this is through the use of automated cell-phone technology (separate from personal use phones) that most cars will have. Currently, however, the cell phone is part of the telematics network of the car, not part of its safety-critical network.

All of these possibilities are taken from current thinking about the network of embedded systems in the car. The outlook for the future complicates the intra-auto network considerably. The major automobile companies plan to change the car from a self-contained network (or pair of networks) into a node in a much larger network. One approach to this is General Motors' immensely successful OnStar offering.[2] OnStar connects the car to the manufacturer, allowing the latter to monitor emergency situations and give on-demand help to the occupants of the car. Not only has this service provided GM with a market differentiator, it has also allowed the company to begin to provide a very profitable subscription service, giving it a revenue stream that is less prone to the fluctuations traditional in the automotive market. The notion of the automobile as a mobile, networked recipient of content is an outgrowth of this seemingly simple beginning.

As envisioned by the automobile companies, the driver of a car will be able to get on-demand directions to anywhere desired, including those locations that are contextually based. From the car's current position, the driver will be able to get directions to the nearest restaurant of a particular type, or the closest automatic teller machine, or an available parking space. The occupants of the car will be able to receive information about the history of the place they are seeing or about its landmarks, or they will be able to get on-demand video or audio stream. The car will be monitored, in real time, to support safe operation, and the driver will be informed of the maintenance needed to keep the car from breaking down. Software upgrades to emission controls or safety systems will be downloadable (obviously at some safe time) to where the car is, making it unnecessary to take the car into the shop. While many of these innovations seem far-fetched, they are in fact being prototyped now;[3] it is likely that new advances and applications will emerge as the technology becomes widely deployed. For example, instrumented vehicles and highways could provide data that would inform a traffic management or control system. Emergency vehicles could be networked to traffic lights to adjust their timing and facilitate passage through crowded areas. Undoubtedly, many new applications of automotive telematics systems connected to larger EmNets are as yet unforeseen.

---

[2] For more information, see <http://www.onstar.com/>.

[3] A presentation to the Computer Science and Telecommunications Board by Akhtar Jameel of DaimlerChrysler Research in January 2001, "The Future of Vehicle Computing," touched on many of these issues.

Example 2: Precision Agriculture

Incorporating EmNet technology into agriculture can be seen as a logical follow-on to the great advances in crop management over the last several decades. Fertilizers, water supply, and pesticides, among other things, have been experimented with and adjusted in order to learn how best to manage crops and to increase productivity. Even with these adjustments, variations in terrain (soil, elevation, light exposure, microclimates, and so on) can make solutions based on large-scale averages suboptimal, especially for highly sensitive crops such as wine grapes and citrus fruit.

This is where EmNets, in the form of precision agriculture,[4] are beginning to play a role.[5] Precision agriculture features the deployment of sensing and actuation at a much finer and more automated granularity than has been available before. This will allow adjusting water, fertilizer, and pesticides to the minimal levels needed for a particular local area, resulting in better yields, lower costs, and less pollution-causing runoff and emissions. The data collected will be analyzed later on (imagine a viticulturist searching for the best places to cultivate grapes for the next vintage).

Adaptation to changing environments will be a crucial component in EmNets used for precision agriculture. Sensors and actuators can be used to very precisely control the concentrations of fertilizer in the soil, based on information gathered from the soil itself, the ambient temperature, and other relevant environmental factors. While there are models for how much fertilizer and water are needed for crops under various conditions, those models are imperfect, mainly because not enough accurate data have been collected across diverse agricultural systems. EmNets can provide that data. Incorporating feedback into the system through the use of sensors, actuators, and adaptation will allow a more fine-grained analysis that could adjust flow rate and duration in a way that is informed by local soil conditions and temperature. One can imagine the use of such precise information in particularly sensitive crops. Sensors that are able to monitor the crop itself (sugar levels in grapes, for example) to provide location-specific data could prove very effective. EmNets will need to be adaptive, multimodal, and able to learn over time in order to solve the problems described above.

Information gathered by sensor networks in a field could be used to

---

[4]For more information on precision agriculture, see BANR (1998).

[5]See Li and Wang (2000) for a description of a wireless sensor network for precision agriculture.

guide planting for maximum yields, in addition to monitoring and reporting on the status of the crops. A future application of EmNets might be to deploy sensors for the early detection of bacterial development in crops or viral contamination in livestock. Another application might be to employ EmNets to monitor flows of contaminants from neighboring areas and send alerts when necessary.

EmNets are also being extended to livestock management. Current computerized feeding systems for dairy cattle, for example, can adjust feed and vitamins for individual animals. Networked sensors, including swallowable sensors, to monitor amounts of food eaten, activity/exercise, and vital signs will provide valuable health information about individual animals and the state of the herd as a whole.

These systems are moderately engineered (along a spectrum from highly engineered to ad hoc), but the need to work under a wide range of unpredictable environmental conditions, as well as to interact with farm vehicles and new elements of the system as they become available, argues for adaptability within the EmNets at multiple time scales.

Example 3: Defense Systems

EmNet applications to defense systems include battlespace surveillance, monitoring the condition and location of materiel and vehicles, monitoring the health status of personnel, and making information accessible to individuals in the field.[6] As efficiency and speed of deployment become more important, the requirements for network access to assets and information become more important too. Each of these application areas is discussed briefly below.

Distributed EmNets in the battlespace will provide seismic, acoustic, magnetic, and imaging tactical information. EmNets can be dispersed by airdrop, inserted by artillery, and/or individually placed by a team securing a building. Military forces are expected to exploit EmNet battlespace surveillance systems to provide capabilities for battlefield shaping and force protection. Battlespace shaping capabilities restrict the movement of an opponent or constrain its advance or retreat. EmNets can provide the critical threat-identification information that enables remote engagement of targets and the halting or redirection of opponent forces. Force protection capabilities provide security on the battlefield and act as a force multiplier. EmNets enable a new force-protection capability by providing threat identification and early warning of an infiltration or

---

[6]EmNet research in these areas will probably prove particularly relevant for DARPA's Future Combat Systems program. See <http://www.darpa.mil/fcs/index.html>.

threatening advance. Force protection may be implemented by distributing EmNets around a protective perimeter or deploying them in advance of maneuvering troop formations. EmNets may allow a small force to operate with the security of a larger force by exploiting densely distributed, autonomous EmNet detection networks.

EmNets offer a new approach to battlespace surveillance. In the past, battlespace sensor systems were large and required large teams for deployment. As expensive assets, they were deployed only sparsely. EmNets, in contrast, involve less expensive, even disposable, devices that may be deployed in large numbers with a high spatial density. This allows the typical EmNet sensor to detect stronger signals from threats than the signals detected by more sparsely distributed sensors, facilitating a response to those threats. Because they are closer to the targets they need to detect, EmNets also engage fewer threats within their area of regard, simplifying signal identification and data association. EmNets can exploit their networking capabilities to cooperatively identify and track the motion of threats.

EmNets in battlespace situations must be highly interoperable and able to accept data from and provide data to other systems. Data from various kinds of sensor platforms (airborne, vehicle-mounted, ground-based, and so on) will need to be integrated and processed. Combining locally derived information with information from remote locations will be important, enabling updates to situational descriptions on a very short time scale. In addition to accruing and processing the data, EmNets will need to make such data readily accessible to personnel, requiring good user interfaces. Such dissemination might involve airborne relays or satellite communications, making communications another major challenge for EmNets in the application. These communications will need to remain secure while resisting jamming, detection, and interception. Challenges are also faced in the implementation of distributed computing for EmNets that must operate at low energy dissipation while maintaining a network for exchanging the appropriate threat signal characteristics.

In addition to battlespace shaping and force protection, EmNets will also be used for asset management. Defense forces rely on diverse vehicles, weapons, and equipment that require a mission-critical, high level of availability.[7] EmNets enable distributed, condition-based monitoring for detecting wear and faults in vehicle chassis systems and vehicle power trains. Applications include wheeled and tracked land vehicles and rotary- and fixed-wing aircraft. Prototype EmNet networks have ap-

---

[7]Large quantities of equipment in many locations create significant logistical challenges that may also benefit from the use of EmNets.

peared in condition-based monitoring onboard Navy ships for power plant monitoring. EmNet condition-monitoring applications require compact, low-power devices that measure and locally evaluate vibration and temperature signatures from rotating and reciprocating equipment. EmNet monitoring also applies to battle damage assessment and fire safety. The challenge of battlespace monitoring for EmNets includes the implementation of low-power, compact devices capable of both high-performance sensing and signal processing, along with networking, self-configuration, adaptation, and collaborative sensing, to exploit the distributed processing capabilities. All are needed to achieve unattended, robust, long-lived systems.

EmNets will also be applied in more tightly coupled systems, such as smart materials and structures. Collections of sensors and actuators on airplane and submarine hulls will enable new modes and efficiencies of operation by adjusting the physical properties of the surfaces to environmental and task conditions. In addition to developing the requisite MEMS components, this application will require many of the developments described in this report, from computational models to distributed coordination and safety evaluation.

EmNets also appear in health status monitoring of personnel. An important emerging requirement is for technologies that provide troops with personal location capabilities to enable security within a platoon and that monitor health, detect injury, and provide notification of injury. Here, EmNets must be wearable and integrated into existing or dedicated networks. The technologies may also be used to detect the use of biological or chemical warfare agents. Challenges include the need for security and low-power operation and the support of multiple biomedical sensor channels. Ultimately, the combination of EmNets for surveillance, condition monitoring, and personnel health status will enable a new tasking, control, and safety capability accessible at multiple command levels.

Finally, making all of the information described above—along with other dynamic, mission-specific information—readily accessible to the warfighter is a task for which EmNets as described throughout this report will be well suited. Vast amounts of information are available in battlespaces that, put to use, could increase the survivability and effectiveness of warfighters. For example, sensors and wireless communications could be used to keep track of the exact location of team members and enemies. Providing warfighters with data on asset locations and readiness, team members' health and capabilities, and overall battlespace information in an accessible, manageable fashion could greatly increase their capabilities and effectiveness.

UNDERSTANDING NETWORKED SYSTEMS
OF EMBEDDED COMPUTERS

With the above examples as starting points, this section describes some of the features of EmNets and issues related to them that should be kept in mind when developing a research agenda. Without attempting a rigid definition of networked systems of embedded computers, this report discusses systems with the following general characteristics:

• *Multiple interacting nodes.* EmNets involve the interaction of more than two embedded computing elements or nodes. The systems of greatest interest are those in which the number of interacting elements is very large (for example, on the order of thousands of nodes).

• *Embedded in control systems operating without human intervention.* EmNets are intended to operate largely without human intervention. Although they may provide information to human operators and require some degree of supervisory control, they are often part of an automated control loop (that is, the system adjusts itself when necessary and directs component behavior), and they tend to interact more directly with their environment than traditional computing systems and to assume a high degree of autonomy. Computation can be local (at the nodes/elements) or centralized or somewhere in between, with localized or regional levels of hierarchical control. In any case, they tend to be tightly coupled to the physical world. They are therefore usually located close to the elements they monitor or control, and they operate in real time.

• *Purpose other than general computing and communications.* The computing elements in EmNets are themselves components of larger systems whose primary purposes are other than general-purpose computing or communications. The elements do not form a general-purpose computer even though particular components of the system may be general purpose. The individual computing elements help to monitor and control the local system, acquiring information from a variety of sensors, implementing changes through a variety of actuators, making decisions locally, and/or possibly relaying processed information to decision makers.

• *Natural or engineered contexts.* EmNets may be incorporated into either natural or engineered systems. The EmNets themselves are engineered, but they may be deployed in a natural system such as the local environment to provide information for scientists, urban planners, or military commanders. They may also be deployed as part of a larger engineered structure such as an aircraft or building.

Within systems that meet these criteria there are useful distinctions to be made. In particular, the following dichotomies characterizing how

EmNets, their requirements, and the applicable technical solutions differ will often be referred to:

- *Energy-constrained nodes versus non-energy-constrained nodes.* Energy-constrained devices are those that are not tethered to an easily replenishable energy source and have a small form factor (size, shape, and total volume), as well as those that exist where heat dissipation is a negative factor. Small form factor implies a fundamental limit on battery size, which in turn sets a fundamental limit on the number of bits that can be processed and/or communicated by the device during its entire lifetime. Other energy sources can be exploited in some cases, but in the general case components will rely on traditional battery technology for the foreseeable future. In this context, energy is the one system resource that is *not* easily renewable. Memory can be reclaimed and bandwidth-consuming data can be delayed to a time when congestion has dissipated, but once a unit of energy has been used, it cannot usually be replenished without intervention beyond the scope of what software can accomplish. When energy is a constraint, communication is often the major consumer of the energy. This, in turn, will have significant influence on the way systems are designed.

- *Fixed topology versus flexible topology.* Virtually all the systems considered here must continue to operate in the presence of node arrival, departure, and failure. That is, configuration will not remain constant throughout a system's lifetime. However, some of the systems are dominated by a fixed topology, whereas others are dominated by a flexible and variable topology that changes significantly during the course of regular operation. A fixed topology facilitates testing and repeatable deployment. Flexible topology introduces a new dimension of variability under which a system's performance must be verified.

- *Safety-critical applications versus non-safety-critical applications.* Some of the systems described will be used in safety-critical applications. When these systems malfunction, property can be damaged irreversibly and people harmed. The implications for designing and engineering such systems are fundamentally different from those for systems in which malfunction produces only degraded speed or visual quality, or even economic harm. Further, many EmNets will utilize general networking protocols. These protocols were originally precluded for safety-critical environments such as aircraft, but newer tools and techniques are starting to emerge and could be greatly enhanced by appropriate research.

- *Highly engineered versus unconstrained, ad hoc systems.* Some EmNets are highly engineered systems, such as those used in ships and aircraft to perform particular functions, like monitoring and controlling the performance of the engine. These are more traditional applications of embedded computing, and they have been the subject of considerable engineering design work. They must, in general, meet strict criteria for system performance, reliability, and safety. They are highly constrained in that system elements are determined during the design and implementation of the system and the configuration of the system is fully controlled. The addition of networking into such systems allows the embedded computing devices to be remotely upgraded (e.g., new code can be downloaded to them to provide new or improved capabilities) or to relay information to a centralized source (e.g., for monitoring performance or use of resources). It also allows information to be shared among embedded devices to aid in local (and global) decision making. Other EmNets are unconstrained, ad hoc systems that have limited a priori system design and limited (or no) control over the overall system configuration, such as in sensor networks deployed in battlefield situations or in public smart spaces.[8] New elements can be introduced into such systems by a number of actors/ participants, and the systems will automatically reconfigure. Such systems can be expected to have a high degree of heterogeneity in the computing elements they contain and a dynamic structure as elements enter and leave the network. A particular challenge is ensuring that the overall system can meet global levels of performance as components are added to or removed from the system. There are, of course, EmNets that fall between the highly engineered and completely ad hoc categories.

HOW EMNETS DIFFER FROM TRADITIONAL SYSTEMS

EmNets are a composite technology, built as aggregations of software and hardware elements. Any given part of a network of embedded computers will look familiar to technologists: the networking constraints will find partial solutions in today's literature; the software controlling the nodes will start out as a variant on today's real-time control code; the hardware at the nodes will be developed from today's best microcontrollers, MEMS sensing devices, and interconnect transceivers. However, as the rest of this report makes clear, *incremental improvement to today's solutions will not suffice to realize the full potential of EmNets*.

The development of packet-switched networks was in a similar nascent period in the late 1960s and early 1970s. Few at the time could have predicted the development of this basic technology into today's Internet,

---

[8]Smart spaces are home or work environments containing information appliances, embedded computers, sensors, cameras, and microphones that allow people to perform tasks efficiently by offering access to information and assistance from computing technology through a variety of input devices and by monitoring on the part of the space itself.

a world-encompassing, ubiquitous communication network that has already eclipsed the telegraph and telephone in the variety of activities and services it supports. By the 1990s, its processing, routing, and interconnection aspects were becoming well understood. The extrapolation to Web sites, search engines, portals, and so on was by no means obvious, even to people working in related fields. The power, universality, and potential of EmNets will stem from combining these components into a system that is more than the sum of its parts. The dangers and difficulties will likewise emerge once the components have been combined, but they will not be immediately visible from any particular piece.

While many of the solutions found for EmNets might apply to other kinds of systems to one degree or another, what is unique about the problems posed by EmNets is the set of constraints on their solutions, several of which are discussed below. While one or even more of these constraints might be present for a traditional system, the combination is what poses one of the largest research challenges for the development of EmNets. More specifically, EmNets present the challenge of building large systems that are

- *tightly coupled to the physical world* and each other in a
- *resource-constrained environment* that will
- *persist for long periods of time* while consisting of
- *many interacting components* and being
- *used and interacted with by nonexpert users.*

Research needs to turn, as it did at the corresponding time for packet-switched networks, to developing the appropriate models, abstractions, and methodologies that will make it possible to build these systems on a large scale, for a wide variety of uses, by a necessarily large collection of people. These factors are elaborated on below.

EmNets Are Tightly Coupled to the Physical World

As noted previously, a major distinguishing characteristic of EmNets is that they interact strongly with the physical world. One EmNet might control all of the major systems of a large battle cruiser. Another might control tens of thousands of actuators based on tens of thousands of sensors to maximize the efficiency of a farm (BANR, 1998). They sense the physical world (e.g., its temperature, air quality, soil factors, or engine vibrations), they communicate and process those sensory data, and in real time they cause physical actions to be taken. Each node of an EmNet might be responsible for, say, one square meter of a farm. In the event of a one-node failure, data from geographical neighbor nodes might be interpolated, so that the affected square meter of farmland does not go unattended until repairs can be made. Accordingly, the precise geolocation of that node is important in a way that is seldom true of today's networks.

An EmNet (hypothetically) controlling a ship will necessarily be held to a much higher standard of performance and trustworthiness than, say, a traditional local area network (LAN) in an office whose primary function is to provide intra-organizational communications capability. If such a LAN goes down, productivity is lost and users become disgruntled. The loss of a ship's control at an inopportune time due to failures in an EmNet physically coupled to critical control mechanisms could result in a collision. This physical coupling of many EmNets means that safety considerations play a paramount role.

EmNets' tight coupling to the physical world also raises issues of usability. Individuals interacting with EmNets are not likely to think of themselves as interacting with a computer or computational device but rather with the objects to which EmNets are coupled (e.g., a sprinkler system as opposed to a digitally controlled irrigation device.) This has broad ramifications for usability research and for safety, reliability, and security as well.

EmNet Nodes Are Often Resource-Constrained

EmNet nodes are likely to be untethered so that they can be deployed in very close proximity to, or even embedded within, the physical systems they are designed to support. This factor places important constraints on the EmNet nodes, organization, system policies, and hardware. Untethered and/or mobile computing elements are usually battery operated, or perhaps they are very low power and run from solar panels. The limited amount of raw power available will have a substantial effect on all aspects of EmNets, from the amount of computation that can be performed on a local physical sensing node to how much bandwidth can be achieved, across what distance, by the EmNet node input/output links (e.g., radio). EmNet nodes may also have important physical constraints, such as allowable thermal dissipation or radio bandwidth limits. For example, an EmNet consisting of a large set of detectors deployed over an area of countryside will have to limit overall radio transmissions in order to avoid massive interference with other EmNets, normal communications traffic, and local regulations. EmNets that include sensors carried by the human body will have to be thermally cool to be practical. There are other kinds of resource constraints aside from power. EmNet components may have limited memory and/or bandwidth available to them. Energy constraints may limit the amount of storage available. Such resource limitations place constraints on the amount of computation and communication that can be accomplished.

EmNets' Long Lifetimes

The artifacts within which EmNets are embedded will undoubtedly have very long lifetimes compared with the lifetimes of the rapidly changing technologies that support the EmNets. Just as it has taken many years to upgrade the basic telephone wiring systems to homes, despite growing demand for bandwidth, EmNets deployed in buildings, on farms, or in the countryside will face this same problem. The longevity of EmNets will thus have to be taken into account during design, as the basic technology will continue to evolve and the previously deployed system will eventually have to interoperate with the new technologies. As networked, embedded devices are scattered throughout the environment, their useful technological life will be determined by Moore's law. Older devices may consume too large a share of valuable resources, so mechanisms for identifying, locating, and replacing or upgrading them will be necessary. The upgradability of today's computing systems is a marketing feature, but for EmNets it is a basic requirement.

The uses to which EmNets will be put may vary considerably over time. A system may have components that are used to measure physical properties and provide raw data that will be elaborated by other components or other systems. It is not always possible in advance to predict what the data will be used for.[9] A change in the application, or in the overall computing structure, may take place while the system and its components persist. In addition, it is very unlikely that entire EmNets will be replaced; instead, individual components may be replaced, upgraded, or decommissioned from time to time. The system lifetime is likely to far exceed the component lifetime.

Complicating long-term planning, EmNets will have to interface with a wide variety of sensors, network gateways, displays, actuators, power sources, antennas, and other EmNets. This heterogeneity, which is itself a major challenge to designing economical EmNets, is multiplied by the longevity requirement. Good interface standards will play a part in solving hardware interconnectivity, but striking a good compromise among cost, performance, and feature set has always been problematic. Solving

---

[9]As an example, consider city buses with sensors that can provide information about their location. This information could also be used to turn the buses themselves into sensors for traffic congestion. Such technology is being developed in several localities (see, for example, <http://www.gcn.com/archives/sl/1998/July/1B.htm>).

the analogous problems in the software domain may be even more difficult.

EmNet Size and Scale Are Significant

Networked systems of embedded computers can grow extremely large. It is easy to imagine deploying sensor technology with which one could sense various conditions within buildings or the environment; such networks might embody thousands or tens of thousands of nodes. In fact, building control systems with tens of thousands of nodes already exist.[10] Networking many of these systems would yield systems of millions of nodes.[11] Economics will allow such large systems to be built, and demand will come from many sources, ranging from environmental researchers to government regulators to the general public. Military applications and battlespace EmNets are also inherently large, encompassing millions of nodes in a three-dimensional space anywhere from the seabed to satellites in space.

Scale matters—systems designed to work properly at one size will often fail at a larger (or even a smaller) size. In systems the size of the EmNets being contemplated here, it is very reasonable to expect that many of the networking, software, and hardware solutions known at present will be unsuitable, or even dangerous. EmNets are particularly vulnerable in this regard, because they appear at first glance to be reasonable extrapolations of current technology. The committee fears that they will be built naively in exactly that way and, worse, that they may even appear to work as desired for a time. The ability to predict accurately how complex engineered systems will behave, especially under unusual or boundary conditions, is limited at best. EmNets will stretch the ability to analyze system behavior beyond current capabilities, making it likely that such systems will exhibit emergent, or unexpected, behaviors.[12]

---

[10]See for example, products made by the Echelon Corporation, <http://www.echelon.com/>.

[11]With just a little more imagination, systems of billions of nodes can be conjured.

[12]Emergent behavior is often described as behavior of a whole that seems more organized and purposeful than that of its component parts. This notion often arises in the context of complex systems, where there are many pieces interacting with one another such that the study of individual pieces in isolation is insufficient to predict the behavior of the entire system (Rapaport, 2000).

EmNet Users Are Not System Experts

EmNets will increasingly be used by people who have little or no systems training. Modern aircraft cockpits have extensive computer-based systems with which the pilot must interface. Even with extensive training, pilots (who are expert users of the systems they operate) make errors a disturbing share of the time.[13] An EmNet that requires extensive user training will have failed in its fundamental promise—computing systems must adapt to users, not the other way around. Yet combining extremely complicated systems with casual or inexperienced users is a potential recipe for disaster. If history is a guide, such users will drive the system into operating conditions that were never considered by the system designers, they will misunderstand what the system is trying to tell them about its own health, and they will put themselves inadvertently at risk by trusting the EmNet when it is no longer trustworthy. An additional complicating factor is that people will less often interact with EmNets per se than with the devices and objects within which EmNet components are embedded. People's expectations of objects in their environment are likely to be very different from their expectations of explicitly computational or communication devices such as PCs or cell phones. The computer industry has a very poor record overall of designing effective user interfaces, much less interfaces that, if misunderstood, can still prevent danger to the users themselves (CSTB, 1997; Laurel and Mountford, 1990; Norman, 1998). Designing for casual interaction (as opposed to explicit use) is arguably an even larger challenge. The change of attitude required of the system designers is profound and infrastructural, and attitudes will need to be quite different from the attitudes that created today's successful networks.

WHY A NEW RESEARCH AGENDA?

This report explores how the characteristics of EmNets demand new kinds of research. It examines the different kinds of applications and configurations in which EmNets may be deployed and identifies technical challenges that have not heretofore been addressed by the research community or resolved in a way that is amenable to EmNets. The report

---

[13]The software in high-tech avionics systems is extremely complex, and most training programs now concentrate on teaching pilots how to use the automation but not necessarily how the automation works. Existing training material is based on a proceduralized, operational model with little attention to causality or the structure of the underlying system. In fact, there have been suggestions that a limiting factor in aircraft automation design may be the level of complexity a pilot's mind can maintain and readily access (Billings, 1996).

attempts to be as far reaching as possible, identifying research challenges in a broad range of areas. The goal is not to specify particular technologies or solutions that need to be developed but to articulate fundamental, underlying research problems that need to be addressed. The areas identified are therefore candidates for fundamental exploratory research that will try as much to understand the problems as to solve them.

To the extent that EmNets represent a continuation of longstanding progress in IT, it is reasonable to ask why special consideration needs to be paid to the research needs for EmNets. In a broad sense, the potential impact of EmNets themselves is justification for an EmNet-specific national research agenda. But as described previously, EmNets present unique technological challenges as well. Research into developing and understanding these systems is vital, for the reasons outlined below.

As EmNets mature and extend into even more areas of society, research will be needed into ways of thinking about designing systems. One can envision systems that are self-monitoring and self-healing—that is, systems that provide active agents to monitor possible problems (as well as their own health) and take appropriate actions, such as to defend against denial-of-service attacks or attempted injection of malicious code. At the same time, continued advances will be needed in enabling technologies. Research will also be needed (1) to make EmNets easy to construct, (2) to make EmNets self-configuring and adaptive, (3) to ensure their performance and safety, and (4) to make them easy to use. These research areas involve system-level issues that arise from the interconnection of large numbers of long-lived information processing devices managed by users who are likely to be experts in a particular application domain but not necessarily in EmNet technology. These users will need to know not just whether the system is working or has failed, they also need to know how close to its safety margins or how healthy the system is so they can make intelligent decisions on whether to use it or take it offline and repair it. While work has progressed in many of these areas over the past decade, it has not generally occurred in the context of embedded computing. Clearly, a number of familiar topics will need to be reexamined, and new topics will need to be addressed.

The potential benefits of EmNets are accompanied by risks that may be exacerbated by the EmNets' very pervasiveness and by the fact that they may be invisible to most who interact with them. The creation and distribution of vast amounts of information about people creates privacy concerns. As EmNets become increasingly critical to our communication, transportation, power distribution, and health-care infrastructures, failures and security breaches will be increasingly dangerous. By the time EmNets are broadly deployed, it will be too late to call them back easily. Therefore, it is critical that we study these systems now, in order to mitigate the risks as much as possible and maximize the benefits.

As this report documents, the technological research issues that are important to EmNets are not unique in and of themselves. Issues of scalability, adaptation, reliability, safety, and performance have all been faced to some extent by other IT systems and have been addressed by research in the more general computing and information technology arenas. What differentiates EmNets and necessitates a new research agenda is that the solutions that have been worked out in areas for more general computing and information technology systems will not work for EmNets. Existing solutions often make a number of assumptions—among them: that energy is readily available, that there is sufficient computing power to allow various layers of abstraction, that the computational elements are generally in static relationships with respect to the physical world, that bandwidth is not terribly constrained, that the computational elements are expensive and therefore rarely duplicated, and that the computational elements are the entities that need to be identified—that simply do not hold for EmNets. While EmNets have many characteristics that distinguish them from traditional systems, it is very likely that the techniques developed to realize EmNets will have enormous positive impact on the design of traditional systems as well; a key example is techniques for self-configuration (see Chapter 3).

It is important to note that networked systems of embedded computers will be and are being implemented, even without the benefit of additional research. Some of these may actually succeed, and others may appear to have succeeded, at least for a time. However, if the maximum benefits are to be gained from EmNet technology at minimum overall risk, much research is needed. It is extremely important that the research community take the lead in this area if there is to be any hope of significant impact. Once systems are established, it is incredibly difficult to upgrade or update them, as has been the case with PCs and the Internet. Designing and deploying them well initially will probably be more cost-effective in the long term, and if the research community can, in a timely fashion, articulate a notion of what is more correct, efficient, secure, safe, reliable, and so on, companies may well adopt it. Once they are deployed, though, history suggests that it will not be possible to effect significant changes or upgrades. It is therefore critical to start addressing the challenges presented by EmNets. Specific research recommendations are provided throughout the remainder of this report.

WHAT THIS REPORT DOES NOT DO

This report is intended to be broad and comprehensive, but there are several topics it does not, by design, treat in depth. These include sensor and actuator technologies that might be used as elements within an EmNet (especially within a sensor network); ethical and policy issues associated with different applications of EmNets and the use of the data they might collect; particular issues of commercialization and market acceptance; and stand-alone (as opposed to networked) embedded systems. These are all extremely important issues—in fact, each is worth its own separate study—that could not be given full consideration here in light of the charge to the committee.

Advanced Sensors and Actuators

The inexorable march of silicon-based technology is making possible the design and deployment of extremely inexpensive, highly capable, low-power sensors (Saffo, 1997). Advances in MEMS technology have already made it feasible to sense odors, vibration, acceleration, pressure, temperature, and many other physical phenomena in ways that will be extraordinarily useful across a wide range of human endeavors. New sensors for sound, visible light, infrared, and extremely low light, combined with ever faster and cheaper digital signal processors, will make large-scale system sensing practical and commonplace. Likewise, new MEMS-based actuators, such as micromotors, will allow EmNets to affect the world in unprecedented ways. The implications of these improving sensor technologies are profound, and this report explores many of them, but the technology of the sensors themselves is largely outside its scope.

Public Policy Issues

There are few, if any, ethically neutral technologies. Powerful technologies such as computing, especially on the scale addressed in this report, have the potential to be utterly pervasive in people's lives. These technologies will be deployed with the best of intentions, but as with all previous technologies, an array of forces will come to bear on them that can be only partially anticipated. These forces will bring a corresponding array of ethical, legal, and policy issues.

The committee believes that the issues will be profound and important. They will require consideration at all levels during the conception, design, deployment, and use of large EmNets. This report can offer no a priori prescription for the ethical, legal, and policy questions posed by EmNets, so its focus has been purposely restricted to technological issues and implications. However, the policy issues are numerous, important, and evident in many contexts. Privacy may be at much greater risk than at any previous time in history, security is a pressing concern when one's attackers can be physically anywhere, and system reliability will become paramount when these new systems have supplanted previous tried-and-true (and simpler) solutions such as telephones, home security systems, agriculture management, and industrial automation. Other issues that will undoubtedly arise concern intellectual property (to whom does the data collected by EmNets belong?), liability (who is responsible when systems fail?), and the "digital divide" (who will have access to what kinds of systems?). There is also an important sense in which the committee believes the technology will permit the easy accretion of large systems—that is, that smaller, self-contained systems will be combined in an ad hoc manner to create much larger systems. The difficulties of engineering a system that is, by definition, unplanned pale in comparison with grappling with its ethical implications.

The reader should not misconstrue the focus on technology in this report to mean the authors believe the policy implications are trivial or benign. The truth is, the committee believes they deserve far more attention than can be given here if the basic task of exploring the technology itself is also to be fulfilled. Powerful technologies can be used for good or ill (or both). EmNets qualify as powerful technology by any definition. The ethical, legal, and policy issues must be addressed during the design and use stages of these systems. In this report the committee raises these issues when they seem particularly pertinent to the discussion in order to draw attention to some of the far-reaching implications of this technology. However, a more in-depth analysis of public policy issues is urgently needed that would lead to appropriate recommendations for solving likely problems.

Commercialization Issues, Standards, Business Models

Deploying very large numbers of anything is unavoidably an exercise in both technology and economics. The technology must be inexpensive enough for large numbers of people to be able to afford it, yet it must be powerful enough to solve some need. And ultimately, there must be enough profit in the venture for the purveyor of the technology to develop products and support them. It is by no means a given that the best technology will prevail, and if there is no economic benefit (or too high a perceived risk, particularly of consequential damages), no vendors may wish to participate. For the purposes of this report, the committee assumed that the technology will be associated with large markets but that part of the research and development challenge may relate to lowering costs for a given level of performance or quality. One area of uncertainty about EmNet markets relates to instances where an EmNet may have a broad public benefit that cannot be easily captured by one or more vendors. Sensors that collect data on individual exposure to toxins whose aggregation could identify the source of the pollution and its distribution patterns are an example of an application with primarily public benefit, and as in other instances of environmental technology deployment, the chief customer (or motivator of purchases by others) may be one or more governmental units. The environment, which is an area where there is an understanding of the economics and a government framework in place, may embrace relevant EmNets as it has embraced other technologies. For public-benefit EmNets that constitute new applications domains, the way forward may be less clear and market development more uncertain. By contrast, for EmNets with inherent commercial value (such as smart office buildings), the committee expects significant markets to develop.

Standards are expected to be important for EmNets because of the fundamental concern about interoperability and the variety of other kinds of interfaces. A dominant producer—and, like other products, most IT products seem to have a small number of major producers once their markets mature—may drive a de facto standard. Alternatively, various groups—industry groups concerned with specific enabling technologies, applications domains that may work through trade associations or focused consortia, or groups such as those convened under the auspices of the National Institute of Standards and Technology (NIST) or even the Internet Engineering Task Force (IETF)—may work to develop standards that may or may not be open. However, it is not a purpose of this report to attempt to identify such standards.

Stand-alone Embedded Systems and Other Networked Information Systems

This report emphasizes the characteristics of EmNets that stem from the embedded, physically coupled aspects of the nodes in combination with the networked aspects of these systems. There are still many research challenges for stand-alone embedded systems, and indeed any progress there will have an important impact on networked embedded systems. Networking allows innumerable new kinds of interactions. It also provides an ability to coordinate across multiple, heterogeneous devices and make use of information gathered by geographically distant actuation devices. In this report, the committee focuses explicitly on networked systems of embedded computing devices, while acknowledging that many of the issues that arise with stand-alone systems will be relevant in the networked arena as well.

While the research recommendations and discussion in this report can and should be seen as part of a larger networking research agenda, the emphasis here is on EmNets that are purposefully built to perform specific sets of tasks, as opposed to ad hoc interconnections of PDAs and laptops for general-purpose application support. Large-scale societal IT systems, such as financial systems, are not included. These systems are engineered, like EmNets, and they have processors and networking capabilities embedded in the fabric of their operation. They are not considered in this study because the computing elements are generally not embedded in devices that have an apparent purpose other than computing and communications. Cellular telephone systems are a particularly interesting case for definitional purposes. They are clearly engineered systems, and they clearly involve embedded processors. They are also, by their very nature, networked, power-constrained, and mobile—as the cell phone moves around in the physical world, real-time handoffs are made between the various transceiver towers so as to keep the user continuously connected to a given phone call. Cellular telephony can provide a number of valuable lessons for the design and operation of EmNets, but there are also circumstances specific to cell phones that the committee believes will cause some of its solutions to be inapplicable to the kinds of EmNets anticipated here. This report tries to carefully distinguish the aspects of cell phone technology that are relevant to EmNets from those that are not.

ORGANIZATION OF THIS REPORT

The remainder of this report elaborates on the themes introduced in this chapter. The report can be read as a progression from very concrete issues involving component technologies such as chips and wireless communications all the way to the abstract computational models that will be used to reason about these systems. Chapter 2 examines several enabling technologies without which EmNets as they are described here would not as easily or as flexibly come to pass. It discusses component technologies used to construct EmNets. Readers who are interested in learning about the larger systems issues related to EmNets should feel free to move directly into Chapter 3, which explores self-configuration and adaptive coordination as these concepts pertain to EmNets and how EmNets organize themselves and respond to changes within the environment and the system. In other words, Chapter 3 examines how the component technologies in Chapter 2 should be arranged to form an EmNet and what kinds of technologies will be needed to achieve this. Chapter 4 moves up another level and examines the features that EmNets will need to have. It explores trustworthiness of EmNets, including the issues of safety, reliability, security, privacy, and usability. Chapter 5 examines the need for better kinds of abstractions and computational models to describe and analyze EmNets that incorporate the features described previously. Finally, Chapter 6 considers the current research infrastructure and how it could be adjusted to better address the challenges that EmNets present.

It outlines several broad areas in which research is needed and makes recommendations to various federal funding agencies.

REFERENCES

Billings, Charles E. 1996. *Aviation Automation: The Search for a Human-Centered Approach.* Mahwah, N.J.: Erlbaum.

Board on Agriculture and Natural Resources (BANR), National Research Council. 1998. *Precision Agriculture in the 21st Century: Geospatial and Information Technologies in Crop Management.* Washington, D.C.: National Academy Press.

Computer Science and Telecommunications Board (CSTB), National Research Council. 1997. *More Than Screen Deep: Toward Every-Citizen Interfaces to the Nation's Information Infrastructure.* Washington, D.C.: National Academy Press.

CSTB, National Research Council. 1999. *Trust in Cyberspace.* Washington, D.C.: National Academy Press.

CSTB, National Research Council. 2000. *Making IT Better: Expanding Information Technology Research to Meet Society's Needs.* Washington, D.C.: National Academy Press.

Joy, Bill. 2000. "Why the future doesn't need us." *Wired,* 8.04. Available online at <http://www.wired.com/wired/archive/8.04/joy.html>.

Laurel, Brenda, and S. Joy Mountford, eds. 1990. *Art of Human-Computer Interface Design.* New York, N.Y.: Addison-Wesley.

Li, Y., and R. Wang. 2000. "Precision agriculture: Smart farm stations." IEEE 802 plenary meeting tutorials, document no. 00362r0P802-15_LRSG-Precision-Agriculture-Smart-Farm-Stations.ppt.

National Institute of Standards and Technology (NIST). 1999. *Testing and Standards for Pervasive Computing.* Gaithersburg, Md.: Information Technology Laboratory, NIST.

Norman, Donald. 1998. *The Invisible Computer.* Cambridge, Mass.: MIT Press.

Rapaport, D.C. 2000. *Computer Simulation Studies in Condensed Matter Physics.* Volume XIII, D.P. Landau et al., eds. New York: Springer-Verlag.

Saffo, Paul. 1997. "Sensors: The next wave of infotech innovation." *1997 Ten-Year Forecast.* Menlo Park, Calif.: Institute for the Future.

Weiser, Mark. 1991. "The computer for the 21st century." *Scientific American* (September): 94-104.

Weiser, Mark. 1993. "Some computer science issues in ubiquitous computing." *Communications of the ACM* 36(7):75-83.

2

Enabling Technologies

To understand the forces shaping networked systems of embedded computers it is useful to look at some of their underlying technologies—the devices used to compute, communicate, measure, and manipulate the physical world. The trends in these devices are what make EmNets such a compelling and interesting research question at this time. The current components are making large EmNets feasible now, and as these components continue to evolve, EmNets will soon become essential, even dominant, parts of both the national and global infrastructure.

Through the economics of silicon scaling, computation and communication are becoming inexpensive enough that if there is any value to be derived from including them in a product, that inclusion will probably happen. Unfortunately, while these "standard" components will enable and drive EmNets into the market, without careful research the characteristics that emerge from these collections of components may not always be desirable. EmNets present many new issues at both the component and system level that do not need to be (and have not been) addressed in other contexts.

This chapter provides a brief overview of the core technologies that EmNets use, the trends that are driving these technologies, and what new research areas would greatly accelerate the creation of EmNet-tailored components. Because the scaling of silicon technology is a major driver of computing and communication, this chapter starts by reviewing silicon scaling and then looks at how computing and communication devices take advantage of scaled technologies. In communications technology, attention is focused on wireless communications technology since this will be an essential part of many EmNets and on wireless geolocation technology since geographic location is a factor in many EmNets. The remaining sections review other components critical to EmNets, namely, the software systems that make EmNets work and MEMS, the new way to build low-cost sensors and actuators. Scattered throughout the chapter are boxes that provide more details on many of the technologies discussed. Readers who are already well versed in these subject areas or who are more interested in understanding the systems-level issues that arise in EmNets should move on to Chapter 3.

SILICON SCALING

Much of the driving force for the technological changes seen in recent years comes from the invention of integrated circuit technology. Using this technology, electronic components are "printed" on a piece of silicon, and over the years this process has been improved so that the printed components have become smaller and smaller. The ability to "scale" the technology simultaneously improves the performance of the components and decreases their cost, both at an exponential rate. This scaling has been taking place for over 40 years, giving rise to eight orders of magnitude change in the size and cost of a simple logic element, from chips with two transistors in the 1960s, to chips with 100 million transistors in 2001. Scaling not only decreases the cost of the devices, it also improves the performance of each device, with respect to both delay and the energy needed to switch the device. During this same 40 years, gates[1] have become 1000 times faster, and the power required per gate has dropped more than 10,000-fold. This scaling is predicted to continue for at least another 10 to 20 years before it eventually reaches some fundamental technical and economic limit (Borkar, 1999).

Silicon scaling continues to reduce the size, cost, and power and to improve the performance of electronic components. Reliability of the basic electronics has also improved significantly. Vacuum-tube electronics were limited by the poor reliability of the tubes themselves—filaments burned out regularly and interconnections were generally made by hand-soldering wires to sockets. Transistors were much more reliable due to cooler operation temperatures and the absence of filaments, but there were still huge numbers of soldered interconnects. As integrated circuits

---

[1]A logic gate ("gate") is the elementary building block of a digital circuit.

have subsumed more and more functionality, they have also subsumed huge amounts of interconnections that are generally much more reliable than soldered pins on a printed circuit board.

Coupling this manufacturing process to the notion of a computer has driven a huge industry. For example, mainframe computers that occupied rooms in the 1980s now can fit on a single chip and can operate faster and at much lower power than the older systems. The scaling of technology has not only enabled the building of smaller, faster computers, it has made computing so cheap that it is economical to embed computing inside devices that are not thought of as computers to increase their functionality. It is this rapidly decreasing cost curve that created and continues to expand a huge market for embedded computing, and as this same technology makes communication cheaper, it will allow the embedded computers to talk with each other and the outside world, driving the creation of EmNets. Just as electronic locks seem natural now (and soon it will be hard to imagine a world without them), it will soon seem natural for embedded systems inside devices that are not typically thought of as computers to communicate with each other.

COMPUTING

The ability to manufacture chips of increasing complexity creates a problem of its own: design cost. While design tools continue to improve, both the number of engineers needed to design a state-of-the-art chip and the cost of said chip continue to grow, although more slowly than chip complexity. These costs add to the growing expense of the initial tooling to produce a chip, mainly the cost of the masks ("negatives") for the circuits to be printed—such masks now cost several hundred thousand dollars. Thus, chips are inexpensive only if they are produced in volumes large enough to amortize such large design costs. The need for large volumes poses an interesting dilemma for chip designers, since generally as a device becomes more complex, it also becomes more specialized. The most successful chips are those that, while complex, can still serve a large market. This conflict is not a new one and was of great concern at the dawn of the large-scale integration (LSI) era in the 1970s. The solution then was to create a very small computer, or microprocessor, and use it with memory to handle many tasks in software that had previously required custom integrated circuits. This approach really created embedded computing, since it provided the needed components for these systems. Over the years the microprocessor was an essential abstraction for the integrated circuit industry, allowing it to build increasingly complex components (processors and memory) that could be used for a wide variety of tasks. Over time, these processors have become faster, and they are now the key component in all computers, from Internet-enabled cell phones to mainframe servers.

The evolution of microprocessors over the past three decades has been unprecedented in the history of technology. While maintaining roughly the same user model of executing a sequential stream of instructions, these machines have absorbed virtually all of the extra complexity that process scaling provided them and converted it to increased performance. The first microprocessor was the Intel 4004, developed in 1971; it had 2300 transistors and ran at 200 kHz. A mere 30 years later, the Pentium 4 processor has almost 42 million transistors and runs at 1.7 GHz. Computer architects have leveraged the increased number of transistors into increased performance, increasing processor performance by over four orders of magnitude (see Box 2.1).

Growing Complexity

Increasing processor performance has come at a cost, in terms of both the design complexity of the machines and the power required by the current designs (on the order of 10 to 100 W). The growing complexity is troubling. When does the accumulating logical complexity being placed on modern integrated circuits cause enough errors in design to begin to drive overall system reliability back down? This is not a trivial concern in an era where volumes may be in the tens or hundreds of millions and failures may be life threatening. Another problem with the growing complexity is the growing cost to design these machines. New microarchitectures such as that for Intel's Pentium 4 processor require a design team of several hundred people for several years, an up-front investment of hundreds of millions of dollars.

Also of growing concern is the fact that continuing to scale processor performance has become increasingly difficult with time. It seems unlikely that it will be possible to continue to extract substantially more parallelism at the instruction level: The easy-to-reach parallelism has now been exploited (evidence of this can be seen in Figure 2.1), and the costs in hardware resources and implementation complexity are growing out of all proportion to additional performance gains. This means that the improvement in instructions per clock cycle will slow. Adding to that concern, it also seems unlikely that clock frequency will continue to scale at the current rate. Unless a breakthrough occurs in circuit design, it will become very difficult to decrease clock cycle times beyond basic gate speed improvements. Overall microprocessor performance will continue to grow, but the rate of improvement will decrease significantly in the near future.

BOX 2.1
Communication Is Costly in Complex Designs

The dominant technology used to build integrated circuits is complementary metal-oxide semiconductor (CMOS) technology. As the integrated circuit shrinks in size, the characteristics of the basic transistors improve—they speed up. Historically the speed of a basic CMOS gate has been roughly proportional to its size. This performance increase will continue, although various problems might slow the rate of improvement in the future (SIA, 1999).

In addition to gates, the other key component on an integrated circuit is the wire that connects the gates. The scaling of wires is more complex than that of the gates and has led to some confusion about how the performance of circuits will scale in the future. As technology scales, the delay of a wire (the length of time it takes for a signal to propagate across the wire) of constant length will almost certainly increase. At first glance this seems like a huge problem, since gate delays and wire delays are moving in opposite directions. This divergence has led a number of people to speak of wire-limited performance. The key point is, as technology scales, a wire of a given length spans a larger number of gates than the wire in an older technology, since all the gates are smaller. A circuit that was simply scaled to the new technology would also shrink in length, since everything has shrunk in size. The amount of delay attributable to this scaled wire is actually less than that of the original wire, so wire delay decreases just as a gate does. While the wire delay does not scale down quite as fast as the gate, the difference is modest and should not be a large problem for designers.

One way of viewing the wire delay is to realize that in any given technology the delay of a wire that spans more gates is larger than the delay of a wire that span fewer gates. Communicating across larger designs (that is, designs with more gates per unit area) is more expensive than communicating across smaller designs. Technology scaling enables larger designs to be built but does not remove the communication cost for these complex designs. So, scaling does not make wire performance proportionally worse per se; rather it enables a designer to build a more complex system on a chip. The large communication delays associated with systems are starting to appear on chips. These growing communication costs of today's large complex chips are causing people to think about smaller, more partitioned designs, and they are one driver of simpler embedded computing systems.

Simpler Processors

Up to this point the focus has been on the highest performance processors, but technology scaling has also enabled much simpler processors to have more than sufficient performance.[2] Rather than adding complex-

---

[2]The words "simple" and "complex" are not used here as a shorthand reference to the Reduced Instruction Set Computing versus Complex Instruction Set Computing (RISC vs.

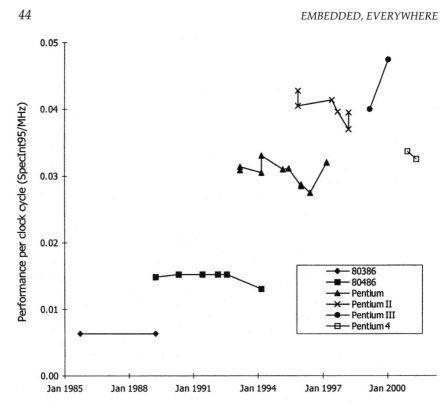

FIGURE 2.1 Instructions executed per cycle.

ity in order to wrest better performance from the chip, it is possible to use the added transistors for other functions, or not use them at all, making the chip smaller and cheaper and, as will be seen in the next section, less power consuming. It is these "simpler" processors that are used in most embedded systems, since they often do not need the highest performance. For many applications, the extra complexity can be and is used to interface to the outside world and to reduce the amount of off-chip memory that is needed to reduce the system cost.

As technology scales, these simpler processors have gotten faster, even if the design does not use more transistors, simply because the gates have become faster. Often a slightly more complex architecture is used, since it is now cheap enough. This scaling trend in the embedded proces-

CISC) debates of the 1980s. They refer to the complexity of a computer's microarchitecture and implementation, not its instruction set.

sor space has dramatically increased the performance of the processors being deployed and will continue to do so (see Box 2.2). The fastest embedded processors have a processing power that is within a factor of four of today's desktop processors (e.g., an 800-MHz StrongArm processor compared with a 1.5-GHz Pentium 4), but most embedded processors have performance that is an order of magnitude worse. With increased processing power comes the ability to build more sophisticated software systems with enough cycles to support various communication protocols. The existence of very cheap cycles that can support richer environments is another factor pushing EmNets into existence.

Power Dissipation

Power dissipation in general-purpose central processing units (CPUs) is a first-order constraint, requiring more expensive power supplies and more expensive cooling systems, making CPU packages more expensive; it may even affect the final form factor of the computer system.[3] Power has always been constrained in embedded systems, because such systems typically cannot afford any of the remedies mentioned above. For example, the controller in a VCR cannot require a large power supply, cannot have a fan for cooling, and cannot make the VCR be taller than such products would otherwise be.

There are two major strategies for taking advantage of the benefits of new processor technology: maximize performance or minimize power. For each new technology, the power needed to supply the same computation rate drops by a factor of three (see Box 2.3). The reason that general-purpose microprocessor power increases with each new generation is that performance is currently valued more than cost or power savings, so increased performance is preferred in the design process over decreased power requirements.

As power has become more important in complementary metal-oxide semiconductor (CMOS) designs, designers have developed a number of techniques and tools to help them reduce the power required. Since in CMOS much of the power is used to transition the value on a wire, many of the techniques try hard to ensure a signal is not changed unless it really should be and to prevent other ways of wasting power. The power saving ranges from simply turning off the processor/system when the ma-

---

[3]For example, microprocessors that dissipate too much heat may require very large fans or heat sinks for cooling. If that physical package is too large, it may be impossible to realize a server in a one-unit-high form factor, drastically reducing the modularity and scalability of the design.

BOX 2.2
Microprocessor Program Performance

While scaling technology allows the building of faster gates, it primarily allows the construction of designs that contain many more gates than in previous iterations. Processor designers have been able to convert larger transistor budgets into increased program performance. Early processors had so few transistors that function units were reused for many parts of the instruction execution.[1] As a result it took multiple cycles for each instruction execution. As more transistors became available, it became possible to duplicate some key functional units, so each unit could be used for only one stage in the instruction execution. This allowed pipelining the machine and starting the next instruction execution before the previous one was finished. Even though each instruction took a number of cycles to complete execution, a new instruction could be started every cycle. (This sort of pipelining is analogous to a car wash. It is not necessary to wait until the car ahead exits the car wash before introducing a new car; it is only necessary to wait until it has cleared the initial rinse stage.) As scaling provided more transistors, even more functional units were added so machines could start executing two instructions in parallel. These machines were called superscalar to indicate that their microarchitectures were organized as multiple concurrent scalar pipelines.

The problem with a superscalar machine is that it runs fast as long as the memory system can provide the data needed in a timely fashion and there are enough independent instructions to execute. In many programs neither of these requirements holds. To build a fast memory system, computer designers use caches[2] to decrease the time to access frequently used data. While caches work well, some data will not be in the cache, and when that happens the machine must stall, waiting for the data to be accessed. A so-called out-of-order machine reduces this delay by tracking the actual data-flow dependency between instructions and allowing the instructions to execute out of program order. In other words, the

chine is inactive, a technique that is used in almost all portable systems, to careful power control of individual components on the chip. In addition, power is very strongly related to the performance of the circuit. A circuit can almost always be designed to require less energy to complete a task if given more time to complete it. This recently led to a set of techniques to dynamically control the performance as little as necessary to minimize the power used.[4] Two recent examples of this are the Transmeta Crusoe processor (Geppert and Perry, 2000) and the Intel Xscale processor (Clark et al., 2001).

---

[4]See DARPA's Power Aware Computing/Communication Program for more information on work related to this problem. Available at <http://www.darpa.mil/ito/research/pacc/>.

machine finds other work to do while waiting for slow memory elements. While much more complex than a simple superscalar machine, out-of-order processing does expose more parallelism and improves the performance of the processor.

Each architectural step—pipelining, superscaling, out-of-order execution—improves the machine performance roughly 1.4-fold, part of the overall threefold performance improvement. Figure 2.1 plots a number proportional to the number of instructions executed each cycle for six generations of Intel processors. The data clearly show that increasing processor complexity has improved performance. Figure 2.2 gives the clock rate of these same processors; it shows a roughly two-fold increase in frequency for each generation. Since a scaled technology comes out roughly every 3 years, 1.4 of the overall performance increase comes from this improvement in speed. The remaining factor of 1.4, which comes from improvements in the circuit design and microarchitecture of the machine, is illustrated in Figure 2.3. This shows how many gates one can fit in each cycle and how this number has been falling exponentially, from over 100 in the early 1980s to around 16 in the year 2000. The decrease has been driven by using more transistors to build faster function units and by building more deeply pipelined machines. Multiplying these three factors of 1.4 together yields the threefold processor performance improvement observed. It should be noted that recent designs, such as the Pentium III and Pentium 4 chips, have not been able to achieve the increases in parallelism (instructions per cycle) that contributed to the threefold increase. This provides some concrete evidence that uniprocessor performance scaling is starting to slow down.

---

[1]An adder, for example, might have been used to generate the instruction address and then reused to do the operation or generate the data address.

[2]In this instance, a cache is a temporary storage place for data on the chip that allows much faster retrieval than accessing the data in memory.

The drive for low power causes a dilemma. (See Box 2.4 for a discussion of micropower sources for small devices.) While processor-based solutions provide the greatest flexibility for application development, custom hardware is generally much more power efficient. Early work in low-power design by Brodersen et al. (1992) and others showed that for many applications, custom solutions could be orders of magnitude lower in power requirements than a general-purpose processor. This is unfortunate, since the economics of chip production, as described earlier, make it unlikely that most applications could afford to design custom chips unless the design process becomes much cheaper. There are a couple of clear reasons why custom chips need less power. Their main advantage is that they are able to exploit the parallelism in the application. While exploiting parallelism is usually considered a way to increase perfor-

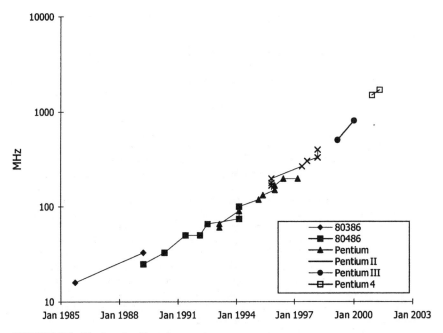

FIGURE 2.2 Clock rate of various processors.

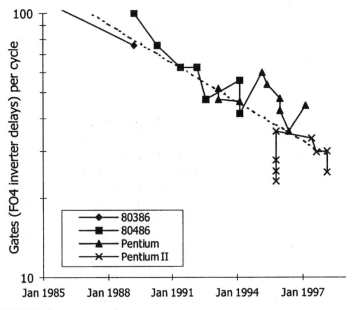

FIGURE 2.3 Gates per cycle.

mance, since performance and power are related, one can take higher-performance systems and make them lower power. In addition to parallelism, custom solutions have lower overheads in executing each function they perform. Since the function is often hard wired, there is no need to spend energy to specify the function. This is in contrast to a processor that spends a large amount of its power figuring out what function to perform—that is, determining what instructions to fetch and fetching them (see Gonzalez and Horowitz, 1996).

As mentioned earlier, the downside of these custom solutions is their complexity and the cost of providing a new solution for each application. This conflict between good power-efficiency and flexibility leads to a number of interesting research questions about how to build the more general, power-efficient hardware that will be needed for EmNets. Some researchers are trying to generalize a custom approach,[5] while others are trying to make a general-purpose parallel solution more power efficient.[6] The best way to approach this problem is still an open question.

COMMUNICATION

As discussed earlier, it is very clear that silicon scaling has made computation very cheap. These changes in technology have also driven the cost of communication down for both wireline and wireless systems. The continued scaling of CMOS technology enables cheap signal processing and low-cost radio frequency circuits. This has been evident in the past several years with the rapid expansion of wireless networking technology, first into the workplace and now into the home (e.g., wireless Ethernet and Apple Airport), which permits laptops and tablets to have a locally mobile high-speed network connection. As the technology improves, more sophisticated coding and detection algorithms can be used, which either decrease the power or increase the bandwidth of the communication. Soon it will be possible to place a low-cost wireless transceiver on every system built, a development that would seem to make it inevitable that these embedded systems will be networked. One constraint is that while bandwidth is increasing and cost is decreasing, the power demands are not becoming significantly lower. Communication

---

[5]See, for example, the work being done at the Berkeley Wireless Research Center, available at <http://bwrc.eecs.berkeley.edu/> or at the company Tensilica, <http://tensilica.com/>.

[6]See, for example, the work being done at the Stanford Smart Memories Project, available at <http://www-vlsi.stanford.edu/smart_memories/> or at the company ARC, <http://www.arccores.com/>.

BOX 2.3
Power in CMOS Circuits

In CMOS circuits, power is dissipated by two different mechanisms: static, resulting from current flow through resistive paths from the power supply to ground, and dynamic, resulting from current needed to change the value of a signal on a wire. Dynamic power is frequency dependent, since no power is dissipated if the node values do not change, while static power is independent of frequency and exists whenever the chip is powered on. In modern CMOS chips, the explicit static power is usually very small, and dynamic power dominates. The static power is never zero, since some leakage current flows when the transistors are nominally off. Today there is a trade-off between leakage current and dynamic power, so in some high-power chips the leakage current can be quite large. This trade-off is described in more detail at the end of this box.

The physical cause of dynamic power is the charging and discharging of the capacitance associated with the wire. Capacitance is a characteristic associated with all physical objects and depends on the shape of the wire. Roughly, the capacitance of a wire is proportional to its length. The dynamic power of a chip is just the sum of the dynamic power of each node on the chip, which in turn is just the energy used per cycle multiplied by the average number of cycles per second. The energy used to change the value of a capacitor is proportional to the value of the capacitance, C, and the square of the power supply voltage, V, used to power the chip. This leads to the common CV^2F formulation for power in CMOS chips, where F is the frequency of the chip (the number of cycles per second).

If an existing design is scaled to a new technology, all of the transistors

---

mechanisms, which are critical for EmNets—they are what make up the networking aspects—are described in this section.

Wireline Communications

The wireline infrastructure is important both because some EmNets will connect to it directly and because those using wireless may generate communications flows with it. The evolution of the wireline infrastructure reflects both a historic emphasis on telephony as the principal application and the rise in data communications applications over the past few decades, a trend accelerated by the commercialization of the Internet in the 1990s. Advances in technology and the entry of new providers of wireline services in competition with traditional telephone companies have combined to lower costs and prices of data communication, in turn stimulating yet more demand for it.

The wireline infrastructure can be divided into segments that involve

become smaller by Δ, and the wires become shorter by Δ. This means that all the capacitances scale by Δ too. Additionally, the power supply is generally scaled by Δ as well, so the energy needed to switch a gate changes by the scaling factor cubed (Δ^3). If this chip is run at the same frequency, it will take about three times less power for a 1.4-fold scaling of the technology. With this scaling, the gates will run about 1.4 times faster, so the machine could run at 1.4 times the frequency and still cut power consumption in half. The power dissipation of high-end microprocessors increases with scaling, since the additional transistors are spent on making a more complex chip (with concomitantly higher capacitance) that runs at twice the frequency rather than the nominal 1.4 times. This overwhelms the gain by scaling, and the power of the resulting processor increases.

To continue to reduce the chip power with scaling, it is very important that the power supply voltage be scaled down. As the supply voltages scale down, another problem occurs. There is a transistor parameter, its threshold voltage, that affects both the transistor leakage current and the gate speed. It is the voltage where the transistor turns on. To maintain gate performance, it would be ideal for the voltage at which a transistor turns on to scale down at the same rate as the power supply voltage scales down. Unfortunately, the leakage current through an off transistor is also set by this parameter and increases rapidly as the threshold voltage approaches 0 V. One needs a threshold voltage of around 0.4 V for low leakage. In some high-performance systems it makes sense to use a lower threshold and deal with higher leakage currents, since the leakage power is still a small percent of the total power. In low-power systems, it is often decided to take the decrease in performance rather than increase the leakage. How to get around this interaction is an open research question.

different technologies and different capacities for communications. Differential improvement of these segments affects the infrastructure's ability to support the increase in communications anticipated from EmNets. Optical fiber has become prominent in the network backbones, and its capacity has been multiplied by the advent of wavelength-division multiplexing, which exploits the ability to communicate through different colors in the optical spectrum and which was enabled by all-optical-fiber amplifiers. Together, these and other advances have lowered the cost per bit of transmission in the backbone and for the wireline infrastructure generally, although the connection from end users (especially residential or small business users) to the backbone remains something of a bottleneck. Digital subscriber line (DSL) and cable modems increase the bandwidth to the end user, but they are unevenly deployed and will probably remain so through at least 2010.

Advances in silicon technology have also improved networking speed inside offices and homes. For structures with good quality wiring,

---

BOX 2.4
Alternative Power Sources

The power requirements of EmNets, like those of embedded and mobile computing environments, present difficult challenges. Some EmNets can, of course, be built with all mains-powered nodes. Others will require portable power, but current batteries will suffice (electronic watches, for example, require little enough power that batteries last for many years). Technology such as lithium polymer batteries already allows one to create energy sources in a wide variety of form factors. However, EmNets will stress power sources because of their need for long operating lifetimes and higher energy density.

One can envision EmNets (as described elsewhere in this report) as consisting of large numbers of very small networked and often wireless components. The low data rates and activity factors will make clever on-chip power-management schemes and low operating voltage essential, but such approaches will not be sufficient to address the energy problem. For some applications that have very low average energy, it might be possible to extend lifetimes by extracting energy from the environment (light, vibration, RF), but further work is needed in this area. Some work in this area has been funded by the Defense Advanced Research Projects Agency (DARPA) and the Jet Propulsion Laboratory (JPL).

Other systems simply need higher energy densities than current batteries provide. While battery technology continues to improve, energy density changes slowly. To obtain much higher densities generally means storing a fuel and supporting a chemical reaction to generate energy. The problem with these chemical solutions is that they generally become more efficient when made larger—building efficient small generators is hard. Fuel cells are an interesting option; however, more work is needed to devise small fuel cells that are superior to batteries and adequate for mobile platforms. A more ambitious approach is to miniaturize a combustion engine/electrical generator. MIT's Micro Gas Turbine Generator Project[1] is looking at the technology needed to create a miniature turbine 0.5 inch in diameter to create 50 W of electrical power. While there are many difficult problems with these combustion solutions, they would provide the best energy density if successful and should be part of the EmNets research program.

---

[1]For more information, see <http://web.mit.edu/aeroastro/www/labs/GTL/>.

Ethernet speeds have been improved from 10 to 100 Mbps and will continue to improve with new gigabit systems. Even in homes without any new wires, signal processing has allowed people to create a network on top of the old phone line infrastructure. One good example of this effort is the Home Phoneline Networking Alliance.[7] Other contexts that may

---

[7]For more information, see <http://www.homepna.org/>.

use wireline infrastructure for EmNets include vehicles and smart spaces; all contexts may eventually use a mix of wireline and wireless communications.

These technologies and infrastructure segments have been developing based on demand associated with conventional computers and telephones. Planning has been informed by speculation about other kinds of networked devices, and there has been some experience with television video being carried on these networks. Because the backbone economics most clearly supports optical systems, the potential for growth in capacity seems greatest there; the in-home network market is developing in part based on speculation about embedded systems in conjunction with computers and phones; broadband access to the home, the so-called last mile, continues to be problematic, however. [8]

Wireless Communications

EmNets will often involve wireless communications, in part because of the ease with which wireless networks can be deployed and connected, and in part because of the wide array of environments in which EmNets will operate. Wireless has been proven inasmuch as cellular telephony and paging networks have proliferated and grown in scale and coverage, both nationally and internationally. Movement beyond conventional telephony and paging to data applications, through personal digital assistants (PDAs) and advanced phones providing e-mail and Web access, has been reinforced by the rise of third-generation technology and standards. However, the new applications and services are limited in their data communications capabilities compared with wireline Internet capabilities. Beyond these larger area networks, where there are large, powerful, energy-rich base stations with large antennas and relatively capable units, much work is being done in short-range wireless systems. There are a multitude of new wireless technologies and accompanying standards that fill this space. For 10 to 30+ Mbps wireless communications, the 802.11b and 802.11a (sometimes known as wireless Ethernet) standards exist in the United States; the corresponding standards outside the United States are HiperLAN2[9] in Europe and Multimedia Mobile Access Communication (MMAC) in Japan. For wireless personal area network (PAN) systems such as Bluetooth (which was initially envisioned as a small form factor, low-cost, cable replacement technology for devices such as cell

---

[8]See CSTB's forthcoming examination of broadband issues, expected in 2001.

[9]HiperLAN2 was created to be a global standard with complete interoperability of high-speed wireless LAN products. See <http://www.hiperlan2.com/>.

phones, laptops, and headphones), IEEE 802.15 is defining new generations of these systems.

Although wireless communication seems to be flourishing, the reality
is that it involves overcoming many problems inherent in over-the-air
communication.[10] The radio-frequency spectrum is a scarce resource and
will need to be shared among a multitude of highly heterogeneous devices with drastically different requirements for bandwidth and communication range. Sharing of the spectrum can occur in time, space, and
frequency. Already, conflicts over frequency are arising between emerging technologies that make use of unregulated bands (e.g., at 2.4 GHz,
802.11 wireless Ethernet conflicts with many new cordless telephones,
and both are now being widely deployed.) Low-cost radio transceivers
are being developed that have very limited range, which isolates them in
the space dimension. This has the beneficial effect of dramatically lowering the power consumption for communication but complicates communication by potentially requiring multiple hops when communicating with
more distant nodes (and thus requiring intermediate nodes to expend
their own power to route packets). An advantage of multihop, however,
is that it provides the opportunity to do data aggregation and collaborative processing at an intermediate node. Many portable devices are also
separating their communication in time to avoid interference, by having
low-duty cycles of transmission. These devices are also trying to avoid
interference by spreading themselves out in the frequency spectrum using spread spectrum techniques. Box 2.5 discusses Bluetooth as it relates
to the need to share the available spectrum.

Two fundamental concerns for EmNets are scaling and heterogeneity. In wireless communication, scaling means maintaining adequate
bandwidth per volume by decreasing the range, dividing up the spectrum, and taking turns using it. Which devices are brought into proximity can have important consequences if they can interfere with each other's
communication or have cumulative bandwidth needs that cannot be met.
An important issue arises with long-lived EmNets: They will occupy a
portion of the spectrum for their lifetime, impacting any other devices
that come within range.[11] It may very well be necessary to consider not

---

[10]For an overview of these challenges, see CSTB (1997).

[11]Consider Vanguard 1, the second U.S. satellite launched in the late 1950s, which had as
its primary function an experiment on the use of solar cells for power supply. Owing to its
small size and capability, it merely broadcast a continuous signal. There was no anticipa-
tion of the need for a cutoff switch, and the satellite operated for years, providing little
useful information but consuming a valuable portion of the RF spectrum.

BOX 2.5
Bluetooth and Shared Spectrum

Bluetooth exemplifies an attempted solution to the need to share available spectrum. It was originally developed by cellular telephone manufacturers to simplify and thus increase the use of the cellular phone for long-range communication by a variety of consumer devices. The concept is simple: provide a replacement for cables that are used to connect laptops, MP3 players, etc., to network services. Bluetooth is short range—approximately 30 m—so that many users can interconnect the same devices within a small geographic area. The idea is to have high bandwidth per unit volume by providing smaller cells packed more closely together. Bandwidth density is just as important as bandwidth—as anyone can attest who has unsuccessfully tried to use a cellular phone in a crowd where hundreds of others were trying to do the same. By having a short range, it is possible for Bluetooth transceivers (now at power consumptions of less than 50 mW) to be included in a wide range of battery-powered devices with minimal impact.

Bluetooth uses frequency hopping to further isolate users. Conversely, devices that do want to communicate must synchronize precisely so that they hop frequencies in unison (the Bluetooth specification includes a discovery procedure for this purpose). Synchronization inherently limits the number of devices that can communicate at any one time. As long as only a handful of devices are being used at one time, this is not an issue. The active devices synchronize, while the others park and conserve power. However, for many of the EmNets envisioned in this report, large numbers of devices will be actively communicating. Bluetooth does not adequately support these needs because it synchronizes devices into small clusters. Although devices can be part of more than one cluster, they and their entire cluster pay a considerable performance penalty in switching between clusters. An important open question for technologies such as Bluetooth is, How will a given device know (or be told) with which other devices it is to communicate? If multiple other devices are in range, how are the important ones for an application identified? Ownership may be important when users want to connect their personal laptop to their personal phone, but this may make it difficult to use a different phone. This problem is much more difficult when what is at issue are embedded elements of EmNets that are deployed as part of an active environment. Moving beyond phones, PDAs, and laptops to applications such as wireless sensor networks and other EmNets, Bluetooth and its ilk may have a role to play. However, significant additional development will be needed.

---

only principled ways to claim a portion of the spectrum but also how to reclaim it when needs change. Heterogeneity means that large EmNets will require multihop networks that will forward data packets between devices that have to exist in different parts of the spectrum (possibly as far apart as radio frequency (RF) and infrared (IR)) or that are limited in range.

Boxes 2.6 and 2.7 describe two areas where EmNets stress wireless communications in new ways. Both focus on short-range, low-power issues, in which there is more uncertainty and need for work than in the other more mature technologies. The first looks at constraints on the circuits used, and the second examines the networking issues.

BOX 2.6
Communications Constraints for
Low-Power, Short-Range Systems

The constraints on communications for low-power, short-range wireless systems stem from environmental effects on radio frequency propagation. These effects, such as spatial separation of the nodes along with antenna gain, multipath propagation, and shadowing, arise from attenuation due to ground scattering effects. The spatial separation issue has both positives and negatives. Spatial, time, or frequency diversity can help with the issue of multipath propagation, and a multihop network can be employed to deal with path loss and shadowing. Each of these is discussed in more detail below.

Spatial separation is an important factor in the construction of wireless communication networks. For low-lying antennas, intensity can drop as much as the fourth power of distance (Rappaport, 1996; Sohrabi et al., 1999b; Sommerfeld, 1949; Wait, 1998; Chew, 1990).[1] This presents a problem when attempting to communicate along the ground. Surface roughness, the presence of reflecting and obstructing objects, and antenna elevation all have an impact on propagation. In general, power fall-off rarely approaches the free-space limit, and particularly in cluttered or near-ground environments a fourth power loss falloff is seen. The losses make long-range communication a power-hungry exercise; the combination of Maxwell's laws (equations describing electromagnetic fields) and Shannon's capacity theorem (describing the connection among error rates, transmission rates, and the capacity of the communications channel) together dictate that there is a limit on how many bits can be reliably conveyed given power and bandwidth restrictions. On the other hand, the strong decay of intensity with distance provides spatial isolation along the ground, allowing reuse of frequencies throughout a network.

Multipath propagation (due to reflections off multiple objects) is also a very serious problem. It is possible to recover most of the loss generated thereby through diversity. Diversity can be obtained in any of the three domains of space, frequency, or time, since with sufficient separation the fade levels are independent. By spreading the information, the multiple versions will experience different fading, so that the result is more akin to the average, whereas if nothing is done it

GEOLOCATION

In many electronic systems the geographic location of objects is not important; instead, it is the network topology, the relative position of objects within a network, that is important. Yet for many systems, geographic data can be very useful—for example, to find the nearest printer

is the worst-case conditions that dominate error probabilities. If the sensor nodes are not physically mobile and the terrain is static, the multipath losses will be invariant with respect to time. Likewise, spatial diversity is difficult to obtain, since multiple antennas are unlikely to be mounted on small platforms. Thus, diversity is most likely to be achieved in the frequency domain—for example, by employing some combination of frequency spread spectrum or hybrid spread/orthogonal frequency division multiplexing systems together with interleaving and channel coding. Networks of embedded computers that may be placed anywhere and that may grow in numbers and density with time will have a critical need for reliable communication; yet the interference among elements will grow proportionally, and frequency reuse may be of little or no value because of mobility and, possibly, uncertainty as to location. For such an application, spread spectrum and direct sequence guarantee a constant flat, wide spectrum for each user and are a good choice for maximizing both the capacity and the coverage of the network. It is not clear, however, whether the inherent inefficiencies will prove too complex and/or too costly. Measures that are effective against deliberate jamming are generally also effective against multipath fading and multiuser interference.

Shadowing (wavefront obstruction and confinement) and path loss can be dealt with by employing a multihop network. If nodes are randomly placed in an environment, some links to near neighbors will be obstructed while others will present a clear line of sight. Given a sufficient density, the signals can in effect hop around obstacles. Multihop also presents opportunities for networking processing and reduction of data. Exploitation of these forms of diversity can lead to significant reductions in the energy required to transmit data from one location in the network to another; such exploitation becomes limited chiefly by the reception and retransmission energy costs of the radio transceivers for dense peer-to-peer networks. In wireless systems there is thus a close connection between the networking strategy and the physical layer. The connection is even stronger when considering the multiple access nature of the channel, since interference among users is often the limiting impairment.

---

[1]The path loss exponent can vary from less than 2 to more than 4 in different environments. See, for example, Parsons (1992) as an introduction to the body of literature dealing with propagation in personal mobile environments.

BOX 2.7
Network Architecture for Low-Power Wireless Systems

In contrast to conventional wireless networks, EmNets must potentially support large numbers of sensors in a local area with short range and low average bit rate communication (fewer than 1 to 100 kbps). The small separation between nodes can be exploited to provide multihop communication, with the power advantages outlined earlier. Since for short hops the transceiver power consumption for reception and listening is nearly equal to that for transmission, the protocol should be designed so that radios are off as much of the time as possible. This requires that the radios periodically exchange short messages to maintain local synchronization. It is not necessary for all nodes to have the same global clock, but the local variations from link to link should be small to enable cooperative signal processing functions. The messages can combine health-keeping information, maintenance of synchronization, and reservation requests for bandwidth for longer packets. The abundant bandwidth that results from the spatial reuse of frequencies and local processing ensures that relatively few conflicts will result in these requests, so simple mechanisms can be used. One such protocol suite that embodies these principles has been developed that includes boot-up, Media Access Control (MAC), energy-aware routing, and interaction with mobile units; see Sohrabi et al. (1999a). It indicates the feasibility of achieving distributed low-power operation in a flat multihop network.

An alternative to a flat architecture is the use of clustering, possibly with clustering at many levels with respect to different network functions. This is particularly convenient if there are multiple classes of nodes, some with special capabilities such as long-range communications, or connections via gateway nodes to the Internet. Different approaches for performing network self-organization into clusters have been developed. Typically, clustering is implemented in ad hoc networks to reduce the number of instances of network reconfiguration in situations of high mobility relative to the messaging rate. It comes at the price of an increased energy burden to the cluster head and some inefficiency in multihop routing. The reduction in routing table updates and the relatively frequent role changes in situations of mobility take care of both concerns. In static networks, hierarchy may be imposed to simplify signal processing—for example, to avoid frequent leader election for processes that must be coordinated over large areas. This could occur even if routing takes place without clustering.

A question that naturally arises is where processing and storage should take place. As indicated previously, communication, while becoming cheaper, costs a great deal compared with processing, so energy constraints dictate doing as much processing at the source as possible. Further, reducing the quantity of data to transmit significantly simplifies the network design and permits scaling to thousands of nodes per network gateway.

in terms of meters, not network connections. In EmNets, this ability to determine one's location in space is often critical—as a way to both name and identify objects and data and coordinate activity within an EmNet.[12] For example, using location information in conjunction with static information about a building would allow the creation of logical location information, enabling an EmNet to determine which objects are in the same room or are cooled by the same air conditioner. Location information can also be used to determine when two (or more) nodes are in close geographical proximity to one another. This would be useful when trying to ensure redundant coverage of a particular area, but needing only one node in the area to be powered on at any given point. Boxes 2.8 and 2.9 provide details of techniques that can assist in determining the location of nodes and, consequently, the larger network geometry (encompassing geographic location, colocation, and proximity information). The first describes the Global Positioning System (GPS) and the second examines alternative geolocation techniques.

COMPUTING SOFTWARE—
OPERATING SYSTEMS AND APPLICATIONS

Embedded systems have been around at least as long as the microprocessor. The software for these systems has been built, more or less successfully, using several different paradigms. Some systems are built from scratch by the manufacturer with all software being created specifically for the device in question. This software may be written in assembly language or may use a higher-level language. Other systems are made using existing software modules and wrapping an application around them. These preexisting modules might include an operating system, network protocols, control algorithms, drivers, and so on. Such modules are available from independent software vendors and in some cases as open source software. Finally, a very few systems are created using formal methods, high-level design tools, and rigorous design methodology.

---

[12]Location systems generally measure the relative geographical positions of objects because measuring absolute positions directly is all but impossible. If one or more of the objects has a known fixed position, then absolute geographic positions can be derived. Measuring relative positions directly is difficult, so most location systems measure the distance between the objects and use the measurements to triangulate the relative locations of the objects. The distance between the objects can be measured in a number of ways, but the most popular is to measure the time delay of a signal transmitted between two objects. This time delay can be measured directly, or it can be measured indirectly by measuring the phase of some oscillating carrier wave (see, for example, the Omega and Decca navigation systems.)

BOX 2.8
Global Positioning System

By far the most common geolocation system in use today is the Global Positioning System (GPS), which was completed by the Department of Defense in 1994. Twenty-four satellites circle Earth in a pattern in which at least five satellites are visible from any location. These satellites contain very precise clocks, and their locations are known to a high degree of precision. They transmit a message that contains both the time on the satellite and the satellite's position. The receipt of four signals provides enough information to solve for the location of the receiver and the time offset of the local clock.[1] What makes GPS reception difficult is that radio frequency (RF) signals from the satellites are very weak. Special coding is used to allow receivers to detect these weak signals, but even with coding, GPS receivers generally work only if they have a direct line of sight to the satellites. Performance inside buildings or in an area covered by foliage is generally quite poor—a severe limitation for EmNets, which will often operate entirely inside buildings. A secondary issue is the large computation needed by current receivers to find the signals from the desired satellite quickly, which can consume considerable resources.

Designing a geolocation system would be much easier if the receiver knew roughly where it was and what signals it should be looking for. This notion of an assisted geolocation system (assisted GPS) has recently been proposed to handle the need to locate a cell phone within a few tens of meters for emergency 911 calls. Assisted GPS leverages the following facts: (1) the nodes have a means to communicate with an outside server (that is, they don't need to be completely self-contained, (2) the position of the nodes relative to the outside server is roughly known, and (3) it is possible (and inexpensive) to build high-quality GPS receivers to the outside servers to assist in determining the location of the nodes.

Revisiting the GPS receiver's task, the hard problem is finding the satellite's signal in the background noise. Yet if the rough location of the node relative to the server is known, the server could calculate the signal that the receiver should see. With this added information, the receiver's search space is much smaller, and the receiver can actually make intelligent guesses about where the signal is. This allows the receiver to integrate over longer sequences of data and improves its ability to find very small signals that are buried in noise. In the cell phone system

These latter systems have been very small in number compared with the more ad hoc designs (Lee, 2000).

Today, as described elsewhere in this report, embedded systems are becoming highly networked and are changing in fundamental ways. This will necessitate important changes in the way the software for these systems is created. For most computers, the software running on a typical embedded system usually consists of an operating system, which is de-

example, the system roughly tracks the location of a phone using signal strength indications to switch between cells. The base station would know the visible satellites and their Doppler frequency shifts, which could be fed to the receivers to make it easier for them to find the needed signals. In many EmNets, the initial position estimate could be even better, which would improve the possibility of finding the weak satellite signals.

Whether an assisted GPS can be made to work for EmNets is still an open research question and needs to be explored.[2] In addition to the obvious issue of signal to noise for the GPS satellite broadcasts, a number of other issues need to be resolved. A critical requirement in these systems is that the time at the receivers be synchronized to the clocks at the server to better than the uncertainty of the signal delay; if it is not, the clock errors will decrease the gain achieved from the server station. This need for good time synchronization is a challenge for many EmNets since for power and cost reasons they may use low-duty-factor networks, which have large latency, and low-power, low-cost clocks, which have higher uncertainty. Another issue is the multipath problem that occurs in urban situations, where a reflected satellite signal can confuse the receiver. Still another concern with incorporating GPS location technology into EmNets is nontechnical: GPS is a creation of the United States Department of Defense, and it may be that many other countries would prefer not to have their positioning systems depend on it as such, notwithstanding the Defense Department's position that it will not interfere with the accuracy of GPS.

---

[1]One way to visualize the problem is to imagine the devices as small balls and the distances measured as sticks that connect the balls together. It takes at least four devices (three distances to each device) to fix the relative three-dimensional locations for each of the objects, and in some cases it takes more than four devices to obtain robust position estimates. Delay must be measured quite precisely given the fast speed of propagation, 3×10^8 m/s. The key to these systems is that they only need stable clocks, not necessarily clocks with extremely high precision (Rappaport, 1996).

[2]The Federal Aviation Administration's Wide Area Augmentation System is an example of a system that incorporates GPS information in a geographically expansive augmentation to basic GPS service. For more information, see <http://gps.faa.gov/Programs/WAAS/waas.htm>.

signed to be useful for many systems with little change, and some application software. (See Box 2.10 for a discussion of requirements in traditional embedded systems.) In today's EmNets, the line between application and operating system often blurs, with reusable components such as communications protocols sometimes considered an operating system and sometimes an application and virtual machines considered neither a true operating system nor an application but rather a sort of middleware.

BOX 2.9
Alternative Geolocation Techniques

The biggest disadvantage of GPS for a robust sensor network is the dependence on the external signal from each satellite and thus the sensitivity to multipath signals, signal absorption, jamming, and satellite loss. Implementing a non-satellite-based RF geolocation framework as part of a sensor network could provide a robust location algorithm and, ideally, would leverage the communication transceiver to limit system redundancy. The biggest hurdle to overcome for RF geolocation is the timing accuracy needed for useful submeter location capability. One-meter position accuracy requires discerning signal-timing differences of 3 ns. Clock accuracies may not need to be this fine if averaging and edge detection are used to compensate for clock error. However, multipath signals in cluttered environments also cause substantial errors in position accuracy to accumulate. Two-way measurements in which relative synchronization is not necessary are one way to get around synchronization problems (McCrady et al., 2000). However, much development remains to be done, as RF systems are still orders of magnitude in price, size, or accuracy from feasible integration in widely deployed EmNets.

Ultrawideband (UWB) shows promise for delivering centimeter-accurate, multipath, integrated communications and position location capability. However, fully developed UWB-based systems with low-cost, compact clocks are not yet commercially available. In addition, the propagation characteristics of UWB signals have not been widely explored, and size, cost, and Federal Communications Commission (FCC) certification issues have not been finalized for developing UWB systems. A working group has been set up that describes some of these issues in more detail.[1]

As an alternative to using RF communication, acoustic signals could be used. Acoustic signals suffer from similar multipath, dispersion, and propagation problems in cluttered environments, but they require a much coarser time scale (six orders of magnitude coarser) for accurate positioning.[2] While acoustic geoloca-

Because in any case EmNets need to work as a whole, operating systems and application software are discussed together.

Traditional embedded systems are often networked, but generally in rather simple ways, or at least the connectivity roles of the embedded systems themselves are rather simple. However, with hardware power increasing rapidly and available bandwidth increasing even more rapidly, new modes of connectivity (both wired and wireless), richer user interfaces, and new standards such as Java, the functionality and resulting complexity are about to increase dramatically. These new EmNets change the rules of the game in a number of ways. They are still embedded systems, but they are also a part of an extremely complex, heterogeneous distributed system. They therefore retain the requirements of tration requires a separate acoustic transmitter, depending on an EmNet's sensing requirements, the receiver may be integrated into existing sensing capability. Acoustic geolocation takes advantage of the relatively slow propagation of sound waves, but it requires development of an alternative subsystem and further exploration of the propagation issues involved before operational use with EmNets can be contemplated.

The methods discussed above first measure distances between objects and then deduce their position; other approaches are possible. In some systems, precise location might not be needed. For example, a few beacons might be able to determine which side of a line an object is on; this might be enough for determining what is in a room but not exactly where. Extending this type of determination might enable the device (or the beacons) to estimate distance and angles between the object. These estimates again provide the basis for calculating geolocation. There are a number of ways to estimate angles and distance other than measuring time of flight. For example most cell phone systems track signal strength as a position estimate (for cell hand-off) and are starting to use antenna arrays to estimate the angle as well. Optical signals can also be used in this manner. For example, laser range finders use a laser and a camera to determine the location of different objects by changing the angle of the laser and measuring when it hits the object. Given the laser angle and the distance between the laser and the camera, one can estimate the distance to the object. These techniques are often much simpler than GPS and merit further research in the context of EmNets.

---

[1]More information is available at <http://www.uwb.org/>.
[2]Acoustic signals travel relatively slowly, moving at roughly 330 m/s. To measure distance this way requires a pair of ultrasonic transducers and some signal processing to detect accurately the signal and measure the delay. It also requires a clear acoustic path between the two devices to propagate the signal.

---

ditional embedded systems, as described above, but also have a number of new requirements. Several of these new requirements are discussed in detail elsewhere in this report: security, safety, reliability, usability, and privacy (Chapter 4); virtual machines and communication protocols (Chapter 3); complexity and analysis tools (Chapter 5); and service discovery (Chapter 3). Boxes 2.11, 2.12, and 2.13 expand upon upgradability, high availability, and the ability to work with new hardware as additional ways in which software will need to be refined to handle the requirements of EmNets.

An additional concern is the cost of correcting failures in EmNet software, which will often far exceed the corresponding cost in more traditional desktop and server environments. This is because the EmNets

---

BOX 2.10
Traditional Embedded Software Requirements

Traditional, non-networked embedded software can be quite complex and have a number of requirements. These have implications both for the application and for the operating system. Several such requirements are the following:

• *Real time.* Because many embedded systems interact intensely with the real world, they often have strict real-time requirements.
• *Portability.* Many different types of CPUs, peripheral chips, and memory architectures may be used in embedded systems. Thus, for low cost, any embedded OS or other reusable component that is meant to be used on multiple applications should be widely portable to custom hardware platforms.
• *Resource-constrained computing.* Since embedded systems may have no disk and little memory and may be power and cost constrained, the operating system must be able to operate in resource-constrained environments.
• *High reliability.* Embedded systems are deployed remotely, often in infrastructure-critical applications. Software faults are thus very problematic and are extremely expensive or even impossible to fix.
• *Safety.* Software can be analyzed on the local system to determine its impact on the system safety objective.

---

will often be deployed in ways that make it difficult to deliver or test corrected software. Also, the costs of the failures themselves may be very high, since many EmNets will perform infrastructure-critical or even life-critical applications. The cost issue is complicated by the fact that the cost of updates and failures may be borne by the end user and not by the developer of the software, which may have no compelling economic rationale for developing reliable software and so may be tempted to cut corners at this critical juncture.

REAL-TIME AND PERFORMANCE-CRITICAL ASPECTS OF EMBEDDED OPERATING SYSTEMS

The new requirements listed above imply more complex, highly functional applications and services to support the systems. These services could be provided by specialized hardware but in most cases will probably be provided by an operating system. However, as mentioned, traditional embedded system requirements do not disappear. In particular, the requirement for real-time response is still critical for many products and remains a challenge, as new functionality must be added without adversely affecting response.

A real-time operating system must enable applications to respond to stimuli in a deterministic amount of time, known as the latency. The actual amount of time is dependent on the application, but the determinism requirement is nonnegotiable. All design decisions in the operating system must therefore optimize system latency. This stands in contrast to most desktop and server operating systems, which are optimized for throughput and for protection of multiple processes, with latency far less important. Critical design decisions as basic as system data structures (queues, tables, etc.), memory protection and paging models, and calling semantics are driven by these very different optimization requirements, making it difficult or impossible to "add" real time to an operating system that was not designed from the beginning with that as a core requirement.

Like any modern operating system, most real-time embedded operating systems are multitasking. Unlike most desktop and server operating systems, however, embedded operating systems are split between those systems in which there are multiple processes, each residing in its own memory, and those in which all tasks live in the same memory map, with or without protection from one another. Furthermore, new systems are beginning to appear based on entirely different memory protection models, such as protection domains. Some of the issues that arise in embedded systems with respect to memory management, tasks, and scheduling are described in Box 2.14.

MICROELECTROMECHANICAL SYSTEMS

Microelectromechanical systems, or MEMS, had their start in a famous talk by the physicist Richard Feynman entitled "There's Plenty of Room at the Bottom" (Feynman, 1960; Trimmer, 1997.) Feynman pointed out that tremendous improvements in speed and energy requirements, as well as in device quality and reliability, could be had if computing devices could be constructed at the atomic level. MEMS represent the first steps toward that vision, using the best implementation technology currently available: the same silicon fabrication that is used for integrated circuits.

MEMS devices generally attempt to use mechanical properties of the device, in conjunction with electronic sensing, processing, and control, to achieve real-world physical sensing and actuation. The accelerometers in modern cars with airbags are MEMS devices; they use tiny cantilever beams as the inertial elements and embody the extreme reliability required of such an application. Other MEMS devices take advantage of the wave nature of light, incorporating regular patterns of very fine comb

---

BOX 2.11
Upgradability

Traditionally, most embedded devices, once deployed, have rarely been upgraded, and then only very proactively and carefully, for instance by physically replacing read-only memory (ROM). In a world of networked embedded systems, and with rewritable, nonvolatile storage widely available, field upgrades will be more frequent and often far more invisible to end users of the systems.[1] This will occur because EmNets may be in service for many years, and the environment to which they are connected and the functionality requirements for the device may change considerably over that time. In some cases, such upgrades are driven by a knowledgeable user, who purchases a new component of functionality and installs it, a nearly automatic procedure. In other cases, updates or upgrades may be invisible to the end user, such as when protocols or device addresses change. Devices like home gateways, automobiles, and appliances may be upgraded online without the consumer ever knowing about it and in ways well beyond the consumer's understanding, raising the issue of usability and transparency to the user.

Transparent software upgrade of deployed EmNets, while probably necessary and inevitable, presents a number of difficulties. The very fact that the upgrades are transparent to the end user raises troubling questions of who has control of the EmNet (the user or the upgrader?) and creates potential security and safety issues if such an upgrade is erroneous or malicious. What if the software is controllable or upgradable by parties that are not to be trusted? Further difficulty is caused by the heterogeneity of many EmNets. Many individual nodes may need to be upgraded, but those nodes may be based on different hardware and/or different operating systems. Deploying an upgrade that will work reliably across all these nodes and EmNets is a challenge closely related to the code mobility issues dis-

---

structures, arranged to refract light in useful ways under mechanical control. A Texas Instruments MEMS device is the heart of a projector in which each pixel is the light bounced off one of millions of tiny mirrors, hinged such that the amounts of red, green, and blue light can be independently controlled.

Microfluidics is an emerging MEMS application in which the fluid capillaries and valves are all directly implemented on a silicon chip and controlled via onboard electronics. Still other MEMS devices implement a membrane with a tunneling current sensor for extremely precise measurements of pressure. The combination of MEMS sensing plus the computation horsepower of embedded processors opens the way to large networks of distributed sensing plus local processing, with communication back to central synthesis engines for decision making.

However, there are challenges to be overcome before MEMS can real-

cussed in Chapter 3. Finally, there may be simultaneity requirements—that is, all nodes in an EmNet, which may be widely dispersed geographically, may need to be upgraded at the same time. This requirement may need to be addressed by multistage commits, similar to those used in transaction processing.

Online update is largely an application issue rather than an operating system issue. However, most system designers will expect the operating system to make the task easier and to handle some difficult problems like upgrade policy, verification, and security. Furthermore, in some cases the operating system itself may need to be field upgraded, a process that almost certainly requires operating system cooperation and that extends beyond the device being updated. A server infrastructure is required to set policies, supply the correct information to the correct devices, manage security of the information, and verify correctness. This infrastructure is likely to be supplied by a few providers, akin to Internet Service Providers (ISPs) or Application Service Providers (ASPs), rather than to be created anew for each individual deployed product.

As of 2001, there is no consensus on how online field upgrade will work for the billions of networked embedded systems components that will be deployed, nor is there any significant move toward applicable standards. Field upgrade is likely to become an important focus of research and development work over the next several years as numerous systems are deployed that challenge the ability of simple solutions to scale up to adequate numbers and reliability.

---

[1]The problem of field upgradability of EmNet elements is similar to the problem encountered in downloading software for software-defined radios, which is being studied by a number of companies and the SDR (Software Defined Radio) Forum, a de facto standards organization.

---

ize this promise. One is in the nature of real world sensing itself: It is an intrinsically messy business. A MEMS device that is attempting to detect certain gases in the atmosphere, for instance, will be exposed to many other gases and potential contaminants, perhaps over very long periods of time and with no maintenance. Such devices will have to be designed to be self-monitoring and, if possible, self-cleaning if they are to be used in very large numbers by nonexperts.

The aspects of silicon technology that yield the best electronics are not generally those that yield the best MEMS devices. As has been discussed, smaller is better for electronics. Below a certain size, however, MEMS devices will not work well: A cantilever beam used for sensing acceleration is not necessarily improved by making it smaller. Yet to meet the low cost needed for large numbers of sensing/computing/reporting devices, the MEMS aspects and electronics will have to be fabricated onto the

---

BOX 2.12
High Availability and Fault Tolerance

Many EmNets must work continuously, regardless of hardware faults (within defined limits) or ongoing hardware and software maintenance, such as hardware or software component replacement. Reliability in an unreliable and changeable environment is usually referred to as high availability and fault tolerance (HA/FT). HA/FT may require specialized hardware, such as redundant processors or storage. The operating system plays a key role in HA/FT, including fault detection, recovery, and management; checkpoint and fail-over mechanisms; and hot-swap capability for both hardware and software. Applications also need to be designed with HA/FT in mind. A layer between the application and the operating system that checks the health of the system and diagnoses what is wrong can be used to control the interaction between the two.

HA/FT systems have not been widely used; instead, they tend to have niches in which they are needed, such as banking, electric power, and aircraft. Those who need them, often communications equipment manufacturers, have built them in a proprietary fashion, generally for a specific product. The first portable, commercial embedded HA/FT operating systems, as well as reusable components for fault management and recovery, are just starting to become available,[1] but they have not yet been widely deployed in a general-purpose context. EmNets will very likely be used in a variety of contexts, and transferring HA/FT capabilities to EmNets is a challenge the community must meet.

---

[1]As examples, see Wind River's VxWorks AE at <http://www.windriver.com/products/html/vxworksae.html>, Enea's OSE Systems at <http://www.enea.com/>, and LynuxWorks at <http://www.lynuxworks.com/>.

---

same silicon. Much work remains to find useful MEMS sensors that can be economically realized on the same silicon as the electronics needed for control and communication.

SUMMARY

This chapter has provided a brief overview of the core technologies that EmNets will use, the trends that are driving these technologies, and the research areas that will accelerate the widespread implementation of EmNets. It has argued that silicon scaling, advances in computing hardware, software, and wireless communications, and new connections to the physical world such as geolocation and MEMS will be the technological building blocks of this new class of large-scale system.

Large systems will comprise thousands or even millions of sensing,

---

BOX 2.13
Ability to Work with New Hardware

Software needs hardware, and the nature of hardware is changing. For decades, the relationship between hardware and software has been well defined. Computer architectures, whether microprocessor or mainframe, have changed slowly, on a time scale of many years. Software has resided in random access memory (RAM) or read-only memory (ROM) and has been executed on an arithmetic logic unit (ALU) on the processor in the computer. New developments in the hardware world will challenge some of the assumptions about this relationship.

Multicore processors—multiple concurrent processing elements on a single chip—are becoming economical and common. They often include a single control processor and several simpler microengines specifically designed for a task such as networking or signal processing. Thus, a microprocessor is no longer a single computer but is becoming a heterogeneous multiprocessing system. Configurable processors, created with tools from companies such as ARC and Tensilica, make it very easy for a user to craft a custom microprocessor for a specific application. These tools can create real performance advantages for some applications. Programmable logic chips are growing larger, with millions of gates becoming available; they are also available in combination chips, which include a standard CPU core and a significant number of programmable gates. These make it possible to create multiple, concurrent processing elements and reconfigure continuously to optimize processing tasks.

All of these advances hold great promise for performance, cost, and power efficiency, but all create real challenges for software. Applications and operating systems must be able to perform well in reconfigurable, multiprocessing environments. New frameworks will be required to make efficient use of reconfigurable processing elements. Interestingly, all of these advances put compilers and programming languages back in the forefront of software development.[1]

---

[1]For examples of this kind of work, see the Oxygen Project at MIT, <http://oxygen.lcs.mit.edu/>, and the Ptolemy Project at Berkeley, <http://ptolemy.eecs.berkeley.edu/>.

computing, and actuating nodes. The basic trends are clear: These large, inexpensive, highly capable systems are becoming feasible because of the cumulative effects of silicon scaling—as ever-smaller silicon feature sizes become commercially available, more and more transistors can be applied to a task ever more cheaply, thus bringing increasingly capable applications within economic range. There are also some countervailing trends, in the form of constraints: Communication is costly, both on-chip and between chips; there are problems looming in the areas of power

BOX 2.14
Operating Systems and EmNets

A multiprocess system uses virtual memory to create separate memory spaces in which processes may reside, protected from each other. A multitasking operating system usually implies that all tasks live in the same memory map, which comes with its own host of security implications. Since many embedded systems have no virtual memory map capability, these simpler systems are prevalent for many applications. A multitask system can also run much faster, since the operating system does not need to switch memory maps; this comes at the cost of less protection between running tasks, however. Those switches can make determinacy difficult, since all planning must take place around worst-case scenarios entailing significant swapping of page tables. A further concern is preemption. Preemption occurs when the system stops one task and starts another. The operating system must perform some housekeeping, including saving the preempted task's state, restoring the new task's states, and so on. The time it takes to move from one task to another is called the preemptive latency and is a critical real-time performance metric.

Not all embedded operating systems are preemptive. Some are run-to-completion, which means that a task is never stopped by the operating system. This requires the tasks to cooperate, for instance by reaching a known stopping point and then determining whether other tasks need to run. Run-to-completion operating systems are very small, simple, and efficient, but because most of the scheduling and synchronization burden is pushed to the individual tasks, they are only applicable to very simple uses. Almost all embedded operating systems assign each task a priority, signifying its importance. In a preemptive system, the highest priority task that is ready is always running. These priorities may change for a number of reasons over time, either because a task changed a priority explicitly or because the operating system changes it implicitly in certain circumstances. The algorithms by which the operating system may change task priorities are critical to real-time performance, but they are beyond the scope of this study.

Preemptive real-time embedded operating systems vary significantly in performance according to the various decisions made—both overt (multitask vs. multiprocess, number of priorities, and so on.) and covert (structure of the internal task queue, efficiency of the operating system's code). Unfortunately, there are no standard benchmarks by which these systems are measured. Even commonly used metrics, such as preemptive latency, interrupt latency, or time to set a semaphore, can be very different because there is no universal agreement on precisely what those terms mean. When the application is added to the system, the resulting behavior is very complex and can be difficult to characterize. It may be very difficult to understand how settable parameters, such as task priority, are affecting system behavior. There are a number of methodologies, however, that can help with these problems.

Other considerations beyond real-time execution and memory management emerge in EmNets. Numerous efforts address the real-time executive aspects, but current real-time operating systems do not meet the needs of EmNets. Many such systems have followed the performance growth of the wallet-size device.

Traditional real-time embedded operating systems include VxWorks, WinCE, PalmOS, and many others. Table 2.1, taken from Hill et al. (2000), shows the characteristics for a handful of these systems. Many are based on microkernels that allow for capabilities to be added or removed based on system needs. They provide an execution environment that is similar to that of traditional desktop systems. They allow system programmers to reuse existing code and multiprogramming techniques. Some provide memory protection, as discussed above, given the appropriate hardware support. This becomes increasingly important as the size of the embedded applications grows. These systems are a popular choice for PDAs, cell phones, and television set-top boxes. However, they do not yet meet the requirements of EmNets; they are more suited to the world of embedded PCs, requiring a significant number of cycles for context switching and having a memory footprint on the order of hundreds of kilobytes.[1]

There is also a collection of smaller real-time systems, including Creem, pOSEK, and Ariel, which are minimal operating systems designed for deeply embedded systems, such as motor controllers or microwave ovens. While providing support for preemptive tasks, they have severely constrained execution and storage models. POSEK, for example, provides a task-based execution model that is statically configured to meet the requirements of a specific application. However, they tend to be control-centric—controlling access to hardware resources—as opposed to data-flow-centric. Berkeley's TinyOS[2] is focused on satisfying the needs of EmNets. Additional research and experimentation are needed to develop operating systems that fit the unique constraints of EmNets.

---

[1]Unfortunately, while there is a large amount of information on code size of embedded operating systems, very few hard performance numbers have been published.
[2]For more information, see <http://tinyos.millennium.berkeley.edu/>.

TABLE 2.1 Characteristics of Some Real-time Embedded Operating Systems

Name	Preemption	Protection	ROM Size	Configurability	Targets[a]
POSEK	Tasks	No	2K	Static	Microcontroller
PSOSystem	POSIX	Optional		Dynamic	PII → ARM Thumb
VxWorks	POSIX	Yes	~286K	Dynamic	Pentium II → Strong ARM
QNX Neutrino	POSIX	Yes	>100K	Dynamic	Pentium II → NEC chips
QNX Real-time	POSIX	Yes	100K	Dynamic	Pentium II → 386s
OS-9	Process	Yes		Dynamic	Pentium → SH4
Chorus OS	POSIX	Optional	10K	Dynamic	Pentium → Strong ARM
Ariel	Tasks	No	19K	Static	SH2, ARM Thumb
CREEM	Data flow	No	560 bytes	Static	ATMEL 8051

[a]The arrows in this column are used to indicate the range of capabilities of the targets.

dissipation, battery life, and design complexity; and many of the areas known to be problematic for today's systems are likely to be substantially more problematic with EmNets.

Networking solutions that work well enough for today's systems are based on many assumptions that are inappropriate for EmNets. For instance, the potentially huge number of nodes, the ad hoc system extensions expected, the extended longevity, and the heavy reliance on wireless communications between nodes will collectively invalidate some basic assumptions built into today's network solutions. Increased needs for system dependability will accompany the use of EmNets for real-time monitoring and actuating, but existing software creation and verification techniques will not easily or automatically apply. Other EmNet requirements, such as the need for software upgradability and fault tolerance,will also require great improvements in the state of the art.

Other technological enablers for EmNets will be MEMS and better power sources. MEMS devices show great promise for real-world sensing (temperature, pressure, chemicals, acoustical levels, light and radiation, etc.). They also may become important for real-world actuation.

EmNet nodes will be heterogeneous. Some will be as powerful as any server and will have more than sufficient power. But system nodes that are deployed into the real world will necessarily rely on very careful energy management for their power. Advances in power management will provide part of the solution; advances in the energy sources themselves will provide the other part. Improved batteries, better recharging techniques, fuel cells, microcombustion engines, and energy scavenging may all be important avenues.

Predicting the future of a field moving as rapidly as information technology is a very risky proposition. But within that field, certain trends are unmistakable: basic silicon scaling and the economics surrounding the semiconductor/microprocessor industry, power sources, and software. Some of these trends will seem almost inevitable, given the past 20 years of progress; others will require new work if they are not to impede the overall progress of this emerging technology.

REFERENCES

Borkar, S. 1999. "Design challenges of technology scaling." *IEEE Micro* 19(4):23-29.

Brodersen, R.W., A.P. Chandrakasan, and S. Cheng. 1992. "Lowpower CMOS digital design." *IEEE Journal of Solid-State Circuits* 27(4):473-484.

Chew, W.C. 1990. *Waves and Fields in Inhomogeneous Media*. New York, N.Y.: Van Nostrand Reinhold.

Clark, L., et al. 2001. "A scalable performance 32b microprocessor." *IEEE International Solid-State Circuits Conference Digest of Technical Papers*, February.

Computer Science and Technology Board (CSTB). 1997. *The Evolution of Untethered Communication*. Washington, D.C.: National Academy Press.

Feynman, Richard P. 1960. "There's plenty of room at the bottom: An invitation to enter a new field of physics." *Engineering and Science*. California Institute of Technology: American Physical Society, February.

Geppert, L., and T.S. Perry. 2000. "Transmeta's magic show." *IEEE Spectrum* 37(5).

Gonzalez, R., and M. Horowitz. 1996. "Energy dissipation in general purpose microprocessors." *IEEE Journal of Solid-State Circuits* (September):1277-1284.

Hill, J., et al. 2000. "System architecture directions for networked sensors." *Proceedings of the 9th International Conference on Architectural Support for Programming Languages and Operating Systems*, Cambridge, Mass., November 12-15.

Lee, Edward A. 2000. "What's ahead for embedded software?" *IEEE Computer* (September):18-26.

McCrady, D.D., L. Doyle, H. Forstrom, T. Dempsey, and M. Martorana. 2000. "Mobile ranging using low-accuracy clocks," *IEEE Transactions on MTT* 48(6).

Parsons, David. 1992. *The Mobile Radio Propagation Channel*. New York: John Wiley & Sons.

Rappaport, T.S. 1996. *Wireless Communications: Principles and Practice*, Englewood Cliffs, N.J.: Prentice Hall.

Semiconductor Industry Association (SIA). 1999. *Semi-Annual Report*. San Jose, Calif.: SIA.

Sohrabi, K., J. Gao, V. Ailawadhi, and G. Pottie. 1999a. "Self-organizing sensor network." *Proceedings of the 37th Allerton Conference on Communications, Control, and Computing*, Monticello, Ill., September.

Sohrabi, K., B. Manriquez, and G. Pottie. 1999b. "Near-ground wideband channel measurements." *Proceedings of the 49th Vehicular Technology Conference*. New York: IEEE, pp. 571-574.

Sommerfeld, A. 1949. *Partial Differential Equations in Physics*, New York: Academic Press.

Trimmer, William. 1997. *Micromechanics and Mems*. New York: IEEE Press.

Van Trees, H. 1968. *Detection, Estimation and Modulation Theory*. New York: John Wiley & Sons.

Wait, J.R. 1998. "The ancient and modern history of EM ground-wave propagation," *IEEE Antennas and Propagation Magazine* 40(5):7-24.

BIBLIOGRAPHY

Agre, J.R., L.P. Clare, G.J. Pottie, and N.P. Romanov. 1999. "Development platform for self organizing wireless sensor networks." Presented at Aerosense'99, Orlando, Fla.

Asada, G., M. Dong, T.S. Lin, F. Newberg, G. Pottie, H.O. Marcy, and W.J. Kaiser. 1998. "Wireless integrated network sensors: Low power systems on a chip." *Proceedings of the 24th IEEE European Solid-State Circuits Conference*.

Bult, K., A. Burstein, D. Chang, M. Dong, M. Fielding, E. Kruglick, J. Ho, F. Lin, T.-H. Lin, W.J. Kaiser, H. Marcy, R. Mukai, P. Nelson, F. Newberg, K.S.J. Pister, G. Pottie, H. Sanchez, O.M. Stafsudd, K.B. Tan, C.M. Ward, S. Xue, and J. Yao. 1996. "Low power systems for wireless microsensors." *Proceedings of the 1996 International Symposium on Low Power Electronics and Design*, pp. 17-21.

Chatterjee, P.K., and R.R. Doering. 1998. "The future of microelectronics." *Proceedings of the IEEE* 86(1):176-183.

Dong, M.J., G. Yung, and W.J. Kaiser. 1997. "Low power signal processing architectures for network microsensors." *Proceedings of the 1997 International Symposium on Low Power Electronics and Design*, pp. 173-177.

Jones, Mike. 1997. "What really happened on Mars?" *The Risks Digest: Forum on Risks to the Public in Computer and Related Systems* 19(49), Available online at <http://catless.ncl.ac.uk/Risks/19.49.html#subj1> .

Lin, T.H., H. Sanchez, R. Rofougaran, and W.J. Kaiser. 1998. "CMOS front end components for micropower RF wireless systems." *Proceedings of the 1998 International Symposium on Low Power Electronics and Design.*

Merrill, W.M. 2000. "Coax transition to annular ring for reduced input impedance at 2.4 GHz and 5.8 GHz." *Proceedings of the 2000 IEEE Antennas and Propagation Society International Symp*osium, Salt Lake City, Utah, July 16-21.

Merrill, W.M. 2000. "Short range communication near the earth at 2.4 GHz." *Proceedings of the 2000 USNC/URSI National Radio Science Meeting*, Salt Lake City, Utah, July 16-21.

Pottie, G.J. 1999. "Wireless multiple access adaptive communication techniques." In *Encyclopedia of Telecommunications*, Vol. 18. F. Froelich and A. Kent, eds. New York: Marcel Dekker Inc.

Proakis, J.G. 1995. *Digital Communications,* 3rd ed. Boston, Mass: WCB/McGraw-Hill, pp. 855-858.

Reed, J.H., K.J. Krizman, B.D. Woerner, and T.S. Rappaport. 1998. "An overview of the challenges and progress in meeting the E-911 requirement for location service," *IEEE Communications Magazine* (April): 30-37.

Reeves, Glenn. "Re: What really happened on Mars?" *The Risks Digest: Forum on Risks to the Public in Computer and Related Systems* 19(49). Available online at <http://catless.ncl.ac.uk/Risks/19.54.html#subj6>.

Yao, K., R.E. Hudson, C.W. Reed, D. Chen, F. Lorenzelli. 1998. "Blind beamforming on a randomly distributed sensor array system." *IEEE Journal of Selected Areas in Communications* 16(8):1555-1567.

Yu, T., D. Chen, G.J. Pottie, and K. Yao. 1999. "Blind decorrelation and deconvolution algorithm for multiple-input, multiple-output systems," *Proceedings of the SPIE*, 3807.

3

Self-configuration and Adaptive Coordination

M any of the anticipated applications of networked systems of embedded computers (EmNets) will be realized only if the systems are capable of configuring and reconfiguring themselves automatically. This chapter focuses on mechanisms needed to achieve automatic reconfiguration. In many EmNets, individual nodes will need to assemble themselves into a networked system, find available resources on the network, and respond to changes in their desired functionality and in the operating environment with little human intervention or guidance.[1]

A set of basic underlying mechanisms will be required to ensure that EmNets are self-configuring and adaptive. For example, components will need to be able to discover other resources on the network and communicate with them. Systems will need to be able to sense changing environmental conditions or changing system capabilities and respond appropriately so that the entire system, as well as individual components, can operate as effectively and efficiently as possible. Both software and hardware adaptability will be important; EmNets will consist not only of elements that can change their software but also of those that take advantage of reconfigurable computing technologies to adapt limited hardware to

---

[1]This requirement is central to DARPA's self-healing minefield program, for example. For more information on this program, see <http://www.darpa.mil/ato/programs/apla/contractors.html>.

the operating environment. Many EmNets will contain components that are constrained in terms of their physical size, amount of memory available, and/or availability of local energy sources. For these system components, both the need for efficiency and the constraints on how it is achieved will be more severe than is the case for more traditional distributed computing systems. Efficient system designs will exploit higher-capacity and resource-rich components where they exist in the overall system and will exploit the redundancy provided by deploying large numbers of inexpensive components. Many current efforts do not focus on systems that operate under these kinds of constraints. Work on the design of personal digital assistants (PDAs) and cell phones, for example, does not need to take into account very large numbers of interacting elements, distributed control, severe energy constraints, or the kinds of physical coupling that many EmNets must accommodate. Approaches taken in the design of smart spaces for homes or office environments are relevant, but such systems generally have more infrastructure to support them than many of the EmNets discussed here.

This chapter examines approaches to providing the mechanisms needed to support self-configuration and adaptive coordination of EmNets. The first section defines these key concepts. The second discusses the elements of self-configuration and adaptive coordination in existing distributed systems, serving as a primer on the state of the art. The final section of this chapter outlines the research needed to realize the vision for robust, scalable EmNets.

TERMINOLOGY

Self-configuration (sometimes referred to as reconfiguration) and *adaptive coordination* (sometimes referred to as adaptation) refer to the spectrum of changes that a system makes to itself in response to occurrences in its environment and internally. Neither of these terms is meant to convey infinite flexibility. The changes that self-configuration and adaptive coordination induce in a system should always be within the constraints of the system's planned functionality (admittedly, one such change might be to modify the functionality of the system). For the purposes of this report, the terms self-configuration and adaptive coordination differ with respect to the frequency and degree of change they induce in or respond to from the EmNet. Making a sharp distinction between the two is not as important as recognizing that some techniques are more relevant to one than to the other. In the rest of this chapter the terms are distinguished in order to highlight the techniques that are more appropriate for each.

Self-configuration involves the addition, removal, or modification of elements contained in an EmNet, along with the resulting process of establishing interoperability among the components and locating essential services (such as data aggregation nodes in sensor networks). Put another way, self-configuration is the process of interconnecting available elements into an ensemble that will perform the required functions at the desired performance level. As such, self-configuration changes the composition of an EmNet and may alter the distribution of functionality across the components that make up the system or may even alter the system's overall function based on which components are available.

Adaptive coordination involves changes in the behavior of a system as it responds to changes in the environment or system resources. For example, to achieve a long lifetime, a system may need mechanisms by which nodes can mediate their actions based on the density of redundant components. Nodes with redundant capabilities might be programmed to alternate responsibility for a given task in the style of sentry duty rotation. Similarly, EmNets could implement multiple levels of service, depending on locally perceived conditions or detected events. Thus, adaptive coordination refers to changes in operational parameters that are made because of variations in available resources or load. Included in these resources are available energy, computational resources, and communication bandwidth. In general, adaptive coordination induces less dramatic changes in system architecture than does self-configuration and does not alter the system's function. The two processes often occur on different time scales. Adaptive coordination tends to take place more quickly than does self-configuration, with a very short lag time between the moment a change is detected in the operating environment and the time the system adapts its behavior.

Another dimension to bear in mind is the level at which the configuration or adaptive coordination occurs. This level can range from reconfigurable hardware to operating systems and run-time environments all the way to application-specific code. Levels vary in the extent of the effect of the reconfiguration and/or adaptive coordination as well as in the amount of code that needs to be stored or retrieved to make the change. A crucial facility that must accompany EmNets' ability to adaptively reconfigure themselves is the facility for self-monitoring. Despite some of the most rigorous testing in existence, many of today's highly complex systems are prone to failure when reconfigured. Telephone switching systems, for example, have suffered severe outages when new software is brought online. Yet this report suggests that EmNets must be able to change along many distinct axes, perhaps without an expert present. New system testing and software update technology will have to be developed. Meeting this challenge has proven to be very difficult, even in more conventional systems; EmNets intensify this need. They will have to be able to convey their current operational state to their users. As argued elsewhere in this study, establishing that state requires far more than just tallying hardware resources. An EmNet will require a way to monitor how well it is performing and to compare this result against its goals; it will also require a means for reporting such information to users.[2]

The nature of the configuration or adaptive coordination depends heavily on the type of application the EmNet supports. In automobiles, for example, the focus of self-configuration would probably be on accommodating the heterogeneity of system components introduced to, and removed from, the system continuously as, for example, the people, conditions, equipment, and procedures vary. Unlike more standard computer networks, such embedded monitoring networks must be built assuming that there is no professional system administration, such that the configuration is highly (if not completely) automatic. Further complicating such networks are two typical requirements (as, for example, would be needed for automobile control): that the overall network be capable of making certain service guarantees and that some operations (such as notifications of life- or safety-threatening events) take precedence over other forms of network traffic.

In sensor networks that might be used for precision agriculture or environmental monitoring, system composition will vary less because the application is more constrained, while more attention must be paid to adapting the nodes' operational parameters to unpredictable and varying environmental conditions. This is particularly challenging and critical in energy-constrained devices that must minimize their expenditure of communications resources on overhead functions and in which opportunistic listening can be relatively expensive because of the dependence on power-consuming communication resources (for example, a radio or other wireless communications device). Extensive capabilities that incorporate both adaptive coordination and reconfiguration will be required in systems such as those used on a battlefield, where changes in both the environment and system makeup can occur rapidly yet certain service guarantees are absolutely required.

SELF-CONFIGURATION AND ADAPTIVE COORDINATION IN DISTRIBUTED SYSTEMS

This section discusses the elements of self-configuration and adaptive coordination in existing distributed systems. These elements include the

---

[2]A long-term trend of diminishing margins against the goal could alert the users to the system's need for attention, for example.

notion of service discovery, as well as the critical issues of interfaces and interoperability. The discussion is primarily applicable to self-configuration; however, it is likely that adaptive coordination will require similar elements (e.g., mobile code). This background is useful in preparing to analyze the issues posed by EmNets. How EmNets differ from other types of distributed systems will become clearer as the analysis proceeds; later in this chapter, research challenges in these areas are examined. In general, EmNets present more extreme versions of the problems encountered in distributed systems, but they also pose a few unique problems of their own, such as low power requirements.

Discovery in Distributed Systems

Automatic self-configuration requires the ability to interoperate with new and old system components without human intervention. System components must be able to automatically discover each other and the services they represent. Building on the interface concepts of network configuration, wire protocols, and code mobility, this subsection discusses the issues involved in device and service discovery and how they relate to self-configuration. How entities on an existing network communicate is generally viewed as the interoperability problem. How those entities find each other, advertise their own services, or join the network is generally taken to be a separate problem, referred to as the discovery problem. Generally, the discovery problem can be divided into four parts:

• How does a network entity join the physical network; that is, how is it authorized and given a network address and a network identity?
• Once an entity is on the network and wishes to provide a service to other entities on the network, how does it indicate that willingness?
• If an entity is looking for a service on the network, how does it go about finding that service?
• How does geographic location affect the services an entity can discover or select for use?

Joining the Network

In traditional computing networks, the task of joining a system to a network has been done by hand: A system administrator configures the system with a particular network identity and then updates the appropriate routing and/or naming tables with the information needed to find the new member of the network. As networks have been scaled up, techniques have been introduced that allow the partitioning of the large network into smaller subnets and the propagation of (manually entered) bootstrapping information from the subnets to the larger networks. However, the advent of larger networks and networks that have little or no professional administration (such as those in the home or in networks of embedded systems) has led to an interest in automating this bootstrapping mechanism.

Mechanisms that automate the joining to a network have been around for some time. The Apollo Domain system, for example, allowed a node (workstation or server) to be connected to the network by finding a location broker with which the new node registered. Then, having completed this registration, the new node could be found by any other node in the network. The Appletalk protocol enabled not only computers but also peripheral devices, such as printers, to join the network and be found automatically by other entities in the network. However, these mechanisms have been confined to particular (proprietary) networks and have not been generally adopted, especially in networks of smaller, embedded systems. One reason is that such mechanisms are based on resource-rich environments as opposed to the resource- and energy-constrained environments that many embedded systems and most EmNets must contend with.

The actual mechanism most generally used for such bootstrapping tends to be conditioned (if not fully determined) by the physical network to which the device is attached. In an Ethernet Transmission Control Protocol (TCP)/Internet Protocol (IP) environment, for example, the Dynamic Host Configuration Protocol (DHCP) is commonly used to hand out addresses to entities that are connected to the network. A part of the Universal Plug and Play (UP&P) specification is a mechanism allowing devices to self-assign a network address to themselves on networks where DHCP is not present. For IEEE 1394 (otherwise known as Firewire), however, a very different mechanism is needed because the network itself will produce the equivalent of a bus interrupt when a new device is plugged in, thus informing every other device of the presence of a new entity. Networks designed for cell phone use have yet another way of allowing the phone to be recognized in the cell. The roaming function allows a phone to register its new location with a central database that then tells the phone's home location how to reroute calls. The range of services achievable by automatic discovery and joining mechanisms is in part determined by whether nodes have unique identifiers or whether at boot time they are literally identical.

Joining the network entails locating essential services as well as obtaining network-level address and routing information. Existing mechanisms make use of multicast[3] and well-known service-location addresses to bootstrap this process.

---

[3]Multicast describes communication on a network between a single sender and multiple targeted receivers.

Advertising and Finding Services

The problem of advertising a service once a physical connection to the network has been established has been approached in a number of different ways. Perhaps the most common approach in general computing systems has been naming and directory services, in which the service that wishes to advertise itself creates an entry in a naming service or a directory service that allows others who know the name or description of the service (or at least the type of service) to get a reference to the new offering. Such mechanisms generally assume that there is a human being somewhere in the loop, because both naming systems and directory servers are string based, with the meaning of the string left to the user. When programs look for services, they need to know the name or description under which the service is registered. Some directory services have evolved rather complex ontologies in the form of description schemas to allow such programmatic access to services.

A different approach has been taken by service traders and the Jini system (Arnold and Waldo, 2000), in which services are identified by the interfaces they support. In a traditional trader system (such as those found in the Distributed Computing Environment (DCE)[4] or the Common Object Request Broker Architecture (CORBA)[5] trading service), a service registers itself by indicating what interfaces it supports; clients look up a service by asking for a reference to something that supports a particular interface. If more than one object has been registered that implements a given interface, then any of the objects can be returned by such a query. In the Jini lookup service, services register by their Java language type; they can be returned to any client asking for something that is at least an instance of the requested class (for example, the returned object might be a subclass of the requested class).

The problem of how an entity finds the place to advertise its services is not always addressed by the systems described above; most naming or directory systems consider this problem to be part of the general bootstrapping mechanism and assume that it is dealt with in some fashion outside their scope. The Service Location Protocol (SLP) is a mechanism that enables either clients or services to find a service directory. Essentially, the entity interested in finding a service directory (either to register a service or find one that has been registered) issues a multicast request

---

[4]DCE is an industry-standard software technology for setting up and managing computing and data exchange in a system of distributed computers.

[5]CORBA is an architecture and specification for creating, distributing, and managing distributed program objects in a network.

that will return the address of a service-finding service. This service supports a well-known interface that allows querying for a service directory, which is much like a standard directory service in which services can be registered under a description or found if they match a description.

The Jini system is similar to SLP in that it begins (on TCP/IP networks) with a multicast request to the local network neighborhood. Rather than returning a directory of service locators, however, the Jini multicast request returns a reference that implements the interface to a Jini lookup service (including the stub code, or driver, allowing communication with the service) that can be used by the service provider (or client) to access that lookup service directly. Universal Plug and Play (UP&P) also makes use of a multicast request, but in UP&P what is multicast is a description (in the form of a Universal Resource Locator (URL) indicating where the description can be found) of the device that is joining the network. All entities that might want to use such a device must watch for such a multicast, and based on the description they will determine if they have the code needed to communicate with that device. There is no central repository of services in the UP&P mechanism. Bluetooth's service discovery protocol (SDP) is specifically for Bluetooth communications and focuses on discovering services available from or through Bluetooth devices and can coexist with other service discovery protocols.

Not all basic networking systems support multicast, so any extension of these types of service-finding protocols to such networks would require that some other bootstrapping mechanism be used to find the initial repository of descriptions or objects. This mechanism could be as simple as a conventionally agreed-upon URL that would be used to identify such a repository or a well-known name of some other form. Such approaches would need to find a way of preventing the entity with the conventional name from becoming a single point of failure (or they would need to determine that such a single point of failure was acceptable in the particular application). Other networks might allow entirely different approaches. An example of this is IEEE 1394 (Firewire), in which, as mentioned previously, attaching a device to the network generates a wire-level interrupt to all other devices attached to the network. On such a network, the service repository could simply notice when a new device was attached to the wire and send to that device the information needed to connect to the service repository.

Location

For systems deployed in the physical infrastructure, a service's location (either absolute or relative to another entity) may determine how it is used or even selected. The mapping between physical location and network connectivity is important. (See Chapter 2 for a discussion of the technologies that enable the determination of geographic location.) In wired or hybrid networks, two devices that are physically close may be, in fact, quite distant in terms of network communication. For example, a desktop personal computer (PC) and a cell phone may both be network-enabled, but for them to communicate, packets must travel through many network segments, including the building's network, the link between the building and local backbone, the connection between the backbone and the cellular phone company, another hop to the appropriate base station, and finally, from the base station to the phone itself. Thus, when a device needs to determine, for example, the closest printer, network proximity is not at all likely to be an accurate measure.

Geographic location is intimately connected to discovery. If each device knows its own geolocation and can provide that information to the discovery servers, then it may be possible to answer the question about "closeness" during the discovery phase. Access to services may also be based on location. If one assumes physical security measures permit a user to enter a particular space, then services locally available in that space can be put at that user's disposal without requiring further authentication. Without location information, users would have to obtain access to the local networks, with accompanying security risks. Thus, location can be quite useful in optimizing service discovery as well as in connecting the physical and virtual worlds so that security measures in one can be applied in the other.

In other types of EmNets, particularly resource-constrained, wireless networks, network organization needs to correspond more closely with geography in order to be efficient in its use of scarce energy resources (since communication over longer distances consumes significantly more energy). In these systems, geolocation may serve as a building block for organization of the network itself—for example, through the use of geographic routing (Karp and Kung, 2000).

Interfaces and Interoperability

Both self-configuration and adaptive coordination require *interfaces*, or standardized ways of communicating between components. An interface is simply a convention that is agreed to outside the scope of the communication of interest but that permits the communication to occur. These interoperability agreements can exist at every level of system abstraction, including electrical, signaling, transport, network, and application levels. Moreover, these agreements extend to code mobility and application adaptation. When EmNets communicate, they must assemble a collection of information that will be interpretable by the receiver. This information may include not only data but also code that the receiver can execute to interpret the data, process it in some way, or forward it to other entities. The format of the information must comply with the interface on which both entities agree in advance.

At the lowest level, interoperability requires the assembling of information (data and code) into a sequence of bits that will be properly interpreted by receivers on the network. At higher levels, this means supporting an abstract machine for which the sender can include instructions within the information it sends. If there is agreement with the receiver on the execution semantics of these instructions, this serves as a powerful model for extending the functions that each device is capable of performing. That is, it becomes possible to move code from one entity to another so that functionality can be modified and extended in ways not predicted by those who originally deployed the device. Other levels of interoperability include transport protocols (e.g., TCP/IP) that permit a sequence of network packets to be generated and reassembled at the other end, as well as remote procedure calls (RPC) and remote method invocations (RMI) that permit one entity to execute an operation on another by sending parameter data and having the result returned.

How interoperability is to be achieved is often one of the major design decisions that needs to be made for networked systems.[6] In traditional distributed systems, methods such as DCE, RPC, and CORBA are implemented to pass a method or procedure identifier to the receiver to indicate the code that is to be invoked on the data by the receiver. Parameters are linearized and included in the RPC packet. More specialized systems can make either or both of these classes of information (procedure identifier and input parameter data) implicit. In a simple system in which data are sent from embedded sensors to a central processing node, only the data need be transmitted, because the operation to be performed on the data is known by the receiving node. In some publish/subscribe systems, even the data that triggered the notification of an event need not be explicitly passed, because the notification itself is enough to indicate the data that triggered the notification. In a more complex, ad hoc sensor

---

[6]This discussion describes interoperability from the perspective of systems that use a call-return or remote-procedure-call model of communication. Networks can also be set up to communicate through message passing by using events in a publish/subscribe fashion or by using various forms of shared memory with adaptive coordination technologies. At some level, however, all of these communication approaches are equivalent with respect to the problems discussed. Although the exact details of the problems may vary from one approach to another, the basic outlines of the problems and the solutions are similar in all of these approaches.

network, intermediate nodes between the originator and its final destination may aggregate the data. Thus, the interpretation of the data may change as it travels from node to node. Each node may want to indicate to the next how to properly interpret and process each data item.

The remainder of this section discusses address configuration, wire protocols, and code mobility as illustrative examples of key interface and interoperability concepts.

Address Configuration

One of the most familiar types of self-configuration is the process by which new devices are added to local area networks. The Dynamic Host Configuration Protocol (DHCP) performs this function on IP networks. A device new to the network must obtain a new IP address in order to have packets routed to it appropriately. A DHCP server for a network allocates a set of IP addresses to acceptable visitors for a limited period of time. DHCP servers do not have to be present on every subnetwork but must be reachable through the standard routing mechanisms. A device finds a DHCP server using a discovery message that is propagated by the network routers to a nearby DHCP server. The server then responds with the IP address for the device to use. This address may be dynamically allocated or determined based on the physical address of the device's network interface card (providing a mechanism for mobile devices to store and later retrieve their network parameters). Devices can easily determine if they need to obtain an address using DHCP if their request packets are not acknowledged. This is an indication that the IP address being used is no longer compatible with the network at which the device is now located.

The DHCP packet format provides a standard interface for devices to use in connecting in a new network environment, thus ensuring interoperability at the level of IP packets. The servers' functions provide a higher-level interface that provides addresses only to authorized visitors and only for limited periods of time.

Wire Protocols

The most common way of ensuring interoperability is to define a standard protocol that all entities on the network will use to identify operations and convert to and from their own internal data representations to the data representation used on the wire. Each entity on the network contains some code that performs this conversion. In a standard RPC system, the code used by a client for this purpose is called the stub code and the corresponding code on the server side is called the skeleton code. This code is often produced by a compiler, which uses as input a description of the interface offered by the server, although handwritten or manually specialized code is often used to improve the performance of the overall system.

This approach to interoperability has a number of advantages. It makes very few assumptions about the devices that make up the network, requiring only that they have the computational power to create the stream of bits and transmit them over the wire (if the entities are sending information) or to recreate information from a stream of bits received from the wire (if the entities are receiving information). Much of the code needed to create the wire stream or recreate the data from the wire stream can be generated automatically from fairly high-level descriptions, allowing a higher level of abstraction to be presented to the human programmer.

There are disadvantages to this approach as well. Because such systems are defined by the wire protocol, the patterns of communication between the various entities are very difficult to change. Such a change essentially requires a revision of the wire protocol, which in turn requires the eventual updating of all of the communicating entities on the network. Such changes are generally needed because of changing hardware or changing requirements, which can be thought of as a scaling of the network over time. The longer the network is expected to run, the more likely it is that changes will be needed to accommodate new hardware (or new software services offered to existing hardware) or that the tasks expected of the network of devices will change or evolve (or, perhaps, a flaw in the original design will need to be fixed). Sometimes these changes can be made using the existing protocols; however, because those protocols define the information sent from one entity to another, it is often necessary to enhance the protocol before such changes can be made.

Mobile Code

Mobile code, or the capability to dynamically deliver and load new code to be installed on network nodes, provides a mechanism for extending the lifetime of a system. The idea is to create a higher level of abstraction, an interface agreement for communicating information that is more complex semantically. By elevating the level at which the common interface is defined, mobile code enables the protocols used by system nodes to be updated over time or modified for specialization or optimization purposes. Mobile code still requires an initial interface agreement regarding how the code will be transmitted and loaded, but given this foundation and a constant physical layer for communication, it provides a graceful upgrade mechanism for network nodes.

Running Mobile Code   In current client-server systems, what is known by each of the communicating entities is the (programmatic) interface used by the client to talk to the service. When the client wishes to use this interface, the client receives from the service a reference, which includes the stub code needed to talk to the service. This code is loaded into the client and presents to the client the programmatic interface that is expected for that service. Because the actual form of the bits on the wire is encapsulated in stub code that comes from the service itself, the wire protocol becomes a private matter between the service and the code it hands out. The client can be, in some sense, far more ignorant; rather than needing code that knows how to translate into a common wire protocol, the client needs only the knowledge of which call method to use. The details of how information is encapsulated into a stream of bits are known only to the code supplied by the service.

The disadvantage of this approach is that it requires considerably more from the entities participating in the network. In particular, it requires that all of the entities be able to load code dynamically and that there be a form of code that all of the participants can understand. For this to be possible there needs to be some platform-level homogeneity in the network that allows code moved from one machine to another to run on the receiving machine. There is a spectrum of approaches to providing this common level. One approach (used in some active networks research[7]) is to construct the network out of devices that are homogeneous at the lowest level, meaning they use the same processor and operating system. Among the advantages of this approach, optimized binary code can be moved and run on another machine, and resource use on the various devices can be controlled. However, the approach limits the flexibility of the overall network, making it difficult to introduce new types of nodes; it also presents problems in scaling over time, because the network of devices will not be able to make use of new processor or binary code environments. It is thus highly impractical. It also requires a large amount of trust in the code being moved, as there are no restrictions on what that code can do and no ways of establishing that the code is either well meaning or well written.

At the other end of the spectrum is an approach that uses a high-level scripting language, such as TCL or Python, as the homogeneity layer.

---

[7]According to a DARPA-funded program at the Massachusetts Institute of Technology, active networks "allow individual users, or groups of users, to inject customized programs into the nodes of the network [and] enable a massive increase in the complexity and customization of the computation that is performed within the network." See <http://www.sds.lcs.mit.edu/darpa-activenet/> for more information.

This approach requires that every member of the network have both the interpreter for the common language and the necessary native libraries available so that the portable scripts can be run. It provides a good layer of insulation from the hardware but requires a fairly large execution environment and set of libraries; it pays the price in performance (most of the scripting languages are between one and two orders of magnitude slower than object code performing the same functions) and, correspondingly, in power consumption. However, this approach is safer than moving binary code, because the scripting language can incorporate limits on what the code can do (as achieved in "safe TCL").

A middle ground between these two divergent approaches is to define a virtual machine and move code that assumes the existence of that machine; this is the method used in systems (such as Jini) built on Java. This approach allows a more compact representation of the mobile code than can be found in most scripting languages, because byte codes are moved rather than text. The environment is far safer than those in which pure binary code is moved, because the virtual machine can make checks on the incoming code and enforce security policies. A rather large environment is still required, but it is often no larger than that required by the scripting approach, and work is being done to make it smaller. The performance degradation is smaller than that found in the scripting approach, although still in the range of 10 to 20 percent.

Resources Newly introduced code may require more resources than does the code already extant at a node. These resources may or may not be available at that node or may be beyond a limit set for the function the mobile code performs. Therefore, negotiation and resource allocation are clearly important aspects of this mechanism. A device seeking to introduce code into another device may first have to negotiate for the necessary resources and must expect to propagate the code only if it is granted those resources. The negotiation will include presenting the appropriate access privileges for modifying the code to be run on another node.

Advantages of Mobile Code Mobile code has many advantages over wire protocols. First, the way services represent information on the wire can be updated without the need to coordinate updates with all clients and services simultaneously. Because the stub code used by the client is obtained, when needed, from the service itself, the service can change the communication protocol used between the client and the service by simply updating the code handed out. The client will receive the new code automatically on an as-needed basis when it next wants to contact the service. Second, this approach allows different implementations of the same service to use different communication protocols. Because the communication protocol is used between the service-supplied stub and the service, the protocol can differ among services, even if those services are implementations of the same interface.

Third, if the method of code movement is combined with a polymorphic language and virtual machine such as Java or Inferno, then the service can evolve in an upwardly compatible fashion to offer new functionality without being incompatible with old clients. If the new functionality can be expressed as an extension or subtype of the existing functionality, then the code handed out by the service to the client can implement all of the existing procedures or methods as well as the new procedures or methods. This design enables old clients to treat the service just as they always did, while allowing new clients (or clients that can reflectively discover and use the new functionality) to use the new aspects of the service. This advantage can be obtained, however, only by requiring a universal type system in addition to code mobility.

Adaptive Coordination in Existing Networks

Making any network of systems adaptive is a challenge, and EmNets increase the challenge by adding constraints not found in other systems. Moreover, the type of adaptive coordination needed in EmNets has only recently begun to be studied in more traditional networks of computing systems, so there is little existing knowledge on which to draw. As background for an analysis of research needs related to EmNets, this section provides examples of how adaptive coordination is handled in more traditional systems. The problems addressed are load balancing, ad hoc routing, and TCP's adaptive congestion control mechanism.

Load Balancing

Load balancing in distributed systems received much research attention in the 1980s as distributed computing became more prevalent. The essential problem is how to distribute processing, storage, or access demand across a set of servers as that demand increases and in some cases as the availability of underlying resources (e.g., servers) increases or decreases (Mullender, 1992). Typical load balancing requires collecting load statistics from servers and assigning new demand based on those statistics. Some approximations may be used in the absence of current load data. Systems may reassign demands based on data or reassign only if there is a failure. Techniques vary with regard to optimization level, robustness, communication cost, and convergence time. The more distributed the system, and the greater the delay and delay variance, the more difficult it is to collect timely statistics and achieve a solution that is both efficient and stable.

Load balancing in networks, usually in the form of adaptive routing, addresses one extreme situation at a time in a highly distributed system. The problem is most challenging when the network is large and covers a wide area, in which case global load information for all network nodes and links is clearly unachievable. Therefore, adaptive routing relies on partial information, which may be partial in scope, coverage, or time (that is, out of date). A classic story of early ARPANET design was the move away from highly adaptive distributed routing to a more stable and slower adaptive routing scheme. The old ARPANET routing scheme (Mcquillan et al., 1980) attempted to move traffic away from congested links, but by doing so it encouraged the congestion to move to the new path in the network, eventually causing all the traffic to move back to the original path! These oscillations are a simple example of the challenges associated with building adaptive systems. Load balancing is applied successfully when the information required can be obtained in a timely fashion and when the rate of controlled change is much slower than the phenomena to which it responds. Within ISP networks (which are really subsets of the larger Internet), such techniques are applied in the form of "traffic engineering." However, even in this more limited context, there is a lot of manual configuration involved.

More recently, very-large-scale distributed services have been proliferating in the context of the World Wide Web. There are Web servers that can be expanded on the fly, by adding more computing capacity without shutting down the existing Web server and then using the added capacity when traffic is heavy.[8] These systems adapt to heavy load by allowing the addition of new machines to the Web server cluster in a way that is transparent to system users. This approach can be viewed as human-assisted configuration of the system; once the administrator adds the system to the physical cluster, the software is able to automatically reconfigure itself to make use of the extra capacity.

Ad Hoc Routing

In recent years, other forms of adaptive behavior have been explored in networked systems. One is ad hoc routing (Corson and Macker, 1997). Traditional routing starts with a fixed location for nodes and links and adapts only to occasional node and link failures and recoveries and to

---

[8]See, for example, the Hosta system from Concept Technologies, Ltd., available at <www.concept-technologies.com>.

variable congestion. Ad hoc routing was developed to provide auto-matic, nonmanual construction of a network when the network routing elements are not in a fixed topology, that is, when they are mobile. Ad hoc routing protocols continually adapt to changing topology, whereas traditional protocols adapt to topology changes much more slowly and less frequently. The form of adaptive coordination required in ad hoc routing is fairly well understood and seemingly manageable, although there are few examples of operational ad hoc networks. There are clearly limits to the ability of any scheme to keep up with continual rapid change, and there is ongoing work to develop methodologies for characterizing such limits, as well as the behavior of adaptive coordination mechanisms as they approach these limits. Related to the work in ad hoc routing is power-aware routing (Sohrabi and Pottie, 1999), which attempts to adapt routes in such a way as to maximize the total network lifetime as deter-mined by battery depletion. This work is indicative of the type of adap-tive algorithms that will be needed to realize the vision of robust, long-lived, and scalable EmNets.

Adaptive Congestion Control in TCP

Another form of adaptive behavior has a completely distributed, lo-cal nature—TCP's adaptive congestion control mechanism. TCP is the transport protocol run in the Internet over the IP protocol. TCP is an end-to-end protocol run on end-system computers (from laptops to desktop PCs to workstations to large servers). TCP provides a virtual connection to the applications that use it, offering in-order, reliable delivery of data. The Internet over which the data are sent exhibits varying data rates due to the heterogeneity of underlying link speeds and variable loading on the links. Van Jacobson introduced adaptive congestion control into TCP (Jacobson, 1988) by which the source of a data stream would reduce its sending rate when it experienced packet loss, an indicator of congestion. When no loss was experienced, the sending rate was slowly increased until all data were sent or additional loss was experienced. In this way, each of the multitude of end systems on the Internet independently adapts its behavior to the dynamic conditions experienced on the network, re-sulting in a more or less stable system—certainly more stable than it was before adaptive congestion control was introduced. The specifics of the TCP congestion control algorithm have evolved over the years, and a sizable body of research has emerged concerned with the characterization of TCP and the aggregate effect of TCP adaptation on the network (Fall and Floyd, 1996). However, this remains an area of active research be-cause of the challenge associated with characterizing such a large system of adaptive elements.

RESEARCH CHALLENGES FOR CONFIGURATION AND ADAPTIVE COORDINATION

This section outlines key research challenges related to configuration and adaptation in EmNets. The subsection on adaptive coordination is the most extensive because the concept is fairly new, especially as it applies to EmNets, and there is still no extensive research base on which to rely.

Research Issues in Self-configuration

As background, it is useful to outline some design basics and criteria. EmNets will appear in hybrid environments of mobile and static networks. Users will expect to connect to networks and services as they enter vehicles, buildings, and outdoor environments. The nodes themselves will be diverse in capability, energy availability, nature and quality of connectivity, and priority. Physical node access will depend on context. Variability in priority will dictate when and if a node is revealed or has services revealed to it at the physical layer. Variability in the node population will introduce further complexity. The addition of new nodes to a local cluster may not be permitted owing to performance constraints. At other times, conversely, it may be desirable or even necessary to incorporate high-priority nodes and their services into the network.

The wireless physical layer is limited by low data communications rates, the sharp decay of radiated power with increasing range, and susceptibility to interference. This implies that network resources may not be consistently available at a given point in the network and may exhibit highly variable performance across space and time. Nodes may appear and disappear according to variations in the wireless channel environment. The wireless physical layer is also diverse. Simultaneously present in the environment are systems ranging from local-area, spread-spectrum networks to wide-area cellular, pager, and even satellite communication systems. Methods are needed for joining these different networks and bridging across adjoining cells. Support for networked embedded systems must include capabilities for low-bit-rate, low-power, low-cost access for virtually all nodes.

Ad hoc sensor networks provide an excellent example of the issues to be addressed. Many applications require the deployment of sensors over wide areas with no predetermined arrangement. The devices must discover each other (or at least their nearest neighbors) and decide how sensor information will flow through the network they collectively form. Different devices may take on different roles as generators, routers, or aggregators. Global efficiency can be achieved only if locally derived information is propagated to other nodes in the network. Devices will need to configure their functions to produce the desired overall effect rather than optimizing for strictly local concerns. Thus, a node may take on the role of router and act as a communications hub, but at the cost of increased energy use. When it eventually loses its ability to perform the function, another device will take its place. Determining how local decisions can lead to efficient global effects is a fundamental challenge for adaptive coordination in ad hoc systems.

EmNets will necessarily be composed of heterogeneous elements. Devices will be optimized for specific functions. For example, some sensors may be small and numerous but also highly constrained, while local aggregators may be more powerful devices with longer-range communications capability and larger power supplies. In addition, the long lifetimes of these systems and the need for adaptation may very well require the ability to upgrade and/or install new code. Trust models need to be developed that will not only control the admission of new code but also police it to verify it works as advertised prior to gaining admission. Finally, these systems must be resilient in the face of failures that occur when devices, communications, or other resources become unavailable. The following paragraphs elaborate on these themes.

Heterogeneity

Configuration via Mobile Code   Given the expectation of a rapid evolution in hardware, networking protocols, and basic networking algorithms in EmNets, an approach to discovery and configuration based on mobile code seems promising. Such an approach allows these components to evolve separately, rather than requiring that the whole EmNet evolve in lockstep. However, interesting and important research issues are still presented by approaches that use mobile code.

Although all of the approaches to implementing mobile code have some advantages and disadvantages, certain issues are common to all of the approaches—a point that often gets lost in the discussion of which technique is best. These issues highlight some of the fundamental engineering trade-offs that will need to be made in constructing networks of embedded systems, especially those made up of devices that are constrained in terms of memory, processor speed, power, and bandwidth.[9]

The most obvious issue is the trade-off that needs to be made between

---

[9]Many of the issues raised by amorphous computing (Abelson et al., 2000) may be relevant to the heterogeneity of EmNets, including how to obtain coherent behavior from large numbers of diverse components and how to develop methods for programming such systems.

memory use and the use of mobile code. For many of the small, embedded components in the systems that are the focus of this report, memory is one of the most precious resources. In some ways, the whole notion of mobile code conflicts with memory conservation; the idea that the recipient of the mobile code needs to know only the interface to the received code, and that all else is hidden behind an interface that is implemented (as needed) by the supplier of the mobile code, means that the recipient of the code has given up the capability to control memory use. Any piece of mobile code may exceed the amount of memory available at the recipient. Even if no single piece of code violates the memory constraints on the recipient, as the network scales up (and more code is moved), there will come a point at which an otherwise acceptable (and perhaps small) piece of code will need more memory than is available.

This issue cannot be dealt with at the component level—even if each piece of mobile code is written to be as small as possible (which might not always be the case)—because it is the sum of the pieces of mobile code that causes the problem. This exemplifies the need to understand how local decisions can affect global properties, and vice versa. The code actually loaded onto a node is determined by the use of the network in a specific situation. Thus, it is an aspect of the design of the network, not the components. On the other hand, the network should not have to know the details and limitations of the components present. Its properties are abstract and implemented by the underlying components. Indeed, one reason for using mobile code is to allow building the network without having information about the individual components.

Protocol-based Configuration   Mobile code offers the opportunity to tailor devices to new applications and evolve their functions over time. However, the resource requirements for mobile code may dictate other approaches instead, especially on the smallest devices used in EmNets. Such approaches, based on prearranged wire protocols used for communication between the various components, present their own research issues.

The first issue is the need to develop an ontology of devices so that they can be described in a way that is natural and consistent across different systems. If services are to be discovered, then they must be discovered with a description that ensures they will be able to use the wire representation sent to them and to generate data in the wire representation expected from them. How such a convention can be described and how it can be reasonably enforced in large-scale systems such as those envisioned in EmNets is an open research question.

Once this ontology has been described, a set of associated wire representations for the data to be transferred to and from devices of each type needs to be defined. These wire representations need to allow queries of data that has been sensed in the environment as well as the transfer of control information from one member of an EmNet to another. How to define these representations in a way that will allow the system to evolve is an open research question. In fact, the research issues surrounding protocol-based, self-configuring systems seem to be the converse of the problems posed by mobile-code-based systems. Each approach can solve some problems that arise with the other but is also subject to problems avoided by the other. Protocol-based approaches allow solutions that apply to devices that are severely resource constrained, but they produce systems that are brittle and lack easy paths of evolution. Mobile-code-based approaches allow easy system evolution, but at the price of abstraction, which consumes what could be scarce resources such as memory and communications capabilities.

A promising area of research might center on combining the two approaches in a hierarchical fashion. Small groups of devices could be built using a protocol-based approach. Together, these groups could possess enough resources to allow utilization of the mobile code approach. This method would allow the overall system to evolve, although groups of nodes in the hierarchy would need to evolve in a coordinated fashion. Such localized, planned evolution is much easier to accomplish than global planned evolution in large-scale systems. At the large scale, shared resources could enable use of the mobile code approach, which allows piecewise evolution of the overall system. Thus some devices in EmNets themselves or in the networking infrastructure to which they are connected can serve as code proxies that can offload computation and memory resources from the more resource-constrained devices in the system. Of course, it will now be necessary to communicate with these proxies or groupings more frequently than if the computation could have been performed locally. This degrades power consumption and reliability but could provide a more flexible evolutionary path than simply over-provisioning every device. In an agricultural context, for example, the irrigation and fertilization system might operate as a sensor network with relatively constrained devices running wire protocols. However, the controller for the systems might be a more capable, general-purpose computing element that would interoperate with the rest of the enterprise's inventory and control processes and would benefit from the long-term flexibility of using mobile code technology.

Discovery Protocols   Current discovery protocols, whether based on wire protocols or mobile code, require that the entity entering the network be able to find, either directly or indirectly, the other entities of interest in the local network neighborhood. Considerable research (and product development) is being done on discovery protocols and join protocols over

Ethernet-based TCP/IP networks. These networks have a number of properties that are assumed to exist, a prerequisite for such protocols to work; in particular, the ability to multicast with limited scope is required by all of the existing or proposed discovery mechanisms. Not all networks that are currently in use or being thought about support these mechanisms, however; how discovery would work over such networks is an open issue.

A research issue that needs to be addressed is how discovery mechanisms of any sort can be scaled to larger networks. For discovery mechanisms that are purely peer to peer (that is, there is no rendezvous entity at any level), it is not clear how this can be done other than by specifying some form of region of interest in the network—a concept that is not well supported in existing network topologies. This issue is further complicated by the potential dissonance between geolocation and network proximity, discussed earlier in this chapter.

For discovery protocols that rely on the collection of entity information in some sort of lookup or directory structure, an approach to scaling could be to form a hierarchy of such lookups, with the leaf nodes of the hierarchy consisting of the lookups contacted by the discovering entities and higher-level lookups consisting of information about the previous level of lookup. This approach is standard in hierarchical naming systems, but it is less clear how the approach would work in systems designed to allow programs to find other programs. In such systems, in which the entity to be found is often represented as something other than a human-readable name, it is not clear how to propagate the information about the contents of a lookup service into upper levels of the hierarchy. Some work has begun in this area, and it may be a scalable alternative to the multicast-based, publish-subscribe mechanisms that are used locally (Yu et al., 1999). In some contexts, this lookup-based approach is preferable to the always-listen approach of multicast because of the energy costs associated even with "listening" on low-power wireless channels (see Chapter 2).

The issue of low-power discovery is key for EmNets with large numbers of small sensor nodes. At this time, low-power discovery emphasizes the assembly of the physical layer at low power. This means, for example, that both the transmit and receive duty cycles are maintained at a low rate. Unique complexities arise when discovery of nodes and physical layer assets must occur in a multihop context. The need for correlation to physical location further complicates this issue. The cluster architecture is often required for typical deployments. For example, in a healthcare environment, individual clinical spaces will form embedded system clusters, which may have weak interactions with neighboring clusters. Energy, bandwidth, synchronization, and information sharing will motivate clustering. Despite the progress that has been made in developing approaches to discovery and interoperability, additional research will be needed to extend these principles to EmNets.

Trust and Failure Models

The ability of EmNets to self-configure brings up a set of issues related to trust among system components, admission and allocation to resources, monitoring and policing, and the ability to deal with failures, some of which may be intentionally inflicted. In addition, means are needed to oversee and administer the status of the whole system; this includes its upgrade status, patterns of resource usage, and overall system health.

Admission Control A critical unresolved issue has to do with how to characterize components and the code they run. Components must be able to make local decisions about what code they will run, whether it resides locally or needs to be imported as mobile code from another node.

The strength of mobile code draws, in part, from the ability to distinguish between the interface (which is all that the client of the mobile-code service needs to know) and the implementation of that service (which gets moved into the client's address space and hides the details of the service from the client). The implementation of the mobile code can change as new hardware, wire protocols, and software services evolve. The client that will run the mobile code knows only about its functional interface. The challenge is that there may well be a set of characteristics important to the client that is normally not discovered. Such characteristics might include the timing constraints or guarantees that the service needs to meet to function properly, the amount of bandwidth or power it requires, and its memory requirements, including the potential downloading of the code of subcomponents.

The problem is that an interface describes only the syntax needed to talk to the service and the broadest notion of the semantics of the service. Other semantic aspects of the service may also be important, but there is a lack of agreed-upon methods for specifying such semantic characteristics. Techniques that have been developed for software abstraction offer no well-defined middle ground between the interface and the full definition of the implementation. An example of a characteristic that might be needed is quality of service. Information about average and worst-case delay bounds might be required for some application domains. Consider the problem of trying to track a vehicle and then collect an image. The nodes that are detecting and exchanging information for localization purposes must do all the tracking in time to trigger the correct imaging device. How to combine a description of the guarantees that a service can provide with the requirements of the client on the service and the requirements of the service on the client is an area open for research.

EmNet elements need to be able to gather this information about the service they want to use so as to make intelligent admission decisions. However, this is not the end of the issue. Once they make the decision to run the code, they need to ensure that it functions as was advertised. Monitoring and policing are therefore needed to verify the service code does not overstep the agreed-upon bounds. Mechanisms are needed to stop code that does not live up to its contract. Admission control and policing decisions are further complicated by negotiations between EmNet elements as to who should run which services. If a device agrees to run a service that other devices are counting on, it has to devise a plan for offloading those functions if it finds itself unable to meet the service's requirements or if the service oversteps its bounds. All of these issues present difficult challenges for the developers of software for EmNets and call for significant research.

Trust and Security   Trust models that can be applied to code (as opposed to people) need be investigated. When code is moved on behalf of a service or device on the network into the address space of a client, the client and service need some way to decide on the level of trust between them. In some embedded systems, trust may not be an issue (for example, when only trusted sensors are allowed into a sensor network). In others, however, several trust issues will be important:

- Whether the receiver trusts the mobile code and allows it to run in any fashion,
- What local resources code can access if it is allowed to run, and
- What rights the local client might want to delegate to the code if it moves on or needs to make calls to other members in the network.

Although some ideas have been developed about notions of trust in principals, it is not clear that mobile code is a principal, or if such code works on behalf of a principal. Indeed, there are cases in which it makes sense to distinguish between different levels of trust—how much the code is trusted to be accurate and nonharmful (which can be thought of as trust in the producer of the code) and what the code is trusted to access (which can be thought of as trust in whoever or whatever the code is running on behalf of). It may well be that all of the problems in the trust model of code can be accounted for with current trust models and an appropriate mapping of the new entities involved in such systems and the entities already dealt with in the trust models. But currently there is no such mapping, nor is there any reason to believe that new problems will not arise.

Security in distributed systems has been investigated for some time. Most security mechanisms, however, rely on the ability to trace an action back to a principal, generally a human being, on whose behalf an operation is performed. In an EmNet, however, most of the requests or resources will be made on behalf of a program, which may not have the full identity of a principal. Even if each program or embedded processor could be treated as a principal, it is not clear how that program or processor should go about authenticating itself.

Beyond these fairly standard sorts of security issues, EmNets can pose security concerns that go beyond those generally thought of in distributed security. For systems in which code is moved from one processor to another, it is not enough to mutually authenticate the interacting entities; the code that is moved from one entity to the other needs to be trusted to some degree and must be given (or denied) access to the resources on the system in which it runs. How this is best done, or even if it can be done, is an unanswered question at this time. Some progress has been made in performing code verification prior to the loading of the code through the use of virtual machines, but the principles behind the code verification mechanism are not well understood. Further, the amount of space taken up by the verifier is large, and it may exceed the benefits offered by code verification on small devices. There have been some investigations into the possibility of performing verification before the code is moved and then signing that code to ensure that it is safe (Gun Sirer et al., 1998), but further research in this area is necessary.

The design of operating systems that can support this type of resource accountability and allocation is also an open research area. Accountability is necessary for resources such as power and bandwidth as well as for the more traditional processor cycles and memory. Allocation may be based on any or all of these considerations, and the code run by the operating system must be guaranteed not to be able to obtain more resources than it originally negotiated.

Failure Models and Monitoring Additional research needed in the area of discovery has to do with the failure models for automatically configured networks. Once a device has joined such a network, how is it discovered that the device has failed? If the automatically configured network has some conceptually central place where members of the network are found, what happens when that place fails? The Jini system has a reasonably well-specified failure model, covering both the failure of components that are registered with a lookup service and the failure of the lookup service itself. This model is implemented using the concept of leases. Leases are granted for a specified period of time. If the device does not return to renew the lease, then it is assumed that the device has failed or left the network and is no longer available. Leases can be used in this manner in both directions, helping a client keep track of a server and—as is more common—helping a server keep track of a client. However, this does not solve all the problems, because the lease server itself may fail and a new node may need to take on this responsibility. The approach taken in the Jini system is not the only possibility; others should be investigated.

An issue related to failure is system health. In many EmNet applications it will be necessary for an administrator or user to know what issues the system is dealing with. For example, a lack of elements in one area (owing to malfunction or outside attacks) could create a low-bandwidth bottleneck or a surplus in another area (owing to malfunction or intentional interference) could cause communications interference. This is important because EmNets are unlikely to be deployed for applications that can tolerate total system failure and be fixed by simply rebooting. A key design goal is thus to have them degrade gracefully (for example, having nodes or elements take over for other nodes and elements when they fail.) The Internet provides a reasonable example of how this might be accomplished, although it is not, of course, subject to the additional constraints that EmNets are operating under.

Additional research is needed in how to characterize systems and their components based on this concept. There may be much to borrow here from the ideas of dual control. In dual control, the behavior of system elements is characterized in situ by stressing them purposefully. What is learned from the interaction can then be used to recognize a problem when it is seen in regular operation. In addition, it will be important to record system behavior so that unintended behavior that emerges when a particular combination of elements or EmNets interacts can be studied and remedied. In fact, doing this automatically might create a sort of immune system that monitors operation and takes corrective actions. Of course, such an immune system as this would itself have to be monitored. This opens up an entirely new area of research that focuses on techniques for restricting the behavior of EmNets within a parameter space that is comprehensible to both humans and machines.

Research Issues for Adaptive Coordination

Several factors make it unlikely that adaptive coordination in EmNets will be mediated or even aided by human operators. One factor is size: EmNets will often be very large, and adaptive coordination will need to take place over a scale (in terms of both numbers of networked elements and size of the covered physical space) that will preclude human involvement. A second factor is the time scale. The time scale over which the adaptive coordination may need to take place is too short to be open to human intervention; by the time a human operator decides what to do, the environmental factors will have changed in such a way as to require a completely different adaptation. A third factor is that the operators, users, and individuals interacting with EmNets may be untrained in the specifics of the system and should not be expected to understand the technology to the depth that would be required to address adaptive coordination. (See Chapter 4 for a discussion of human factors and the usability of EmNets.) The rest of this discussion focuses on the technical considerations mentioned above.

The large number of elements in such systems suggests a brute force method of achieving adaptive coordination: adding more elements to the EmNet to allow high levels of redundancy without modifying the designed behavior of the nodes. However, this method would require communication bandwidths that would drain the available energy of battery-powered elements. Simple replication is predicated on the idea that bandwidth (and the power needed to use the bandwidth) is an abundant resource, which is not the case in many of the EmNets of interest. In addition, issues of stability might arise with increasing numbers of nodes in the network—additional work in control for EmNets is required to characterize and manage stability.

Monitoring system health is a critical issue for two reasons. First, many envisioned applications of EmNets have reliability and safety concerns that are more severe than those for traditional desktop distributed systems (see Chapter 4), so it is critical that system degradation and signs of imminent failure be detected. More germane to the discussion in this chapter is the need for resource-poor components to adapt to variations in available resources in other components so as to achieve overall system efficiency. However, these same resource constraints make extracting information on dynamic system state expensive. Variations in available resources could arise in the context of normal operation or be due to intruders or malicious attacks. System health monitoring will thus need to incorporate intrusion detection and antijamming facilities.

There are some promising avenues for obtaining the adaptability needed. The low cost of the elements in many applications will enable the use of large numbers of elements in ways that supply redundancy when needed, while lowering or at least limiting the amount of communication required over the system itself. However, this approach will work only if nodes are designed to be adaptive to their environment and to the behavior of other elements in the system. For example, a node might set the frequency of periodic sample communication or its transmit power based on the density of nodes observed within its proximity.

These large numbers of system elements might also allow the system to monitor itself much more carefully so that adaptive coordination can be predicted or expected in new and interesting ways. For example, traffic generated by a node could be monitored by the nearest neighbor, which could quickly determine when that pattern changed or ended abruptly, indicating failure or loss of power. Such continuous monitoring would permit nodes to react quickly to losses in the network.

Exploiting Redundancy

One general area for research is how to exploit the redundancy that may exist in many EmNets. Especially in sensor networks and other systems based on large numbers of inexpensive nodes, some degree of redundancy can be expected. In sensor networks, for example, multiple nodes may provide coverage of overlapping geographic areas. In a smart space, multiple printers, displays, or databases might exist. Not only can this redundancy improve reliability, but it might also ease the process of self-configuration. For example, when nodes need to be upgraded, only a small percentage of the nodes might be upgraded manually, and the others could be instructed to check the new nodes for updates. With inexpensive components, the possibility exists of deploying multiple solutions rather than focusing on finding a single optimal one. In this section, the discussion is primarily about systems in which components are relatively inexpensive, allowing large numbers of them to be deployed.

In some cases, the cost of deployment is fixed within a certain range and grows only slowly as the number of deployed nodes increases. In these contexts, redundancy can be exploited to help achieve long system lifetimes (offering both robustness in the face of environmental dynamics and energy efficiency) if algorithms can be identified for nodes to use in self-configuring. For example, nodes can identify when they need to be operational and when they can sleep, thereby conserving energy to be used when other nodes go to sleep or use up their energy reserves. Such methods of exploiting redundancy require new computational models and abstractions so that elements have the information needed to determine the steps they should take to maintain system performance in the near term while preserving long-term capabilities.

Over the years, a number of approaches have been developed to help information technology systems make more efficient use of available resources. Indeed, some key issues in system scalability can be thought of as a set of methods for determining how nodes should take turns, share system resources, or coordinate actions to boost their efficiency and effectiveness. Clustering is an approach in which a single node collects information from other nodes and takes on the task of communicating that information to other clusters on behalf of individual nodes. Time division multiple access (TDMA) is an example of nodes taking turns using communication slots. Ethernet is an example of the use of carrier sensing and collision detection to coordinate use of the shared channel. It uses randomization to help coordinate system operations. TCP/IP congestion control scales in the sense that the users of a shared, congested resource use signals (dropped packets) to coordinate their respective use of the channel, thereby taking turns sending packets through the bottleneck. Multicast transport protocols such as RTP/RTCP[10] and SRM[11] expanded the use of Ethernet randomized and localized techniques for scalably sharing a resource (see Box 3.1).

The systems in which these techniques will be most useful have a large potential solution space. In other words, if there is just one or a very small number of acceptable solutions (for example, if just a few particular nodes out of hundreds or thousands need to take an action), then completely distributed, localized techniques alone are unlikely to provide a good solution. However, if there are many satisfying solutions, then one can envision energy-efficient techniques based on localized algorithms that find satisfying solutions in unpredictable contexts.

The generalizations of the RTCP and SRM techniques, referred to as adaptive fidelity, have potential for uses beyond simply achieving robustness. For example, in a smart space application, wall panels might be manufactured with very large numbers of sensors and actuators embedded. Adaptive fidelity schemes could be used to arrange for smaller numbers of these elements to be active during times of relative inactivity, conducting relatively long-duty-cycle scanning and offering relatively slow response. Triggered by detection of greater activity, additional nodes would move into the low-duty cycle mode and focus on a smaller area of interest; in this way, the collection of nodes would achieve higher fidelity behavior when there was more action to be observed or managed.

Another technique for exploiting redundancy might be to program or design EmNets to take advantage of opportunistic behaviors. For ex-

---

[10]RTP (real-time transport protocol) (Internet RFC 1889) is the Internet-standard protocol for the transport of real-time data. The data part of RTP is a thin protocol providing support for applications with real-time properties such as continuous media (e.g., audio and video), including timing reconstruction, loss detection, security, and content identification. RTCP (real-time transport control protocol) provides support for real-time conferencing of groups of any size within an intranet. It offers quality-of-service feedback from receivers to the multicast group as well as support for the synchronization of different media streams.

[11]SRM is scalable reliable multicast, one of many proposed transport protocols proposed for multicast (Floyd et al., 1997).

BOX 3.1
Exploiting Redundancy/Long-Lived Systems

RTP/RTCP is a pair of protocols used to facilitate networked multimedia applications (Floyd et al., 1997). RTP provides timing information in application-level data to allow smooth and possibly synchronized playback of data types that must be played back to the user in a smooth manner. RTCP is the control channel for RTP. RTP/RTCP was designed to support potentially very large groups where a small number would be transmitting simultaneously but a large number could be simultaneously listening. One of the scaling issues that arose was how to keep the control traffic (the periodic session messages sent by each receiver) from consuming too many resources. The designers developed a technique later referred to as scalable session messages in which each receiver monitors the number of other session participants currently sending session messages and adjusts the period of session message transmission so as to maintain the combined average session message transmission below a defined small percentage of overall data traffic being sent/received in the session. This technique was applied again in the reliable multicast transport protocols, SRM. The potentially very large set of data recipients must send session messages to communicate successful/unsuccessful receipt of packets. The same local algorithm for determining the frequency of session message reporting is used. SRM went on to use localized randomized algorithms more extensively as a means of achieving scalability. In particular, SRM uses localized algorithms for determining who should send requests for retransmissions and who should send repairs for retransmissions. This is an example of exploiting redundancy in that all members of a session that have lost a packet are potentially redundant in their role of requesting a retransmission. Similarly, all members who correctly received the lost packet are potentially redundant senders of the message repair. SRM elaborated on Ethernet distributed, randomized, resource usage techniques to identify local algorithms for each node to run that would result in efficient sending of requests and replies. Note that SRM does not result in perfect efficiency. A centralized scheme with global knowledge will always do better in any particular case. But SRM, by defining localized algorithms for each node to run, allows the collection of members to self-configure to an efficient state. It is more scalable than centralized approaches when the location of packet loss is unpredictable and nonstationary.

ample, they could delay some basic reporting functions (for example, transmitting, reorganizing, calibrating, and reporting system health) until greater bandwidth, energy, or processing capabilities become available. Some nodes could enter a sleep mode when redundancy is detected, thereby saving power and contributing to longer system lifetimes. Self-configuration itself could take competing paths in which mobile code may be distributed at times when, or to locations where, the combination of circumstances (bandwidth, operational real-time constraints, etc.) enables a self-configuration operation. Distribution of self-configuration commands, code, and verification acknowledgements may all adapt accordingly. This type of capability will require nodes to contain algorithms that provide flexibility in operating conditions.

An important part of adaptive coordination is the capability of individual nodes to monitor their own status and that of their operating environment. Nodes will need to gather information about changes in the status of other nodes (for example, that a nearby node has failed or entered a different operating state), changes in the availability of resources (for example, limited power or loss of a communications link), and changes in the environment that are being sensed and responded to. The nodes will need to rely on a variety of sensing modalities. For example, they may need optical sensors to indicate whether they have lost line of sight to another node with which they communicate frequently. They will need checks on their power levels. One of the most critical areas of research, as yet unexplored, will be the characterization of large-scale distributed systems composed of physically coupled, autonomous and/or adapting elements and operating under unpredictable, highly resource-constrained environmental conditions.

Centralized Versus Decentralized Control

An issue that needs to be addressed with regard to both self-configuration and adaptive coordination is control of the system configuration. If individual elements of an EmNet can change their technical characteristics, capabilities, and operating modes—either through upgraded hardware or software or through adaptive coordination—how can the system guarantee its overall performance and stability or be sure that individual elements have access to the bandwidth, quality of service, or other properties they need in the system? Conversely, if a system contains large numbers of nodes, how can a central node control the overall configuration of the network in a timely fashion?

Issues of adaptive coordination, configuration, and, more generally, control can be addressed through any of several schemes. At one end of the spectrum are centralized schemes in which individual components are not self-configuring but the overall system is. At the other end of the spectrum are decentralized schemes in which individual components are themselves self-configuring. All cases require that some policy be expressed at the time the system is deployed (and probably afterward) that guides and focuses the self-configuration, with respect to not only the humans involved and the self-configuring system but also the centralized controller and the distributed elements. (See Box 3.2 for a discussion of cooperative behavior and control.)

The viability of a centralized versus a decentralized scheme depends on several factors, including the scale of the system and the rate of anticipated change. Central control across a large network may be impossible to implement in a time-bounded fashion. (For a brief discussion of traditional control and systems theory as it relates to EmNets, see Box 3.3.) Local functions need to be optimized and reconfigured as the environment changes. If environmental conditions are not predictable and change faster than information can be extracted and analyzed, then a decentralized scheme is needed. But decentralization introduces issues of adaptive coordination and overall system performance. How can overall system performance be optimized if decisions are made locally? How can requirements for overall system performance be specified from a single point?

To provide for a degree of centralized control in a large EmNet with numerous elements, some sort of hierarchical, tiered structure will be needed. Many EmNets will be composed of heterogeneous collections of elements, each with different sets of capabilities and constraints. Some elements may be far less restricted than others in terms of, for example, the amount of power available to them; the system ought to be able to adapt by making such elements bear the brunt of power-intensive tasks. Other elements may be less restricted in terms of available memory or bandwidth, or they may have persistent storage easily available. Adaptive mechanisms can exploit system heterogeneity by using extra power where it exists in the overall system to offload work from elements with lower energy capacity.

Even when all nodes start out with equivalent capabilities, it may be efficient from a system-lifetime perspective to have the system select a small number of nodes to execute higher-power operations using higher-power resources (for example, long-range radio). Robustness can still be achieved by arranging for the "hierarchy" to self-configure using automated mechanisms for selecting which nodes will run the higher-energy resources. Automated hierarchy formation and clustering imply a need for automated reelection and selection in the face of failures. The adaptive coordination can take place efficiently and rapidly as the various elements adapt based on local measurements of environmental conditions and available resources.

As such systems adapt by reconfiguring the tasks that each element performs based on its capabilities, the distinction between configuration and adaptive coordination may begin to blur. How those capabilities are communicated and allocated is an open area of research, as are questions

---

BOX 3.2
Cooperative Behavior and Control

A possible approach to distributed control is directed diffusion. Directed diffusion amounts to controlling a system by means of activation and inhibition messages, the sum of which can either reinforce or discourage a course of action.[1] As an example, consider a sensor network in which multiple nodes have access to the outside world through a specialized node with long-range communications capabilities and that communicates to the rest of the nodes by passing messages from one node to another (that is, via multihop connections). If several nodes observe an event, then directed diffusion can help determine which nodes should be involved in deciding whether to report the event, which one should do the processing, and what information should flow to the long-range link given a desire to minimize energy expenditures.

If latency (delay) in making a decision is not an issue and the probability of a node accurately detecting an event is related to the strength of the signal it receives relative to background noise (the signal to noise ratio, or SNR), then the nodes can wait a period of time based on the SNR before alerting or inhibiting neighbors. The node that receives the signal with the highest SNR will send its alert first, communicating a message to the long-range link and sending short inhibition signals to its neighbors. The other nodes then avoid transmitting their decisions or activating one another to engage in cooperative detection. If the signal at the node with the highest SNR is still below the threshold for reporting the event, the node could instead activate its neighbors, asking for their decisions and the relative certainty of those decisions. These activation messages will propagate outward with reduced intensity (that is, they will require progressively higher certainties to respond), and nodes with higher SNRs will reply sooner. When enough replies have been combined to allow the original node to make a decision with the desired

---

of how groups of machines with different capabilities could be organized to perform a set of activities that are presented to the rest of the system as a single unit. Similar hierarchical organizations have been used in more traditional systems, but they are not based on the capabilities of the individual components in the manner described above. How to adapt the overall system configuration (or subsystem configuration) to maximize the information obtained while minimizing the use of scarce resources is a promising area for future research.

Some systems may benefit from decentralized control schemes, which also require further research and analysis. The minimum number of bits that must be communicated to make a reliable decision is unknown for all but the simplest of problems involving more than one sensor node. Given the high power cost of communications, it would be useful to know what the threshold is and thus to learn whether particular algorithms are any-level of certainty, that node can issue inhibition signals to its neighbors while propagating its decision to the long-range link.

This procedure progresses through several distinct phases of operation: detection of a stimulus, formation of subnetworks of communicating nodes, gathering and processing of information, destruction of subnetworks, and long-range communication of results. To minimize energy expenditures, it avoids using complicated set-up signals to establish subnetworks, instead employing the natural decay of communications signals with distance to establish a perimeter. Although perhaps failing to pick the optimal fusion center or routing of information, this approach can dramatically reduce the overall amount of sensor information transmitted within the system and help conserve energy. Varied behavior can be obtained with a few control signals (with feedback), with no need to designate a central controller before the procedure starts. Of course, the long-range link could also serve as a master node, commanding different thresholds to become active or inhibiting their behavior. In this way, behaviors can be adapted over time to meet changing global objectives. Human operators could perform this adaptive coordination, but as understanding of the system grows, networks could be designed with increased autonomy.

NOTE: Some work in this area has been done by the chair of this study committee (Intanagonwiwat et al., 2000).

[1]This approach is similar to that used by ants for a variety of highly complicated functions, such as establishing trails to food and removing them when the food supply dwindles. Successive use of a trail reinforces it, but small random deviations that provide a more direct route to a food can alter (e.g., straighten) the trail and lead to increased energy efficiency. Other signals can terminate an activity and focus attention on other tasks.

---

where near optimal. (For a discussion of local computation vs. communication as related to EmNets, see Box 3.4.) If the processing problem is cast as a rate-distortion problem, in which (weighted) false alarm and missed detection probabilities constitute the distortion and the communications energy takes the role of rate, then additional questions can be explored. For instance, What is the effect of array density on the rate-distortion region for a given communications and signal propagation law and set of source statistics? This is a deep and difficult problem (for example, under what conditions is there a convex rate-distortion region?), but its solution could have a large payoff. Preliminary progress has been achieved with simple versions of this problem, but a huge problem space remains to be explored.

The interaction between a system element and its neighboring elements is not typically considered in control theory but is essential to

---

BOX 3.3
Control Theory

EmNets bring together two established research communities—distributed systems and control. Control is a rich research area that studies how to use feedback to optimize the behavior of electromechanical systems. Control has its roots in simple servo control systems but is now used in the design and operation of a wide class of electronic and electromechanical systems. Often these systems have hundreds of processors and components from multiple vendors. Some of these systems run chemical plants, manufacturing plants, and even buildings. By bringing together these two areas, EmNets create a number of new research areas.

Control theory is used to solve a number of difficult problems. For example in flight control systems, the dynamics of the plane are carefully studied, creating an optimal controller for this system. Often this controller is combined with a number of estimators that produce an estimate of what the measured parameters should be. The estimator can be used to provide input from sensors that might not be read each cycle (for example, the computation might require 25 data points while only 10 are being collected at any given time) or check that the current model of the system represents the actual system. In some highly critical situations, banks of estimators can be used to model how the system would behave under various fault conditions. During normal operation, these estimators will poorly match the system, but under a fault condition one of these estimators might become a better match than the original system. Thus, when a fault does occur (such as the loss of an engine in an aircraft), that fault's estimator has current information and can be used to update the control equations for the plan, to allow it to continue to function at some reduced performance until the error is repaired.

Rather than using a fixed system model, *model predictive control* adapts the system model and the control formulation. It solves an optimal control problem at each step, using current sensor data and measured system performance. This type of control was initially used in large-scale refineries, where cycle times are very long (tens of minutes), providing sufficient control for the required computation.

---

modeling EmNets. The interaction between a node and its immediate neighbors is critical, because physical stimuli are often correlated to physical space and because the communications costs and latencies to near neighbors are likely to be less than average. Centralized control rules can be devised for such a group, but the complexity of the decision-making process, even for a relatively small collection of nodes, will demand some decentralization and probably hierarchy as well. Layered control hierarchies are notoriously difficult to optimize, but perhaps by scaling to large numbers designers can reduce the demand for efficient use of the individual components. In any scheme, the fundamental issue of stability arises. Once the design moves away from centralized control, the theory

Both types of system rely on getting sensor measurements at fixed time increments. While networks are often used in control systems, their properties are not considered in the problem formulation. For high-performance control loops, sensors are given logically separate networks (or even physically separate wire) to collect the data, making variable packet delay and possible data loss nonissues. In addition, in almost all cases the control algorithm is centralized and not run in a distributed fashion. The long cycle time of many process control systems makes the issue of networks in these systems uninteresting, and in any case existing technology meets the requirements of these systems. While robust operation is critically important, with commands being issued to individual pumps, valves, heaters, and the like (in a factory setting), the long cycles provide time to consider and reject outlying data and every actuator is likely to have a secondary sensor for redundancy and prediction checking.

While the notion of fixed time samples is fundamental to most control theory, there are some methods that might migrate to network-based systems more easily. One possibility is to use Lyapunov methods, where the idea is for each unit to greedily minimize a value function that serves as a coordinator. This transposes to asynchronous systems very nicely. In general, the actions of each unit would have to be coordinated carefully (simple examples show that activating two feedback systems simultaneously can lead to disastrous loss of performance or instability), but if there is a value function that each is separately minimizing, the actions are automatically coordinated.

To the standard control issues EmNets add the issues of resource constraints, distributed systems, and networks. In control environments, networks are assumed to be stable, not to lose information, and not to have delays. All of these are likely to be violated at some point for EmNets posing new research challenges.

NOTE: The committee thanks Stephen Boyd of Stanford University for his guidance in developing this description.

for characterizing the system and guaranteeing stability is not well developed. Note that actuation, signal processing, and communications (or more likely, a combination of these) all raise fundamental questions of resource allocation in response to a physical stimulus. Accordingly, a solution in any one of these domains may well have applications to all the rest. The problem of cooperation thus appears to offer an excellent opportunity for multidisciplinary research; there are probably lessons to be learned from diverse disciplines, with a potentially high payoff. (An example of an area in which multidisciplinary approaches are used is distributed robotics, described in Box 3.5.)

BOX 3.4
Local Computation Versus Communication

One of the design choices that must be made in EmNets is the balance between local computation and the communication of data back to a more centralized processing node. In other words, to what extent should an individual node process the data it has collected or been sent when it also has the option of communicating raw, unprocessed data to another node for processing? This issue is particularly important in EmNets that operate with limited stores of energy and must therefore minimize energy consumption. It is extremely important in systems that rely on wireless communications to transport data because of the energy requirements of wireless systems. Many sensor networks will be in this category, as will mobile elements of other EmNets, such as smart spaces.

The high energy consumption of wireless communications systems leads to unique conclusions about the distribution of tasks in the distributed embedded system network. For example, in a typical wireless sensor network, the network's task is to identify events that occur in the network environment and communicate these occurrences to a remote user. Conventionally, this would be done by transmitting received sensor information to a remote asset for processing. EmNets composed of many distributed devices become collectively more capable if significant computation is performed locally, with the goal of recognizing local events and communicating only event identification codes, as opposed to complete data sets.

As an example of the trade-off between computation and communication in an EmNet, consider a wireless sensor system that is distributed over a large surface. Communication between devices occurs between nodes in a multihop architecture in which information is passed from the source node to the destination node by traveling through a number of intermediate, proximate nodes. Under these conditions, the power transmitted from any one node declines rapidly as the distance from the transmitting node increases.[1,2]

The severe decay of wireless communications has a profound influence on the balance between communication and computation resources. System designers must decide between communicating data directly for remote processing or performing local processing and communicating a shorter message or perhaps none at all to a remote node. The energy required to transmit even short messages could power significant amounts of computational processing locally. The large computation budget is available for potentially quite powerful information processing that could reduce the amount of information that needs to be communicated. Hence, considerable design and development effort will need to be directed to the deployment of EmNets that leverage powerful local computation and cooperative processing to identify local events and even command local action. Low-power wireless embedded systems will therefore create demands for a rich set of novel network and distributed computing solutions that have not been previously needed in conventional wireline systems.

---

[1]See, for example, Parsons (1992) as a starting point into the total body of literature dealing with propagation in personal/mobile environments.
[2]See also Sohrabi et al. (1998).

Collaborative Processing

A sensor network is an example of an EmNet that illustrates the benefits of using system architectures and adaptive coordination to improve overall system performance in the face of stringent resource constraints. Sensor networks generally require constant vigilance by at least a subset of the sensors so that desired events can be reliably detected. At the same time, the system must avoid generating false alarms when a particular event has not occurred. Sensor networks can employ a power-conserving hierarchical detection scheme to meet these objectives. For example, individual sensors may use energy-efficient procedures for detecting acoustic, magnetic, infrared, or other forms of energy and then attempt to make a detection decision independently. If the sensor cannot reliably make a decision, it could employ some processing and sensing to seek information from nearby sensors. These processes involve larger expenditures of energy, especially if the sensor and its neighbors must communicate. Additional processing, using a large neural network or some other sophisticated procedure, could be used to provide greater assurance if necessary. In the worst case, raw data might be transmitted back to a remote site where human operators analyze the data and determine whether an event has been detected. This step consumes large amounts of energy and must be avoided, except when absolutely necessary.

As this example illustrates, there are trade-offs to be made with regard to the extent of processing to be conducted by individual sensors and the amount of information communicated among them. In many applications, there will be no events to report much of the time and no need to apply the most expensive algorithm, which is transmitting data to human operators for analysis. But, there may be too many circumstances in which the least expensive detection algorithm will fail. A processing hierarchy can lead to huge reductions in energy consumption while assuring the required level of reliability. Processing hierarchies are intertwined with networking and data storage issues. How long and where data are stored (or queued) will differ at different levels in the hierarchy; the decision on whether to communicate with neighboring nodes—and which ones—will depend on the signal-processing task. The amount of energy consumed by communications and the degree to which energy is scarce will affect the processing strategy (that is, the willingness to communicate and whether processing is centralized or distributed). All of this, in turn, depends on the physical constraints that the system faces, allowing the physical layer to intrude.

Given the amount of energy needed to communicate a short message, it often pays to process the data locally to reduce the volume of traffic and make use of multihop routing and advanced communications techniques,

BOX 3.5
Distributed Robotics

Distributed robotics is the study of algorithms for the control and coordination of groups or teams of robots. A multirobot group is a superb example of a networked embedded system that embodies challenges in control, communication, and coordination as it faces uncertainty in sensing and action, unexpected failures, and a dynamic environment. The notion of a single, centralized controller coordinating a distributed robot group is considered untenable, as it is neither scalable nor robust. Thus, control must be distributed to the individual robots, which must communicate and adapt as necessary to produce globally efficient behavior of the system as a whole.

Several key methodologies are relevant to multirobot control, as they are to individual robot control. Reactive control involves the lookup and execution of precompiled, stateless collections of rules, with no looking into the past or planning for the future. Deliberative control uses centralized world models and planning but scales poorly with the complexity of the control problem and the group size. Hybrid control attempts a compromise between reactive and deliberative approaches by employing both and compromising between them as necessary; this is a dominant paradigm in robotics. The other dominant paradigm is behavior-based control, which is of particular relevance in distributed robotics.

Behavior-based controllers consist of collections of behaviors, time-extended processes or control laws that achieve and maintain goals. For example, "avoid obstacles" maintains the goal of preventing collisions, and "go home" achieves the goal of reaching some destination. Behaviors can be implemented in software or hardware and as processing elements or as procedures. Each behavior can take inputs from the robot's sensors (for example, camera, ultrasound, infrared, tactile)

such as coding, to reduce energy consumption. Collaborative processing can extend the effective range of sensors and enable new functions. For example, consider the problem of target location. With a dense array of networked sensors, one means for tracking the position of an object (for example, a target or a detected event) is for all nodes that detect a disturbance to make a report. The centroid of the reporting nodes is one possible estimate of the position of the target. This approach requires the exchange of very few bits of information per node.

Much more precise position estimates can be achieved with a technique called beam forming, in which individual sensors exchange information about detected events and the time they were detected. Although this approach consumes more energy, it offers several benefits: higher quality data for subsequent classification decisions, long-range position location, and even some self-location and calibration possibilities for the

and/or from other behaviors in the system and send outputs to the robot's effectors (for example, wheels, grippers, arm, speech) and/or to other behaviors. Thus, a behavior-based controller is a structured network of interacting behaviors. Behaviors themselves embed state and can form arbitrary representations when networked together. Thus, behavior-based systems are not limited in their expressive and learning capabilities, and they are well known for their real-time response and scalability. The metaphor of a robot being controlled by a collection of behaviors scales well to systems of robots being themselves behavior collections. Currently, behavior-based control appears to be the de facto standard for distributed multirobot control, owing to its robust and scalable properties.

As EmNets evolve to include actuation and mobility, lessons can be learned from the area of distributed robotics. The significant open problems in distributed robot control include the synthesis and analysis of adaptive group behavior, group coordination, and communication strategies that facilitate dynamic, run-time, efficient resource allocation within a distributed system. Distributed robots need to be self-configuring and will usually be unattended. Latency is also an important concern for both types of systems. Both are likely to interact with humans at some points or on some level, and it may be the case that usability and interaction issues will overlap. However, the constraints on EmNets differ in some ways. Many EmNets will have severe power limitations, whereas many distributed robots may be large enough to incorporate more than adequate battery power. In addition, EmNets will probably consist of many more components and nodes than distributed robots would need to incorporate.

NOTE: The committee thanks Maja Mataric and Gaurav Sukhatme of the University of Southern California for their guidance in developing this description.

nodes.[12] In some applications, sparse clusters of nodes that use beam-forming techniques might be preferable to dense deployment of less-intelligent nodes, or it might be better to enable both sets of functions. For example, a dense network of less-intelligent sensors deployed in conjunction with a less-dense array of intelligent nodes could capture information on demand for beam forming. Such collaborative processing can be regarded as a further extension of the signal processing hierarchy to multiple nodes, with the collaboration being extremely expensive in terms of energy use but performed only rarely, such that its marginal energy cost may be acceptable.

Key to any network collaboration is the idea of *synchronization* among

---

[12]See, for example, Parsons (1992) as a starting point into the total body of literature dealing with propagation in personal/mobile environments.

elements of the network. Synchronization depends on both the accuracy of the local clocks and the ability of the network to coordinate local clock accuracy. Both long- and short-term clock drift are important for providing various levels of functionality. For spread-spectrum communication, high-accuracy clock synchronization with the received signal is necessary to decode the information sent. However, only relative synchronization is needed for node-to-node communication, because the propagation delay is not quantified at each node. In addition to enabling communication, coordinated synchronization is important as a means to enhance power savings, enable collaborative sensing, and allow multisensor self-location.

Local power requirements on a remote EmNet must be reduced to the bare minimum needed to supply continuous sensing and a minimum level of event detection, while incorporating functionality to expend power as needed for communications or more intensive processing. This is appropriate for situations in which the frequency of events is expected to be high enough that every EmNet in a network needs to be ever vigilant. For longer-lifetime sensors in environments with a lower event probability, support communication and processing may be set up to operate intermittently. If the network is operating in a form of TDMA communication, then for low latency event reporting, each sensor must stay synchronized. In addition, to coordinate sensing times and enable coherent collaborative processing, each EmNet needs to be synchronized to a global time scale. Thus, clock drift on each sensor limits the length of noncommunication between sensors or the power savings achievable by powering down the radio. Additionally, if a sensor field is put in a somnolent state in which only selected sensors are powered down, total network power savings will be greater if the multiple sensors coordinate their sleep time (requiring synchronization) as opposed to randomly powering down to provide a reduced alert state overall.

Collaborative sensing (by, for example, using beam-forming algorithms) benefits from synchronizing all the sensing inputs. The combining of results from multiple sensors at different locations to counter jamming, enhance resolution, or enable distributed sensing requires relative timing information. On the coarsest scale, timing is required to coordinate which event occurs where. Finer resolution of timing allows recognizing coordinated events by coherently combining results from multiple sensors, thereby fully realizing the utility of a distributed sensor system. In fact, the effective resolution of coherent combinations of inputs from multiple sensors is limited by the time synchronization of the sensors.

Programming EmNets to achieve significant collaborative processing raises some of the same challenges as are faced in parallel computing and distributed databases. Neither model adequately addresses the combined constraints of EmNets, however. For example, in contrast to parallel computing environments, the data in an EmNet will be inherently distributed. And in contrast to distributed databases, EmNets are much more resource constrained. An assumption in distributed databases is that moving the data from place to place is relatively inexpensive. In EmNets, the emphasis will be on performing the processing where the data are located. Some techniques from each of these models may prove useful, however, and their applications to EmNets merit further investigation.

Finally, the cooperative and collaborative nature of EmNets might frequently create requirements for configuration actions that are implemented across all or nearly all the nodes in a network. If a system is self-configuring, at times there may be a need to clearly identify the subsets of the system that have changed or been upgraded. This is referred to as a need for "atomicity," in which the system as a whole is considered a single, atomic (indivisible) entity. Specifically, the configuration of network protocols or security functions may be an action that must be applied with complete assurance across all nodes in a network. Errors in configuration for one node in a vast area may have unbounded impact. Atomicity of some kind may be needed when a change must be collective or coordinated, but it might not be achievable using standard techniques because there is no enumeration or unique identification of individual components. Moreover, there is a possibility that not all elements need to be upgraded; some components may be disconnected or obstructed for significant periods of time. If a piece of the system is changed, there must be a way for the system to detect whether the resulting final state is workable. How does one determine that enough components have been upgraded to take on the new behavior? How do old components detect that they should change their behavior when they encounter new ones?

SUMMARY

Self-configuration involves the addition, removal, or modification of elements in an EmNet and the subsequent process of establishing interoperability. In contrast, adaptive coordination addresses changes in the behavior of a system as it responds to changes in the environment or system resources (such as remaining energy). Together, these processes are critical for creating robust and scalable unattended EmNets. The state of the art in self-configuration is fairly well developed, with well-understood approaches to address assignment, service discovery, and mobile code. However, significant research progress is needed to achieve automatic self-configuration among large numbers of distributed nodes, while still conforming to well-defined trust and failure models, which are critical to embedded systems applications. Adaptive coordination is a well-developed discipline for centralized systems, and distributed coordination is widely applied outside of embedded applications (for instance, in Internet applications and protocols), but there is much work to be done in the area of distributed adaptive coordination to support embedded applications. Promising directions include techniques for exploiting system redundancies and localized processing and collaborative signal-processing techniques. Such techniques are particularly critical for unattended, resource-constrained systems.

REFERENCES

Abelson, Harold, Don Allen, Daniel Coore, Chris Hanson, George Homsy, Thomas F. Knight, Jr., Radhika Nagpal, Erik Rauch, Gerald Jay Sussman, and Ron Weiss. 2000. "Amorphous computing." *Communications of the ACM* 43(5). Also as MIT Artificial Intelligence Memo 1665, August 1999.

Arnold, Ken, and Jim Waldo, eds. 2000. *The Jini Specifications*, 2nd ed. Cambridge, Mass.: Addison-Wesley.

Corson, M. Scott, and Joe Macker. 1997. Presentation of draft entitled "Mobile Ad Hoc Networks: Routing Protocol Performance Issues and Evaluation Considerations," IETF. RFC 2501.

Fall, K., and S. Floyd. 1996. "Simulation-based comparisons of Tahoe, Reno, and SACK TCP." *Computer Communication Review* 26(3):5-21.

Floyd, S., V. Jacobson, C. Liu, S. McCanne, and L.A. Zhang. 1997. "Reliable multicast framework for light-weight sessions and application level framing." *IEEE/ACM Transactions on Networking* 5(6):784-803. An earlier version of this paper appeared in *ACM SIGCOMM '95*, August 1995, pp. 342-356.

Gun Sirer, Emin, Robert Grimm, Brian Bershad, Arthur Gregory, and Sean McDirmid. 1998. "Distributed virtual machines: A system architecture for network computing." Eighth ACM Sigops European Workshop.

Intanagonwiwat, Chalermek, Ramesh Govindan, and Deborah Estrin. 2000. "Directed diffusion: Scalable and robust communication paradigm for sensor networks." *Proceedings of the Sixth Annual International Conference on Mobile Computing and Networks (MobiCOM 2000)*, Boston, Mass. Available online at <http://lecs.cs.ucla.edu/~estrin/papers/diffusion.ps>.

Jacobson, V. 1988. "Congestion avoidance and control." *ACM SIGCOMM '88*.

Karp, B., and H.T. Kung. 2000. "GPSR: Greedy perimeter stateless routing for wireless networks." *Proceedings of the Sixth Annual International Conference on Mobile Computing and Networks (MobiCOM 2000)*.

Mcquillan, J., I. Richier, and E. Rosen. 1980. "The new routing algorithm for the ARPANET," *IEEE Transactions on Communications* 28(5):711-719.

Mullender, Sape. 1992. "Kernel support for distributed systems." *Distributed Systems*, 2nd ed. S. Mullender, ed. Cambridge, Mass.: Addison-Wesley.

Parsons, David. 1992. *The Mobile Radio Propagation Channel*. New York: John Wiley & Sons.

Sohrabi, K., and G.J. Pottie. 1999. "Performance of a novel self-organization protocol for wireless ad-hoc sensor networks," *IEEE VTS 50th Vehicular Technology Conference* 2:1222-1226.

Sohrabi, Katayoun, Gregory J. Pottie, and Bertha Manriquez. 1998. "Near-ground wideband channel measurement in 800-1000 MHz." *IEEE 1998 Vehicular Technology Conference*.

Yu, H., D. Estrin, and R. Govindan. 1999. "A hierarchical proxy architecture for Internet-scale event services." *Proceedings of WETICE'99*, June.

4

Building Trustworthy Networked Systems of Embedded Computers

U sers of networked systems of embedded computers (EmNets) will demand certain characteristics, including *reliability, safety, security, privacy,* and ease of use (*usability*). These features can be encapsulated in the term "trustworthiness."[1] Such features must be built into a system from the start; it is difficult, if not impossible, to add them in an adequate and cost-effective manner later on. A large challenge to adding these sorts of features to EmNets is the combination of an open system architecture with distributed control.

The need for high *reliability* in almost all EmNets is obvious, but how to ensure it is less obvious. Today's techniques for designing reliable systems require knowledge of all components of a system—knowledge that cannot be ensured in the rapidly changing environments in which EmNets will be used. Testing mechanisms that apply to standard networks of computing devices may well fail to apply in the context of EmNets, where components may shut down to conserve power or may be limited in computing power or available bandwidth. These and other reliability questions will need to be studied if EmNets of the future are to be trusted.

Some EmNets may operate unattended and be used to control dangerous devices or systems that, through either normal or flawed opera-

---

[1]For an in-depth treatment of trustworthy networked information systems that incorporates many of these aspects, see CSTB (1999).

tion, could lead to significant human, economic, or mission losses. Similar problems were encountered early on in manufacturing automation; here the systems are potentially larger, certainly more distributed, and operate in much less controlled environments. The constraints on EmNets—including long lifetimes, changes in constituent parts, and resource limitations—strain existing methods for evaluating and ensuring *system safety*. In addition, many EmNets will be operated—and perhaps even configured—by end users with little technical training. New designs may be needed that allow untrained users to operate these systems safely and effectively. Accidents related to software already are starting to increase in proportion to the growing use of software to control potentially dangerous systems (Leveson, 1995). Networking embedded systems together, as envisioned for many new applications, will only add to these problems by enabling a larger number of potentially more complex interactions among components—interactions that cannot be anticipated or properly addressed by system users. New system and software engineering frameworks are needed to deal with these problems and enhance the safety of EmNets.

Security and *privacy* will also be required in many systems. The amount of information that can be collected by EmNets is staggering, the variety is wide, and the potential for misuse is significant. Capabilities are needed to verify that the information cannot be compromised or used by those who have no right to it and/or to cope with the likelihood that misuse or other problems are going to occur. In addition, these systems will need to be protected from tampering and attacks mounted from outside the system. New networking technologies will introduce the potential for new types of attacks. Security can help with elements of reliability and safety as well since it involves not only satisfying objectives but also incorporates protective mechanisms.

Finally, EmNets need to be *usable*. The systems must be easy to learn, easy to use, and amenable to understanding, often at different levels of detail by different types of users. As these systems become more complex and open to more varieties of computer-mediated interaction, they need to be designed in such a way that end users and operators understand what a system is doing. Systems that violate users' expectations lead to frustration at best and errors at worst; it will be important to keep user expectations in mind in design decisions as these systems become more complex and pervasive. In addition, many of these systems will not be directly used by individuals—rather, individuals will *interact* with EmNets in various contexts, often without realizing it. Understanding how such interactions will take place and what people's conscious and even subconscious expectations might be is an additional challenge for usability design in EmNets.

The unique constraints on EmNets raise additional concerns; this chapter discusses the challenges inherent in designing EmNets to be reliable, safe, secure, private, and usable, and suggests the research needed to meet these challenges.

RELIABILITY

Reliability is the likelihood that a system will satisfy its behavioral specification under a given set of conditions and within a defined time period. The failure of a particular component to function at all is only one form of unreliability; other forms may result when components function in a way that violates the specified behavior (requirements). Indeed, a component that simply stops functioning is often the simplest to deal with, because such failure can be detected easily (by the other components or the user) and, often, isolated from the rest of the system. Far more difficult failure cases are those in which a component sends faulty information or instructions to other parts of the networked system (examples of so-called Byzantine faults); such a failure can contaminate all components, even those that (by themselves) are functioning normally.

Systems need to be designed with great care to address the expected failures. Because EmNets will often be unattended or operated by nonexpert users, operator intervention cannot be relied upon to handle most failures. Current failure models for distributed systems revolve around the ways in which individual components or communications infrastructure can fail (Schneider, 1993). Fault-tolerant designs of such systems generally assume that only a small number of failures of any type will occur. It is not at all clear that these models apply to EmNets, in which the individual components are assumed to be easily and inexpensively replaceable, and the usual mechanisms for detecting faults (such as a request for a keep-alive message) may be prohibitively expensive in terms of power or bandwidth or may generate false failure notifications (in the case of components that shut down occasionally to conserve power.) The development of techniques for fault-tolerant designs of systems in which the individual components are resource-bound and easily replaceable is an area ripe for investigation.

Nor are current techniques for verifying the reliability of design implementations readily applicable to EmNets. While significant work on the hardware verification of nontrivial systems dates back to at least the mid-1980s (see, for example, Hunt's work on the FM8501 microprocessor (Hunt, 1994)), it is more appropriate for individual components and may not be applicable to EmNets. Each component, to be reliable, must correspond to its specification, and the overall system will be considered reliable if it adheres to the system specification. Experience has shown, however, that merely confirming the reliability of individual components of a system is insufficient for understanding the behavior of the overall system. Existing methods for ensuring reliability are tied to tests of system implementations against the appropriate specification. It should be noted that testing traditionally occurs after design and implementation. While testing and validating complex designs after the fact tends to have more appeal than building in reliability and assurance from the beginning (which calls for greater rigor and costs more), it is an extremely difficult task that already consumes a large fraction of the overall expense, schedule, and labor of an engineering project. Microprocessor design teams typically allocate one validation person for every two designers, and the trend is toward parity with future designs. Many software projects report deploying one validation person for every software writer. Companies are investing heavily in testing because (1) shorter product development schedules no longer permit a small set of testers to work on a project for a long time, (2) the overall complexity of the designs is making it increasingly difficult to achieve the product quality necessary for introducing a new product, and (3) the volumes of product being shipped today make the possible expense of product recalls intolerable to most companies.

"If you didn't test it, it doesn't work" is a general validation philosophy that serves many hardware or software design projects well. The idea is that unless the designer has anticipated the many ways in which a product will be used and the validation team has tested them comprehensively, then any uses that were overlooked will be the first avenues of failure. But the problem is not as simple as listing the product's features and checking them one by one (although that is indeed one aspect of normal validation). Design flaws that manifest themselves that simply are usually easy to detect. The more insidious product design flaws appear only when multiple product features are combined or exercised in unusual ways. The complexity of such situations hampers efforts to detect flaws in advance.

For EmNets, the challenge of testing every system feature against every possible real-world usage will be daunting, even for an accurately configured system in initial deployment. But what happens a few months later when the system owner begins to extend the system in ad hoc ways, perhaps upgrading some nodes and adding others supplied by another vendor? The central challenge to EmNet reliability is to extend today's tools and validation methods—for example, the Willow project on survivable systems[2] and Easel (Fisher, 1999), a simulator for modeling

----

[2]For more information, see <http://www.cs.colorado.edu/serl/its/>.

unbounded systems,[3] may offer insights—to the much more difficult scope of large-scale EmNets.

Reliability Research Topics Deserving Attention

The following research topics deserve attention:

• *Fault models and recovery techniques for EmNets that take into account their scale, long life, open architecture, distributed control aspects, and the replaceability of their components.* Appropriate models of failure and how to deal with failures in systems that are distributed and have the scale, longevity, openness, and component characteristics of EmNets have yet to be investigated. Until such investigations take place it will be difficult to design reliable systems, much less test implementations of those designs. Such research should be linked to research into the computational models appropriate for such systems (see Chapter 5).

• *EmNet monitoring and performance-checking facilities.* Over the past several decades, considerable research has gone into monitoring and system health management, but EmNets pose unique problems owing to their potential scale and reconfigurability and the scarcity of component energy.

• *Verification of EmNets' correctness and reliability.* The size and distributed nature of EmNets may preclude complete system testing outside of simulation. Advances in analysis and simulation techniques would increase confidence in cases where complete testing is virtually impossible before the system is used in the field.[4]

SAFETY

Safety refers to the ability of a system to operate without causing an accident or an unacceptable loss.[5] Many EmNets (for example, a home entertainment system) will not present significant safety problems even if they fail, although such failures might frustrate or inconvenience users. Other failures may raise significant safety issues.

Safety and reliability do not necessarily go hand in hand. An unreliable system or component is not necessarily unsafe (for example, it may

---

[3]For more information, see <http://www.cert.org/easel/easel_foundations.html>.

[4]See *Making IT Better* (CSTB, 2000c) for a discussion of the limitations of the simulation of complex systems today.

[5]"Accident" is not an engineering term; it is defined by society. In the aviation community, for example, the term "accident" is used to refer to the loss of the hull of an aircraft; anything else is considered an incident, even though human life may be at risk.

always fail into a safe state or an erroneous software output may not cause the system to enter an unsafe state, or a system that stops working may even decrease safety risks), whereas a highly reliable system may be unsafe (for example, the specified behavior may be unsafe or incomplete, or the system may perform unintended functions). Therefore, simply increasing the reliability of the software or system may have no effect on safety and, in some systems, may actually reduce safety. Reliability is defined in terms of conformance with a specification; accidents usually result from incorrect specifications.

Whether viewed as a constraint on, or a requirement of, the system design, safety concerns limit the acceptable design space. Like the other desirable characteristics addressed in this chapter, safety cannot effectively be added onto a completed design, nor can it be tested or measured "into" a design. Safety constraints need to be identified early on in the design process so that the system can be designed to satisfy them. Testing and measurement simply provide assurance on how effectively the design incorporates already-specified safety considerations.

Engineers have developed a range of techniques for ensuring system safety, many of which have been extended to systems with embedded computers; however, much more research is needed (Leveson, 1995) in this area, which has attracted comparatively little attention by computer science researchers. In system safety engineering, safety efforts start early in the concept development stage. The process involves identifying system hazards (i.e., system states that can lead to accidents or unacceptable losses), using them as the basis for writing system safety requirements and constraints, designing the system to eliminate the hazards and their effects, tracing any residual safety-related requirements and constraints that cannot be eliminated at the system level down to requirements and constraints on the behavior of individual system components (including software), and verifying that the efforts were successful.

EmNets introduce added difficulties to this process. They greatly increase the number of states and behaviors that must be considered and the complexity of the interactions among potentially large numbers of interconnected components. Although all large digital systems experience similar problems, EmNets are unusual in that many operate in real time and with limited direct human intervention. Often they are either unattended or managed by human operators who lack technical skills or are untrained. Furthermore, EmNets afford the possibility of more dynamic configuration than do many other types of systems. Many EmNets are likely to arise from ad hoc extensions of existing systems or from several systems tied together in ways unanticipated by the original designers.

Historically, many accidents have been attributed to operator error.

Indeed, a common reason for automating safety-critical systems (apart from increasing efficiency) is to eliminate operator error. Automation has done this, but it has also created a new type of error, sometimes called technology-induced human error. Many of these new errors are the result of what human factors experts have labeled technology-centered automation, whereby designers focus most of their attention on the mapping from software inputs to outputs, mathematical models of required functionality, and the technical details and problems internal to the computer. Little attention is usually given to evaluating software in terms of whether it provides transparent and consistent behavior that supports users in their monitoring and control tasks. Research on various types of system monitoring, including hierarchical monitoring and standards thereof, may prove useful here.

Without the kind of support mentioned previously, technology-centered automation has changed the reasons for accidents and the types of human error involved. Humans have not been eliminated from most high-tech systems, but their role has changed significantly: Often, they are monitors or high-level managers of the automation, which directly controls the system. On modern fly-by-wire aircraft, for example, all pilot commands to move the control surfaces go through a computer—there are no direct mechanical linkages. Automation designs seldom support the new roles humans are playing. And yet, when the inevitable human error results from what aircraft human factors experts have called clumsy automation (Wiener and Curry, 1980), the accident is blamed on the human rather than the system or automation design. All of the recent Airbus accidents and some of the recent Boeing accidents involved pilot confusion arising from the design of the automation (Leveson et al., 1997). Examples include mode confusion and the lack of situational awareness (both related to inadequate feedback, among other things), increased pilot workload during emergencies and high stress periods, automation and pilots fighting over control of the aircraft, increased amounts of typing, and pilot distraction. Human factors experts have tried to overcome clumsy automation by changing the human interface to the automation, changing user training, or designing new operational procedures to eliminate the new human errors resulting from poor automation design. These efforts have had limited success. Some have concluded that "training cannot and should not be the fix for bad design" (Sarter and Woods, 1995) and have called for more human-centered automation. Currently, however, coping mechanisms are required until such automation becomes more widespread.

If researchers can identify the automation features that lead to human error, they should be able to design the software in such a way that errors are reduced without sacrificing the goals of computer use, such as increased productivity and efficiency. EmNets complicate the process of error reduction simply because of their increased complexity and the opacity of system design and operation. Today what can be automated easily is automated, leaving the rest for human beings. Often this causes the less critical aspect of performance to be automated, leaving to humans the more critical aspects. Worse, the systems often fail just when they are most needed—when conditions are complex and dangerous, when there are multiple failures, or when the situation is unknown. Unfortunately, if the routine has been automated, the human controller has been out of the loop, so that when the automated systems fail, it takes time for the human operator to regain a sense of the state, time that may not be available. EmNets increase the likelihood that human intervention will not be readily available. Approaches to automation should be changed from doing what is relatively easily achievable to doing what is most needed by human operators and other people affected by system behavior. This principle is, of course, applicable to more than just EmNets. The solution will need to incorporate the economic and institutional contexts as well as the technology.

Safety Research Topics Deserving Attention

Widespread use of EmNets will compound the existing challenges involved in designing safety into systems. These challenges will need to be addressed quickly to avoid future problems and to ensure that the potential of EmNets is effectively tapped. To address problems of safety in EmNets adequately, greatly expanded research will be needed in a number of areas, including the following:

• *Designing for safety.* Safety must be designed into a system, including the human-computer interface and interaction. New design techniques will be required to enforce adherence to system safety constraints in EmNet behavior and eliminate or minimize critical user errors. In addition, designers often make claims about the independence of components and their failure modes to simplify the design process and make systems more amenable to analysis, but they lack adequate tools and methodologies for ensuring independence or generating alerts about unknown interdependencies. The system itself, or the design tools, will need to provide support for such capabilities. This may well require changes in the way computer scientists approach these sorts of problems as well as collaboration with and learning from others, such as systems engineers, who have addressed these issues in different domains.

• *Hazard analysis for EmNets.* The deficiencies in existing hazard analysis techniques when applied to EmNets need to be identified. Designers and implementers of EmNet technology who may not necessarily be familiar with such techniques will need to understand them. Hazard analysis usually requires searching for potential sources of hazards through large system state spaces; EmNets will complicate this search process for the reasons already discussed. The results of hazard analysis are critical to the process of designing for safety and verifying that the designed and implemented system is safe.

• *Validating requirements.* Most accidents related to software stem from requirements flaws—incorrect assumptions about the required behavior of the software and the operational environment. In almost all accidents involving computer-controlled systems, the software performed according to specification but the specified behavior was unsafe (Leveson, 1995; Lutz, 1993). Improved specification and analysis techniques are needed to deal with the challenges posed by EmNets. These techniques should take into account that user needs and therefore specifications will evolve.

• *Verifying safety.* In regulated industries, and even in unregulated ones in which liability or costly recalls are a concern, special procedures are required to provide evidence that fielded systems will exhibit adequate levels of safety. EmNets greatly complicate the quest for such assurance, and new approaches will be needed as the complexity and potential number and variety of potential failure modes or hazardous system behaviors increase.

• *Ensuring safety in upgraded software.* Even if the software is designed and assured to be safe in the original system context, software can be expected to change continually throughout the life of a system as new functionality is added and bugs are fixed. Each change will require assurances that safety has not been compromised, but because it will not be practical to redo a complete software system safety analysis for every change, new techniques will be needed to minimize the amount of effort required to verify safety when potential system and software design changes are proposed and to cope with the consequences of safety failures. Users can be expected to extend the system in ways unanticipated in the original design, adding new components, trying out new functions, and so on.[6] In addition, the system and software design may become unsafe if there are unanticipated changes in the environment in which the

---

[6]Further complicating the situation is the fact that backup safety features, meant to be invoked only in emergencies, are often discovered by human operators and used as primary resources. Thus, if the system automatically detects a human error and produces an automatic correction, the human will soon learn always to make the error; oftentimes it is easier to do the task wrong and let the system correct it than to go through the laborious act of getting it right.

software is operating (a likely occurrence in a battlefield situation, for example). Methods are needed to audit the physical components of the system and the environment (including system operators) to determine whether the changes violate the assumptions underlying the hazard analysis. Approaches to software upgrades must address safety concerns in hardware components, too (for example, component audits could include calls to hardware components to validate their IDs).

SECURITY

Security relates to the capability to control access to information and system resources so that they cannot be used or altered by those lacking proper credentials. In the context of EmNets, security relates to controlled access to the subnetworks, the information stores, the devices that are interconnected, and the computing and communication resources of a given network. Many of the research issues that were raised with respect to safety in EmNets also apply to security. In addition, security analysis needs to assume that an adversary is actively trying to abuse, break, or steal from the system (an assumption not usually made for safety analysis.)

Security can be difficult to achieve in information systems of all types, but will perhaps be especially so in EmNets. Not only will the deployment of EmNets containing various sensor technologies allow the physical world to become more tightly interconnected with the virtual world, but the networking of embedded computers will also tend to increase the vulnerability of these systems by expanding the number of possible points of failure, tampering, or attack, making security analysis more difficult. The range of products into which processing and networking capabilities may be embedded will greatly expand the number of nodes at which security will need to be explicitly considered and influence the expectations at each node. Many of these nodes will consist of presumably ordinary everyday devices in which security is not currently a concern (thermostats, audio equipment, and so on); however, mischief will become an increasing risk factor. Their close connection to the physical world and interconnection with larger networks accessible by more people with unknown motives will make lapses of security potentially more damaging, increasing the risks associated with EmNets. In a military context, of course, the compromise of even fairly prosaic devices (such as food storage equipment or asset monitoring systems) that are part of a larger EmNet could have serious security implications.

EmNets' configurations will be much more dynamic, even fluid, than typical networked systems. EmNet user interaction models may be quite different from those in traditional networks. These properties have significant impact on security (and privacy). For example, as one moves from place to place, one's personal area network may diffuse into other networks, such as might happen in a battlespace environment. Interactivity may not be under an individual's direct control, and the individual may not understand the nature of the interactivity. Various nodes will engage in discovery protocols with entities in contexts they have never encountered before. Some EmNets may be homogeneous and their connectivity with other networks may be straightforward. In such cases, traditional network security techniques will suffice, with policy and protection methods executing in a gateway device. In heterogeneous, diffuse, fluid networks, traditional network security methods will not be effective. Rather, trust management and security policies and methods will be the responsibility of individual nodes and applications. This may put demands on the operating system (if any) that runs on those individual nodes. They may need to distinguish between secure operating modes and more permissive modes (especially during discovery, configuration, and update procedures).

Protecting System Boundaries

A key problem is how to protect the network from outside attack. The physical world has a number of well-understood and easily recognizable protective barriers and security structures. Retail stores, for example, have a physical structure to protect valuables. Even though these stores are open to the public, shoplifters can be thwarted by a well-defined notion of inside and outside and sensors used to overcome attempts to conceal goods. Such approaches have few analogues in the virtual world. Further, in the case of shoplifting, a risk management calculation is performed: that is, some level of security breach (shrinkage) is acceptable to merchants because absolute security would be unacceptable to customers. Risk management is also required for EmNets; however, calculating the risk is extremely challenging and variable because there are so many unknowns in these systems. The physical isolation of a network, together with extremely rigid and secure protocols for attaching terminals, is the only highly reliable method for protecting networked information systems from external threats (that is, attacks from outside hackers and others without access privileges), but this approach is not viable in many systems that need to be interconnected to be useful. In EmNets, physical boundaries and remoteness are effectively erased by the presence of sensors and network connectivity, and notions of entry and exit begin to fade. Except in physically isolated networks, the concepts of inside and outside generally do not exist. Yet this is one way in which users, and even designers, think about security problems—a mindset that, in itself, is extremely problematic. Two further factors complicating the notion of inside versus outside are that components of EmNets will change over time (perhaps all of the components, many times, over the life of an EmNet) and that much of the communication will take place over wireless networks. The wireless aspects of EmNets make them prone to interference and jamming (intentional interference), which affect both reliability and security.

The most common way to establish boundaries between the inside and outside of a networked information system is to use firewalls that control communications at the juncture between two networks. Firewalls do not, however, establish true boundaries; they merely limit the exchange of packets between networks according to policies that are increasingly difficult to understand and assure, especially on networks that need to invite access by growing numbers of users, as in the case of so-called extranets. Although new technology, such as the suite of IPSec protocols,[7] seems to offer opportunities to define boundaries (for example, virtual private networks), what it actually provides is access control. The controls apply to arcane objects (such as packet headers) that are difficult to understand for most users. Furthermore, it is almost impossible on most networks to understand all of the means by which objects may be stored or accessed, making the effectiveness of access controls unclear. In EmNets, the system perimeters are even more difficult than usual to define and may change over time. To the extent that EmNets are used over ever wider areas encompassing space (satellites), land, and ocean (seabed and submarines), between large numbers of vehicles, or spread throughout a large battleship, the difficulties of developing and implementing robust access controls will only grow.

Managing Scale and Complexity

The large scale and high degree of complexity in EmNets will further frustrate the attempt to identify boundaries and improve security because these characteristics will tend to make system security more difficult to analyze. What are the threats to a given EmNet? How are security risks evaluated? What should be the public policy regarding completion of a security threat analysis preceding deployment of an EmNet, if "deployment" can even be considered an actual, discrete event? It is becoming very difficult to offer even simple answers to these questions as the physi-

---

[7]Internet Protocol Security (IPSec) is a framework of open standards for security at the network or packet processing layer. Earlier security approaches have usually been at the application layer.

cal and logical connectivity of networks increases.[8] Methods for evaluating threats and assessing security risks in complex systems whose elements are tightly coupled to physical-world artifacts are lacking. As recent events on the Internet indicate, some types of threats, such as denial-of-service attacks, have a high success rate, and many system users naively hope that the motivation for such attacks is slight.

The virtual world remains difficult to contain. Although cryptographic techniques enable engineers to build arbitrarily secure system *components*, assembling such elements into secure *systems* is a great challenge, and the computing research community does not yet understand the principles or possess the fundamental knowledge necessary to build secure systems of the magnitude necessitated by EmNets. It will be increasingly important to ensure that security issues are addressed at the outset of system design, so that notions of network isolation can be dealt with in a straightforward manner. Historically, however, networks are designed and often deployed before security issues are addressed. With many—perhaps most—EmNets, that sort of approach will result in problems. If security design is an afterthought, or a security hazard has already produced consequences, then the system is usually much too complex to even analyze from a security perspective. At present, it appears likely that systems whose evolvability is already hard to predict will be deployed without a full understanding of the security implications. This suggests both the need to accelerate relevant research and the need for coping and compensating strategies.

Mobile Code and Security

The use of mobile code in EmNets will create another potential vulnerability with implications for security.[9] The networking of embedded computers allows for remote updates to the programs that run on those computers as well as the use of mobile code. If either capability is implemented, then the system is open to a significant security hazard—namely, that the code that eventually runs on these computers may not be code that is legitimately intended to be run on them. Furthermore, even if the code is legitimate, it may have unintentional security flaws. A number of mechanisms can be used to deal with this problem—examples include

---

[8]These questions apply to the other elements of trustworthiness described in this chapter as well. The size, scale, and complexity of EmNets complicate issues of privacy, reliability, safety, and usability along with security.

[9]Mobile code and its implications for self-configuration and adaptive coordination were discussed in Chapter 3.

secure boot loaders and secure class loaders that check code authentica-
tors and compliance with security policies—but such mechanisms are not
generally used in today's embedded computers, let alone in conventional
computing and communication systems. As embedded computers become networked, it will be necessary to deploy these and other features
much more routinely.

Of course, EmNet resource constraints, whether of memory, computational capability, or power, will make it difficult to use some of these
techniques in their current forms. Their use will also require deployment
of the infrastructure necessary to support and maintain the policies by
which these systems abide. In some cases this process will be straightforward, but in other others it will be far more complex. An automobile
manufacturer, for instance, may be able to deploy tools comparatively
easily that assure that code updates originate from the manufacturer.
What is less clear is how to meet the challenge raised by open-air contexts,
such as a battlespace, where there is less control over the environment
and more opportunities for and likelihood of malicious activity.

Denial of Service

Denial-of-service attacks on EmNets could be of significant concern
if they are widespread or involve safety-critical systems. Indeed, if society relies more on EmNets and allows them to be involved in many daily
human activities, the invitation to disrupters grows. The wireless aspects
of EmNets will be particularly susceptible to jamming attempts, for example. Denial-of-service attacks are very difficult to defend against if
they are not anticipated in system design and taken into account in each
system service protocol, at both high and low levels of communication.
Because EmNets are often characterized by a lack of "excess" computing
resources, extraneous requests, as found in flooding-based distributed
attacks, will more easily swamp these systems. Moreover, they will often
be constrained in terms of the power available to them, so the mere act of
receiving requests in a denial-of-service attack can cause long-term damage to an EmNet, well beyond the duration of the attack. (For more traditional systems, denial of service is a transient attack; when the attack
stops, the damage usually stops accumulating. This is not the case with
battery-powered EmNets.)

The above observations may pose significant challenges to the design
of high-integrity networks such as are found in the military. Traditional
techniques that ensure the integrity of executables, such as credentialing
and integrity checks, are subject to denial-of-service attacks in the form of
very simple, otherwise innocuous, easily concealed, network-borne vi-
ruses that do little more than append themselves to files or memory im-

ages, invalidating credentials. Systems that rely on precise integrity techniques can turn out to be highly fragile. Certainly, operating-system-level techniques may be employed to thwart such denial-of-service attacks, but it remains to be seen how effective they will be.

Security Research Topics Deserving Attention

The security issues discussed above raise a number of research issues that need to be addressed, including the following:

- *Network access policies and controls.* How does one devise, negotiate, deploy, and renew network access policies that address the various threats that may be of concern to a given EmNet? How can this be done in an environment in which the EmNet itself is reconfigured, often on an ad hoc basis? Access controls need to be devised that will be easily understood, able to protect the wide variety of information that may be collected under widely varying and often unforeseeable circumstances, and perhaps even self-configuring.
- *Enforcement of security policies.* How should security policies be observed on individual network elements as well as on the network operating system? How are these policies devised and enforced when there are multiple "owners" of various parts of an EmNet?
- *Critical infrastructure self-defense.* Mechanisms need to be identified that are useful for ensuring mobile code safety, defeating virus attacks, and preserving function in spite of the failure or compromise of one or more nodes. What types of safe operating modes can be devised that allow for the secure update of an EmNet, reducing the risk of attack while maintaining performance? This will be especially important for EmNets that control critical infrastructures and support military applications and battlespaces as well as for more civilian-oriented applications such as electric power systems, financial systems, and health-care systems.
- *Preventing denial-of-service attacks.* Mechanisms are needed that preserve the inherent capacity to communicate over EmNets yet effectively defend against denial-of-service attacks.
- *Energy scarcity.* Security in the face of energy scarcity is a significant challenge. New authentication and data integrity mechanisms are needed that require less communication overhead. It may be possible to exploit heterogeneity and asymmetry within the network to allow smaller system elements to do less than larger ones. Further, when there is redundancy in the EmNet, it may be possible to exploit the redundant components in order to detect outliers and possibly sabotaged nodes.

PRIVACY

The anticipated broad deployment of EmNets in public spaces and private homes could allow the collection of considerable information about individuals. In many cases, individuals may be unaware of sensor networks deployed in the public spaces or commercial environments they enter and the associated information being collected about them. Even in their own homes, many users may be unaware of the types of information that embedded processors are collecting and possibly transmitting via networks to vendors or other recipients.[10] The embedding of information technology into a growing number of devices will increase the amount of personal and personally identifiable information that can be collected, stored, and processed.

Achieving consensus on privacy and confidentiality policies continues to be a vexing problem and will only become more problematic as EmNets become more pervasive and interconnected. It should be noted that most of the issues involved here are not strictly technical but rather issues of public policy. The question is not necessarily, What *can* be done technologically but rather, What *should* or should not be done? The technical challenges lie in designing systems that facilitate support of the policies once they are decided.[11,12]

Consideration of the privacy implications of EmNets cannot be limited to these systems alone but must extend to the larger networks of more powerful computers to which EmNets connect. Information about transactions and events collected through networks of simple computers and sensors can be and is analyzed for links and correlations in much more powerful computers, both online and offline. It is these more powerful computer networks that can turn relatively innocuous data collected on EmNets into detailed data shadows that allow the reconstruction of complicated personal profiles. How, in the face of these prodigious capabilities, can systems provide anonymity whenever it is useful and appro-

---

[10]Few automobile drivers, for example, are currently aware that many cars collect and store information about the way a car has been driven (e.g., driving speed, acceleration, engine speed). This information can be used by manufacturers to better analyze accidents and, hence, improve safety but could also be used to disallow warranty claims or to prove that an automobile was operated in an unsafe manner.

[11]Alan Davidson, of the Center for Democracy and Technology, briefed the committee on privacy issues for EmNets, saying, "Privacy should be a critical design value as [these] systems are conceived and implemented."

[12]For more information on the notion of designing systems that are sensitive to policies and human values, see *Value-Sensitive Design: A Research Agenda for Information Technology* (Friedman, 1999).

priate? What are the limits of the protocols and technologies that assure anonymity and prevent linkages between events and transactions? With more and varied data being collected, it is becoming increasingly difficult to avoid the linking of these data and, more specifically, associations of data with real identities even when protocols that assure local anonymity are used.

Conceivably, policy-controlled, secure systems can collect data and policy-controlled, secure systems can dispense them. But who sets the policies, and who enforces them? Numerous legal and public policy questions need to be addressed. Who owns the personal data collected either with or without the knowledge of the person? Should ownership be negotiable? If so, how can people extract value from their own personal data in an equitable fashion? What is practical and enforceable in systems in which interactions are fleeting and take place very quickly? Can and should protocols be provided whereby people can exchange their data for other value, and how can people avoid being unfairly coerced? These are broad issues that are also applicable to the Internet. In the United States, regulation has limited the use of customer proprietary network information (CPNI) on telephone networks.[13] Should there be similar limitations for other networks? Or will it be too difficult to define what is proprietary to the customer? How might the government gain access to such information, or should there be ways of protecting the information from access?

A related issue that will need to be resolved is how (and sometimes whether) to advise people when their actions are being monitored. Many EmNets, for example, will be difficult to detect, and users may be unaware that they are being tracked. This issue has already arisen in the context of electronic commerce, where consumers have expressed concern about the monitoring of their Web surfing and online purchasing. In most cases, consumers are unaware that their actions are being monitored, stored, and compiled into individual profiles even though individuals are usually aware that they are interacting with a system and are actively providing it data. EmNets may become so ubiquitous and so invisible that people are no longer aware that they are interacting with a networked system of computers and will often unknowingly and passively provide data. One part of the issue is notification: making people aware of the fact that they are being monitored. As experience with

---

[13]See the Code of Federal Regulations, Title 47, Volume 3, Part 64 (GPO, 1998). In 1999 an appeals court vacated the FCC's CPNI order on First Amendment grounds in US West v FCC, available at <http://www.fcc.gov/ogc/documents/opinions/1999/uswestcpni.html>. The Supreme Court let this ruling stand.

online profiling has demonstrated, however, notification is not a simple process. Many questions need to be answered. When should notification be mandatory? How can users be effectively signaled? Given individual differences in sensitivity and awareness, it may be difficult to provide adequate notification to some without annoying others. This may especially be the case in smart spaces, where all sorts of information may be collected and possibly linked to an individual. More research is needed to address issues like these.

Additional means may also be needed to control the disclosure of information. The issue of disclosure arises when information is collected for one purpose but used for other purposes (often referred to as mission creep). Disclosure is often provided in privacy policies for Web sites, but EmNets often involve more passive interactions in which disclosure is less convenient. For example, a smart space may collect information about an individual and provide it to others with the intention of providing a useful service, but the individual being probed may not be appreciative. Are there techniques that would allow users to control the flows of information about them? How can a user answer questions such as, Where is my information? Who has it? How did it get there? Who is responsible if something goes wrong? In addition, What conditions are needed so that users trust others not to misuse their data, and can EmNets be designed to engender an atmosphere of trust that is not due solely to ignorance of their existence in a given situation? Considerable work has begun on technologies that allow consumers to express privacy preferences[14] and purveyors of intellectual property to control the dissemination of their work.[15] However, these approaches are being developed in the context of Web-based electronic commerce; whether or not they are extendable to a broader set of EmNet-based applications is unclear.

It would seem to be very difficult for anyone to avoid giving up personal information to these networks. There are risks even when everyone's intentions are well understood. It would be useful to have some general principles whereby the risk of inadvertent privacy violation can be minimized. These might include disposing of information as soon as possible after it is used; storing information near the point of use; and avoiding the removal of such data from local control whenever possible. Use of anonymity or pseudonymity and of protocols that prevent the linking of data sets could also be considered.

---

[14]For example, see the Platform for Privacy Preferences Project (P3P) at <http://www.w3.org/P3P/>.

[15]See Chapter 5 of CSTB (2000a), a report on intellectual property in the information age.

The fundamental issue is the ability of individuals to control the collection and dissemination of information about them in an environment in which daily transactions and events—and the events associated with their personal environment—involve EmNets or are controlled or monitored by them. Research is needed to better understand people's expectations about their rights and abilities to exercise such control and resist intrusion. What are the expectations about privacy, and how are they evolving as people become more exposed to and familiar with various technologies? Can one outline the privacy rights that people either expect or legally possess, and can one identify ways in which different types of EmNets threaten those rights and run counter to those expectations? Conversely, as EmNets become ubiquitous, are there ways to use the technology to defend privacy rights, or will privacy necessarily be lost? As the FTC has recognized (Thibodeau, 2000), many privacy questions will need to be rethought in a world of increasing automation and instantaneous wireless communication. Both privacy expectations and case law are evolving. It will be necessary to clearly understand the trade-offs involved. EmNets have more of a propensity to be ubiquitous and enveloping, unavoidable in our environment, where individuals are not in control of their interaction. In these cases, privacy issues cannot be addressed by education and personal policies alone. Rather, they become (even more) a matter of public policy.[16]

Privacy As Related to Security

While security and privacy are very distinct properties, they are related (for example, security can provide mechanisms with which to protect privacy). Privacy is often said to involve the right or desire to be left alone. In the context of EmNets, it more often has to do with the right or intention of a person to keep certain personal information confidential. A breach of security may result in breach of privacy by someone without proper credentials who gains access to private information; a breach of privacy may also occur when information that is freely shared over a network is abused or when EmNets are deployed into various environments without notification, consent, or full disclosure. Breaches of security may also involve the dissemination, through an EmNet, of information that is intended to be shared for a narrow purpose but is used nonetheless for broader purposes because of an inability to precisely con-

---

[16]CSTB anticipates a policy-oriented study on privacy in the information age to begin sometime in 2001. In addition, Chapter 5 of the CSTB report *The Internet's Coming of Age* (CSTB, 2001) examines implications for broad public policy, including issues related to privacy and anonymity on the Internet.

trol data flows or the use of information collected for one purpose for a completely different purpose.

Security and privacy are related for another reason, too: both may be studied and understood in a given context by analyzing threats and risks. The security threats to a given network can be catalogued; countermeasures for those threats specified; and then residual risks of failure, oversight, and inadequacy identified. Similarly, the threats to privacy from the deployment or specific use of EmNets may be catalogued, means for protecting and preserving privacy specified, and the residual risks analyzed and managed. Privacy issues may be somewhat more challenging to deal with than security issues because they entail varying expectations and values and because access control practices often call for conveying personal information. Privacy seems far more malleable than security, because what counts as private is socially negotiated; privacy violations may occur when individuals have different understandings about the boundaries and contexts of privacy (this will be especially true with new technologies and where the technology moves information across multiple social contexts). Expectations are in flux, as the Internet is demonstrating that there is less privacy than may once have been assumed. Further, people differ with respect to the types of information they wish to keep private, the conditions under which they might allow access to different sorts of information (for example, health records, financial information, and online purchases), and the degree to which they value privacy.

Privacy Research Topics Deserving Attention

While the privacy issues discussed above raise many public policy questions, they also raise several technical research issues that need to be addressed. Both the policy and technical issues demand much additional research, but this research need not be EmNet-specific. In addition, while many of the policy and technical issues may not be directly applicable to defense and military situations, the need in such situations for identification (for example, friend or foe?) and for need-to-know classification of information make some of these points relevant. Privacy has largely been dealt with by advocacy, legal, and political processes; however, it will increasingly involve and require technical mechanisms and contextualizations. The committee strongly encourages additional research in the many policy issues surrounding privacy and makes the following recommendations with respect to technical concerns:

• *Flexible policy management.* EmNets, and indeed all information systems, do implement some form of privacy policies. Often, however, this is by default not by design. Research is needed to develop a calculus of privacy[17] and ways to enable flexible, configurable privacy policies in systems so that as external situations or policies change, the system can be easily adjusted to reflect that. Systems should be designed to allow incorporating a wide range of potential privacy policies.

• *Informed consent.* Implementing informed consent in technological systems is a difficult challenge. EmNets seem likely to make this problem that much harder. Owing to the passive and ubiquitous nature of many of these systems, users will often not be aware that information about them is being gathered. Notifying users who may not even be aware of the existence of the EmNet is a difficult problem. Even more difficult is acquiring meaningful informed consent from those users. Research into these and related issues is essential.

• *Accountability research.* Research into possible legal requirements for the protection of personal information may be needed to ensure adequate accountability. The goal should be to ensure that specific individuals or agents, probably those who deploy EmNets and will use the information gained therefrom, are deemed responsible and accountable for the protection of an individual's private information collected on those networks.[18] Privacy and/or anonymity preservation techniques need to factor in accountability. Accountability, like privacy, is not absolute (Lessig, 1999). What is needed is technology to support a range of preferences, which may vary with users and contexts, for enhancing privacy, accountability, and other values.

• *Anonymity-preserving systems.* Research in designing systems whose default policy is to preserve individual users' anonymity is needed. It is an open question to what extent these systems would need to allow completely untraceable use rather than just strict identity protection except in the presence of authorized agents. Another possible avenue of investigation would be to enable anonymity-preserving authentication[19]— for example, to enable systems to determine that individuals are members of a certain group (say, doctors in a hospital) but not to allow more fine-grained identification.[20]

---

[17]A calculus of privacy can be thought of as a method of analysis, reasoning, or calculation that takes into account the many factors relevant to privacy (people's expectations, the characteristics of disclosed information, ease of access, etc.) and the relationships among them.

[18]P3P can be seen as the early stages of a technology that gives people more control over their data and provides information about how Web sites handle personal information.

[19]Another CSTB committee is currently investigating authentication technologies and their privacy implications.

[20]CSTB's report *Summary of a Workshop on Information Technology Research for Federal Statistics* (CSTB, 2000b) has a section on limiting disclosure, which addresses some of the inherent difficulties in protecting identities in the face of extramural information.

USABILITY

Usability refers to the effectiveness and efficiency of a system in meeting the goals and expectations of its users. All complex systems raise usability issues, and EmNets are no exception. Usability is not a single trait of a system but rather an umbrella term encompassing a number of distinct (and often conflicting) traits, including learnability, efficiency, effectiveness, and satisfaction. Moreover, these traits are not intrinsic to the system but must each be evaluated with respect to specific classes of users. For example, what is intuitive and therefore effective for a casual or beginning user may be tedious and verbose to an experienced user. Further, in the case of EmNets, it may not be accurate to refer to people who interact with them as "users" per se. Consider the case of an EmNet controlling various systems of a building; generally the EmNet will be essentially invisible to the people interacting with its features. An important distinction must also be made between users who are outside the system boundary and operators who are within the system boundary and are, in effect, essential components of the system. Users and/or others interacting with the system will usually have little formal training, whereas operators will almost always have some training because they are hired and trained specifically to operate the system. Operators, in addition, often are required to monitor the automation and take over its functions, if necessary, or to share the control function in various ways. The presence of trained operators allows the system designer to engineer specific training requirements into the system—a luxury that is not generally available in the case of end users. On the other hand, the quality of administration for many systems is very low, and it is not clear that the "users" who will insert components into EmNets are any less qualified than many of the administrators.

Usability and safety are very different—and potentially conflicting—features. Straightforward attempts to improve one negatively affect the other. For example, usability often dictates that operations carried out frequently be convenient and perceptually salient in order to maximize learnability and efficiency. But if such actions are also potentially hazardous, safety concerns may suggest that they be hidden or rendered difficult to execute by accident, for example, by requiring redundant inputs or repeated confirmation. Usability concerns, by contrast, would dictate that a user enter the data only once. One way to address this might be to devise a data encoding scheme that uses error correcting and detecting codes. This would allow detecting simple data entry errors of the sort known to be most common by humans (for example, transposition of adjacent items or missed elements) and, upon such detection, producing either nonsense or correctable states. Such design conflicts are not necessarily insurmountable, as suggested above, but they are unlikely to be dealt with satisfactorily in complex real-world systems in the absence of design methodologies that explicitly give both issues their due. Such efforts are important even where safety has absolute priority over usability, since safety measures that ignore usability are far more likely to be circumvented or otherwise subverted than are those that take usability into account.

It should be noted that although complex systems tend to present more usability challenges than simpler systems, complexity per se is not the main deterrent to learnability or other aspects of usability. There are vastly complex systems (for example, the telephone network) for which high levels of usability have been achieved; and there are relatively simple devices (such as the alarm clocks found in most hotel rooms) that are consistently baffling to all but the most determined user. Usability of complex systems is maximized when (1) complexity that does not need to be exposed to the user is kept hidden and (2) when complexity that must be exposed is exposed according to an underlying cohesive, understandable, conceptual model that maximizes the predictability of the system's behavior, supports the user's efforts to generalize about those behaviors, and minimizes special cases and arbitrary actions.

Creating Mental Models

Mental models are a convenient concept for examining problems of usability. A mental model of a device can be thought of as an individual's idea of the expected behavior of the system as a whole (that is, how the system works) plus information about the current system state. Thus, the mental model amounts to a user's expectations about the behavior of the devices he or she is using. Users form mental models of systems—how they operate or are internally organized—even if they know virtually nothing about the systems. Different users will form different models of the same device; indeed, research shows that a single individual may have several (even contradictory) models of a system (Leveson, 1995; Norman, 1998). An automobile mechanic will have a much more detailed (and hopefully more accurate) model of a car than will a casual driver who has never learned how a car works. Products aimed at mass markets and untrained users must be designed with these mental models in mind to ensure easy operation and commercial success.

Users often generate a mental model for a newly encountered device by analogy to other devices perceived to be similar. In many cases, this analogy may be loose and casual. For example, a first-time user of a digital videodisk player probably will attempt to treat it like a videocassette recorder or a compact disk player. In other cases, the match between the old and new may be quite deliberate on the part of the designer. For example, antilock brake systems (ABS) were deliberately designed to be as indistinguishable as possible from conventional braking systems. The ABS example provides an interesting illustration of the pitfalls of user-model analogies and the conflict between usability and safety. Although most users tend to think of ABS systems as exact functional replacements for conventional brakes (and new-car user manuals tend to describe them in these terms), the analogy breaks down under poor traction conditions, in which conventional systems should be pumped whereas ABS systems should not. The analogy has been drawn to enhance usability and learnability (no special training is required and the driver need not know which type of brakes the car has), but it also has led to serious accidents.

Usability may also be enhanced by designs based on standard metaphors. A familiar example is the desktop metaphor used in the design of graphical user interfaces for personal computers. In this paradigm, files and other abstractions defined by the computer's system architecture are presented to the user as graphical metaphorical objects on the screen. These objects are imbued with certain consistent behaviors. For example, screen icons can be dragged around, they stay where they are placed, double-clicking on them opens the program, and so on. In effect, the user interface is endowed with a consistent physics more or less analogous to the physics of the real world and, to the extent that the analogy is appropriate and consistent, the user is able to apply schemata developed in dealing with real-world things to the metaphorical "things" behind the glass. It is important to realize, however, that metaphor is a means and not an end. When metaphors are clean and well chosen, they can become a powerful means of providing consistency in support of user models. But it is the consistency that ultimately has the greatest value, not the metaphor per se, and often the causes of consistency and ease of learning are better served by other techniques.

An example of a usability technique is the use of idiom in interface design (see Cooper, 1995). Idioms are design conventions that, unlike metaphors, cannot readily be guessed but rather must be learned, by either instruction or experiment. For example, many computer interfaces that use graphical interfaces require the user to double-click the mouse while the pointer is at a particular location on the screen to effect a desired action, such as opening a document. Unlike the process of dragging an icon or window to reposition it, there is nothing metaphorical about the double-clicking operation—that is, it does not obviously correspond to anything the user has encountered in the real world. Nonetheless, if implemented consistently and with proper attention to human factors issues, the technique is easy to learn and use. In effect, this arbitrary behavior becomes an important part of the physics of the interface without ever having been part of the physics of the real world.

In designing for usability, good designers will require a grasp of the probable models that users will tend to bring to (or infer from) the device. As obvious as this may be, such understanding is difficult to achieve, in large part because designers typically know things that users do not. They are inevitably better informed about the true nature of the device than a normal user is, and designers cannot easily act as if they are typical users. Yet, this is exactly what is required to design against a user model that may be imperfect.[21] There is a large literature on methods that help a designer take the user's perspective, most notably various approaches to user studies and so-called heuristic analysis techniques (Nielson and Molich, 1990; Nielson, 1994). More work is needed on developing good conceptual models of systems.

EmNet-Specific Usability Issues

Many of the usability issues raised by EmNets are common to all complex information systems. However, there are characteristics of ubiquitous computing in general and EmNets in particular that present new and unique challenges to the usability engineer. In particular, the distributed nature of EmNets and their often intimate coupling with the physical environment represent a fundamentally new relationship between device and user. A personal computer is a thing one sits in front of and uses. How will end users think about EmNets? Probably not as "things." They may think of them as capabilities, as smart spaces, or as properties of the built environment. They may think of them as magic. Often, they will not think of them at all. The usability of such systems will not be the sum of the usability of their component parts. It will instead be an emergent property of the behaviors of the visible nodes and their invisible counterparts, of their interactions, and of the physical environments to which they are coupled. What is the source of global coherence in a system that may be spatially distributed, incrementally designed, and implemented using heterogeneous and independently developed components? Although the existence of such system-level behavior, as a superset of the behavior of the individual components, is not new, it is nonetheless

---

[21]The relationship between implementation models and user models is discussed at length by Cooper (1995) and Tognazzini (1992).

difficult to address. What is new is that the very existence of the complex system may be unknown to the end user.[22]

Usability Research Topics Deserving Attention

EmNets raise interesting challenges related to the usability of systems with emergent properties. When large networks of devices are used to create smart environments, for example, the process of designing these networks to enhance usability and of ensuring helpful effective models will be complicated by the very complexity of these systems. More research is needed in the following areas:

• *Design for users and interaction.* Approaches need to be developed for designing EmNets of increasing complexity that are usable with minimal training and without detailed knowledge of the system design or of the complex interconnections among system components. EmNets should be designed to accommodate users with varying skill levels and to accommodate the fact that they will often be invisible to the individuals interacting with them.

• *Appropriate conceptual models.* Further study is needed on the construction of appropriate conceptual models—that is, models that describe

---

[22]A further consideration is the relationship between EmNets and their operators. One could speculate that the experience might be less like running a specific machine than participating in a confederation. A lot will be going on, couplings will often be loose. One could also imagine the operator finding himself or herself more in the role of influencer than absolute controller. For example, EmNets widely coupled to the outside world may have severe responsiveness constraints that prevent the immediate execution of operator commands. In spatially distributed systems, communications cannot be instantaneous, and in bandwidth-constrained situations may be extremely sluggish. This, too, may contribute to the operator's sense of being only loosely coupled to the system. Efforts should be made to generalize lessons learned from the control of existing EmNets or EmNet-like systems, such as the telephone network and the power grid, both of which have benefited from a great deal of rigorous human factors research. Research synergies may also exist with areas of distributed control being worked on by DARPA and other agencies, such as collaborations between humans and confederations of agents and control of robot swarms.

In many cases, the locus of interaction design is likely to shift from user/device interactions to user/information interactions. The emerging disciplines of information architecture and human information interaction (Gershon, 1995, Lucas, 2000) shift the focus of design from devices as such to the information that those devices mediate. Examples of research topics in this area include architectures for universal identity of data objects, replication architectures, techniques for maintaining perceived constancy of identity across heterogeneous display media, tangible interface techniques (Ishii and Ullmer, 1997), and information-centric user interfaces and polymorphic rendering (Roth et al., 1997).

the critical aspects of the system and that are understandable and usable by people. Further study is also needed on developing appropriate specifications. People need to learn how to design for both novice and expert use of EmNets and for situations where the person interacting with the system is not aware of any interaction. Furthermore, attention needs to be paid to the different types of assistance that various users will need. System maintenance personnel will have a different and often deeper understanding of the system than will system operators.

REFERENCES

Computer Science and Telecommunications Board (CSTB), National Research Council. 1999. *Trust in Cyberspace.* Washington, D.C.: National Academy Press.

CSTB, National Research Council. 2000a. *The Digital Dilemma: Intellectual Property in the Information Age.* Washington, D.C.: National Academy Press.

CSTB, National Research Council. 2000b. *Summary of a Workshop on Information Technology Research for Federal Statistics.* Washington, D.C.: National Academy Press.

CSTB, National Research Council. 2000c. *Making IT Better: Expanding Information Technology Research to Meet Society's Needs.* Washington, D.C.; National Academy Press.

CSTB, National Research Council. 2001. *The Internet's Coming of Age.* Washington, D.C.; National Academy Press.

Cooper, A. 1995. *About Face: The Essentials of User Interface Design.* Foster City, Calif.: IDG Books.

Fisher, David A. 1998. *Design and Implementation of EASEL: A Language for Simulating Highly Distributed Systems.* Pittsburgh, Pa.: Carnegie Mellon University. Available online at <http://www.sei.cmu.edu/programs/nss/design-easel.pdf>.

Friedman, B. 1999. *Value-Sensitive Design: A Research Agenda for Information Technology.* No. SBR-9729633. Washington, D.C.: National Science Foundation.

Gershon, Nahum. 1995. "Human information interaction," Fourth International World Wide Web Conference, December. Boston, Mass.

Government Printing Office (GPO). Code of Federal Regulations. Title 47, Vol. 3, Parts 40 to 69, revised as of October 1, 1998. Available online at <http://frwebgate2.access.gpo.gov/cgibin/waisgate.cgi?WAISdocID=177665407+1+0+0&WAISaction=retrieve>.

Hunt, Warren. 1994. "FM8501: A verified microprocessor." Ph.D. dissertation, LNCS 795. Heidelberg, Germany: Springer-Verlag. Abstract available online at <http://www.cli.com/hardware/fm8501.html>.

Ishii, Hiroshi, and Brygg Ullmer. 1997. Presentation at CHI 97 Conference on Human Factors in Computing Systems, March.

Lessig, Lawrence. 1999. *Code and Other Laws of Cyberspace.* New York: Basic Books.

Leveson, N.G. 1995. *Safeware: System Safety and Computers.* Reading, Mass.: Addison-Wesley.

Leveson, N.G., J.D. Reese, S. Koga, L.D. Pinnel, and S.D. Sandys. 1997. "Analyzing requirements specifications for mode confusion errors," Workshop on Human Error, Safety, and System Development, Glasgow.

Lucas, Peter. 2000. "Pervasive information access and the rise of human-information interaction." *Proceedings of ACM CHI '00 Conference on Human Factors in Computing Systems.* Invited session, April.

Lutz, R.R. 1993. "Analyzing software requirements errors in safety-critical embedded systems." *Proceedings of the IEEE International Symposium on Requirements Engineering,* January.

Neisser, U. 1976. *Cognition and Reality*. San Francisco, Calif.: W.H. Freeman and Co.

Nielsen, J. 1994. "Heuristic evaluation." *Usability Inspection Methods*. J. Nielsen and R.L. Mack, eds. New York: John Wiley & Sons.

Nielsen, J., and R. Molich. 1990. "Heuristic evaluation of user interfaces." *Proceedings of ACM CHI '90 Conference on Human Factors in Computing Systems*.

Norman, D.A. 1998. *The Invisible Computer*. Cambridge, Mass.: MIT Press.

Roth, S.F., M.C. Chuah, S. Kerpedjiev, J.A. Kolojejchick, and P. Lucas. 1997. "Towards an information visualization workspace: Combining multiple means of expression." *Human-Computer Interaction Journal* 12(1 and 2):131-185.

Sarter, N.D., and D. Woods. 1995. "How in the world did I ever get into that mode? Mode error and awareness in supervisory control." *Human Factors* (37) 5-19.

Schneider, Fred B. 1993. "What good are models and what models are good." *Distributed Systems*, S. Mullender, ed. Reading, Mass.:Addison-Wesley.

Thibodeau, Patrick. 2000. "'Huge' privacy questions loom as wireless use grows." *Computerworld*, December 18.

Tognazzini, Bruce. 1992. *Tog on Interface*. Reading, Mass.: Addison-Wesley.

Wiener, Earl L., and Renwick E. Curry. 1980. "Flight-deck automation: Promises and problems." *Ergonomics* 23(10):995-1011.

BIBLIOGRAPHY

Card, S.K., T.P. Moran, and A. Newell. 1980. "Computer text-editing: An information processing analysis of a routine cognitive skill." *Cognitive Psychology* 12:32-74.

Card, S.K., T.P. Moran, and A. Newell. 1983. *The Psychology of Human-Computer Interaction*. Hillsdale, N.J.: Lawrence Erlbaum Associates.

Fowler, M., and K. Scott. 1997. *UML Distilled: Applying the Standard Object Modeling Language*. Reading, Mass.: Addison-Wesley.

Gray, W.D., B.E. John, and M.E. Atwood. 1993. "Project Ernestine: Validating a GOMS Analysis for Predicting and Explaining Real-World Task Performance." *Human-Computer Interaction* 8(3):237-309.

Kieras, D., and P.G. Polson. 1985. "An approach to the formal analysis of user complexity." *International Journal of Man-Machine Studies* 22:365-394.

Minsky, M. 1974. "A framework for representing knowledge." MIT-AI Laboratory Memo 306. (Shorter version in *Readings in Cognitive Science*, Allan Collins and Edward E. Smith, eds., San Mateo, Calif.: Morgan-Kaufmann, 1992.)

Perrow, C. 1984. *Normal Accidents: Living with High-Risk Technology*. New York: Basic Books.

Schank, R., and R. Abelson, 1977. *Scripts, Plans, Goals and Understanding*. Hillsdale, N.J.: Erlbaum Associates.

5

Models of Computation

As discussed in Chapter 2, advances in circuit design, packaging, power management, and networking (especially wireless networking) provide the components needed to construct large networked systems of embedded computers (EmNets) for a wide range of applications. The opportunities are, in fact, overwhelming, because these components will be incorporated into systems of increasing complexity on which society will depend in unprecedented ways. The effort needed to design systems so that they can be maintained, configured, and trusted will be substantial. If EmNets are to be designed in a principled way rather than being assembled using techniques determined on a case-by-case basis and specialized to the system being built, computational models will be needed to provide a conceptual framework in which the designs can be created, thought about, and tested.

Designers of complex systems use a range of conceptual models to help them construct and reason about systems. These conceptual models are built out of a set of abstractions that hide those aspects of the system that are considered to be either irrelevant or sufficiently unimportant. By not being part of the model, these irrelevant or unimportant aspects need not be thought about in the design of the system, and a variety of ways of implementing the abstractions they correspond to can be used when constructing the system. Thus, the right computational model will simplify the system as well as allow different implementations of the design. Further, the computational model provides the designer with the conceptual mechanisms that allow trading off one aspect of a design against other aspects. When given the appropriate abstractions, the designer of a system can decide to maximize certain features of the system at the cost of others, or decide to design a system that trades functionality in one area for functionality of some other part of the system.

The adequacy of a computational model is determined by two measures. The first measure is the suitability of the abstractions that have been chosen: They should allow those aspects that are important to the system to be represented in the model and not require the designer to think about those aspects of the system that are not important. The second measure of adequacy is the implementability of the computational model on the environment it is meant to encompass. A model may incorporate abstractions that make the design of a system easy, but that is no help if the abstractions cannot be implemented in the target technology of the system. On the other hand, a set of abstractions might be straightforward to implement but not allow the designer to focus on the properties that are needed, because the abstractions do not simplify the system enough to make the design tractable, or they might simplify it in the wrong way, making it impossible to attain some important aspect of the design.

Computational models are not required to build working systems. Indeed, since one of the questions that needs to be answered in evaluating a computational model is whether it is possible to implement the abstractions of the model, some systems must be built before a model is completely fleshed out and fully validated. In particular, functioning EmNets have been and will continue to be built without complete computational models for them. However, without such models, these systems must be built in an ad hoc fashion, and problems that are not addressed by the existing models must be addressed while the system is being constructed. These problems need to be solved anew by each system implementation, making the process more costly and more time consuming. In short, coherent, well-thought-out computational models will eliminate these problems and will facilitate analysis of systems (for example, to ensure trustworthiness) as they evolve over time.

A number of existing computational models might be applicable to EmNets. Because these systems are built with multiple processors used for a particular task, models of parallel computation could be extended to them. EmNets also share characteristics with storage area networks and distributed databases, so models that have been used in those arenas could also provide insights. However, the computational model most often used in thinking about an EmNet treats it as a distributed system, focusing on the interaction of computation and communications. In distributed systems, these models describe both how the various processors carry out the computation and how they communicate with one another.[1]

---

[1]This discussion intentionally avoids using the word "process" because it is possible that the units of computing are parallel, and a process is typically assumed to be sequential.

Because all computational models are really contracts—that is, particular abstractions can be used given that they can be adequately implemented and particular functionality can be reflected in the abstractions— it is important to examine the models when the problem domain, the properties that the system needs to maintain, or the hardware configuration changes. All of these changes come into play with the design of EmNets. Hence, it is important to ask the following questions:

- What abstractions used in traditional computational models might be applied to EmNets, and are those abstractions rich enough to allow a model that is sufficient for the properties that are needed in EmNets?
- Are there new abstractions that must be created, either in addition to or replacing those of a traditional computational model, when computational models for EmNets are built?
- Is it possible, given the abstractions that can form a coherent and adequate computational model for EmNets, to implement those abstractions in the technology that will be used for EmNets?

This chapter examines these and other key modeling issues. The first section provides a primer in models of computation. The second section examines the models of computation already developed and in use for describing distributed computing systems. The third section identifies ways EmNets might strain or require extensions in existing models and describes potentially fruitful avenues of inquiry that could lead to the development of new or enhanced models appropriate to these systems. The last section suggests an overall approach to pursuing this type of research.

WHAT ARE MODELS OF COMPUTATION?

Existing computational models function at many different levels of abstraction; often, high-level abstractions build on simpler ones. The abstractions can involve data, computation, and communication. The most familiar computing model is probably that of a sequential processor, which states that the output of the system can be modeled by a simple sequential execution of the instructions in the program. Although almost all processors execute instructions in parallel to enhance performance, and some modern processors execute instructions out of order (see Chapter 2), the computational model used by programmers assumes that the processors obey a set of constraints that allow this simple, sequential computational model to be retained.

Computational models evolve over time, as abstractions are introduced to eliminate unnecessary details and clarify the important design points of the systems being modeled. In the early days of computer science, the data aspects of a computational model were thought of in low-level terms, such as bit strings or integers. Such low-level abstractions were often tied to particular machine architectures, which used data words of different sizes, and they were difficult to use in different environments or to reason about. This led initially to the notion of simple data types (for example, 8-bit bytes and byte streams) and ultimately to the introduction of the higher-level data abstractions that are used today, such as abstract data types or objects.

Abstract data types, rather than focusing on the data structure implementation, model the data and operations at a higher level in terms of the desired response. One way of implementing these abstract types is through objects, which represent information in terms of the operations (often called methods) that can be performed on that information and which associate with that information the code needed to manipulate it. Thus, rather than representing a geometric point as a pair of integers indicating the x and y coordinates, an object representation would define methods that returned the x and y coordinates and would allow the point to be drawn or moved. How the object actually represents the information is left up to the implementation of the object (for example, it can use a pair of integers, polar coordinates, or some other scheme). Such objects allow functionally equivalent representations of information to be treated as identical from the point of view of the user, allowing the user or a higher-level model to concern itself with the use of information rather than the representation of it.

Computational models for distributed computing have followed a similar evolution. Early models were concerned with the communication of data from one cooperating computer to another. For example, the Open Software Foundation's Distributed Computing Environment (DCE) Remote Procedure Call (RPC) (Zahn et al., 1990) system centered on describing data and communicating them from one machine to another, no matter what the internal representation of that data might be. Abstract data types in the form of interfaces were introduced in the Common Object Request Broker Architecture (CORBA) (Object Management Group, 1991), allowing definitions of the types of information that could be exchanged from machine to machine without reference to the way the machine represented or computed that information. Object-based systems, such as those in Modula-3 Network Object (Birrell et al., 1994) or the Java Remote Method Invocation (Wollrath et al., 1996), allow objects and associated methods to be communicated from one machine to another in the system. These systems can be seen as extensions of the techniques used on a single machine, adding the communication aspect to the model for the distributed system case.

Such innovations represent important progress because they allow a change in the level of detail, from how bits or other groups of entities are managed, to behavior that can be depended on by the rest of the system. This shift enables a modular decomposition of functionality that is critical for keeping system complexity under control. Thanks to these additional layers of abstraction, reasoning about the system needs to take into account only the information supplied by the abstract data type or object, not how that information is represented in the underlying execution engine. This specification of what information is supplied (or required) acts as an interface, stating only what is necessary for the information and not the incidental features of the particular representation of that information. As discussed previously, an increase in the level of abstraction of the interfaces on which the system relies also greatly reduces system fragility, because a system can adapt and change some of the lower-level mechanisms while maintaining the higher abstractions needed for system operation.

By supplying these abstractions, the computational model also limits what can be expressed within the computing model. Each abstraction limits the detail that is considered important in the model, simplifying reasoning about the system at the price of limiting the vocabulary of the designer. When applying a computational model for one discipline, such as distributed computing, to the domain of EmNets, the overriding question is whether the trade-off between abstraction and expressive power has been accomplished correctly. If not, the computational model will need to be extended or replaced by one that gives the proper vocabulary to the designer of the systems in the new domain.

Whether or not a particular computing model can be implemented is often determined by the set of presuppositions on which the model is based. Building an abstraction may require certain properties in the underlying system that are not explicitly part of the model. For example, one of the major differences between the distributed computing model articulated by the CORBA abstractions and the model articulated in Java Remote Method Invocation is the latter's ability to pass objects, including their methods, from one participant in the network to another. This, in turn, is implementable because the system presupposes the existence of the Java Virtual Machine on all members of the system, allowing both behavior and data to be passed in the distributed system. The CORBA system does not make this presupposition, so it can only allow the passing of behavior in very limited circumstances, since a general model of mobile behavior, while useful, would be unimplementable.

Models of computation also allow the precise definition of notions of resource complexity. In more conventional systems, this has often meant time, space, and communications bandwidth. In EmNets, trade-offs between energy, latency, memory, processing, bandwidth, and persistent storage will be necessary. As algorithms are constructed to work within the computational models created for EmNets, it will be necessary to evaluate them with respect to these various complexities and the trade-offs between them.

DISTRIBUTED COMPUTING MODELS: CURRENT PRACTICE

While there are several models for distributed computing, nearly all of them are based on one of two underlying abstractions: distributed objects and distributed shared memory. Both provide a basis for under-standing computing systems in which elements are distributed across a network and, as such, can offer a starting point for thinking about EmNets. Other models can be built on top of these basic models, offering higher levels of abstraction when necessary. These two models, however, form an expressive base that is carried through in the models built on top of them. If these basic models lack a way of expressing concepts that are needed for thinking about EmNets, models built on top of them will be unable to add the concepts at a higher level. If these basic models cannot be implemented in the environment presented by EmNets, it will not be possible to implement computational models built on top of them. As will be seen, both models have serious deficiencies when used as a base for EmNets.

As interesting as the concepts used in building the traditional compu-tational models of distributed systems are the concepts that have been abstracted out of such models. The traditional model has concentrated on the mechanisms for passing information from one network component to another (RPC, message passing, shared memory). However, the tradi-tional model has abstracted away notions such as communication timing, resource use, and memory requirements for the underlying system. These are not important concepts in traditional distributed systems, since those systems assume that the entities that are connected by the network are sufficiently powerful computers, plugged into an adequate source of long-term power, with few limits in terms of the amount of memory available or the ability to store persistent information. However, a number of these concepts that do not appear in traditional computational models of dis-tributed systems are vital to the design and understanding of EmNets. A similar example has to do with the failure models that have been devel-oped for distributed systems (Schneider, 1993), which range over a vari-ety of ways in which the communication between systems can fail but have a simple model of failure in terms of the components of the system themselves. This simple model of failure may be inadequate for EmNets, where there are likely to be large numbers of networked systems that may fail (or turn themselves off) often.

Differences such as these call into question the use of traditional distributed computing models in the domain of EmNets. At the very least, it seems clear that certain concepts that have been abstracted out of the computational model for other kinds of systems will need to be added to reach a model that is adequate for reasoning about EmNets.[2] The rest of this section elaborates on some of the assumptions made in traditional models and explores why such assumptions may not be adequate for EmNets.

Both distributed shared memory and distributed objects are based on attempts to abstract over many of the details for the communication needed in a distributed system. Sometimes this is achieved by assuming that a robust network is used in the system that can deliver information to the desired destination. Other systems may attempt to mask communication failures or reflect such failures to the next layer or even the application. The goal, in both cases, is to allow the system designer to concentrate on the way the system works without having to worry about the reliability of the underlying communication framework.

In the distributed objects model, the entire system is composed of objects, or combinations of information and the functions or methods used to manipulate and access that information. These objects can reside on different machines; in some of these systems, the objects can migrate during the computation. In this model, objects are created with the knowledge of how to communicate with certain other objects (that is, they are provided with references to these objects when they are created) or types of objects (that is, they are provided with references to these objects as the result of a method call), and they do so by calling the methods associated with those objects. When objects call the methods of other objects, the object being called can be on either the same machine as the caller or on a different machine. The call mechanism abstracts away the details of the communication needed to make a remote call, thus simplifying the model. This means that in the implementation of the model, the call mechanism must handle all the communication issues, such as dealing with an unreliable network by retrying the call as appropriate. Some systems try to supply a call mechanism that can deal with all forms of failed communication, but some forms of failure break this abstraction. Other systems attempt to reflect such failures to the caller, perhaps by an error message indicating communication failure. However, in all of these systems the

---

[2]In a similar fashion, *Trust in Cyberspace* (CSTB, 1999) discussed the limitations of security models for networked computer systems.

assumption is that communication rarely fails and that the cost of communication is at worst the time it takes for the communication to take place.

In the distributed shared memory model, individual computation units do not communicate directly with one another. Instead, an area of memory is provided to each unit and made to appear to be common to all units. Computation units use this area of shared memory to communicate indirectly, by calling methods of objects in this shared system state. A typical way of using this model is to make the objects in this system state very simple, so that their only methods are read and write; but the model can also be applied to objects that allow any kind of method. Note that this technique does not require an actual area of physical memory to be shared by all computation elements; rather it is an abstraction of a possible, more complex interconnection network that provides this illusion. As in the case of the distributed object model, the communication mechanism must "do the right thing" in the presence of network problems and failures and convey the right information to users when problems cannot be masked. The shared memory model attempts to present a model to the programmer in which there is no communication, only the invocation of methods on local (but shared) objects. With such a model, either the underlying system must be able to mask all communication failures from the participants or the computational model of shared memory must be compromised to allow information about such possible failures to be visible. Implementing the model without accommodating failures requires a network that can be made as reliable as memory access, and again the cost of communication is represented as (at most) increased latency in the access to shared memory.

Other models can be and have been built on top of one of these two models. An example is the class of models built on the idea of a shared whiteboard, which can be seen as an extension of either the shared memory model or the distributed object model. In such systems, there is a single shared repository of information objects that is accessible to all participants in the distributed system, and communication involves writing information into such spaces and allowing it to be read out by some other member of the distributed system. The shared space can be viewed as shared memory with special access operations or as a special type of distributed object. In either case, the new model is a further abstraction on one of the more basic models. Rather than adding new concepts to the model, it builds new abstractions on the old models. Lessons may also be drawn from higher-level parallel programming models, such as NESL,[3]

---

[3]For more information on NESL, see <http://www.cs.cmu.edu/~scandal/nesl.html>.

BSP,[4] and HPF,[5] where a rich set of aggregate operations is provided to the programmer and compiled down into code for the constituent nodes and components. However, with EmNets the collection of nodes may be unstructured, constantly changing, and oriented toward real time. This problem is also related to database query processing, if one views the data being collected from the pool of sensors as a fine-grained distributed database. This view is attractive, because data are identified by key, rather than by address. However, the model for EmNets will not be working with regular tables and records but with a changing collection of data streams, where aggregate query operations must be spread across many tiny nodes and must be placed as close as possible to the data so as to minimize energy-consuming communication. A third and related viewpoint is that the EmNets are an extremely fine-grained tuple space, as in Linda[6] or JavaSpaces (Freeman et al., 1999). Linda-like systems can be seen as a shared whiteboard in which a particular naming system is used that has been extended to deal with both communication and concurrency issues. Many operation sequences take place in the tuple space concurrently, with associative operations utilizing the inherent parallelism. A unique element of EmNets is the opportunity to exploit redundancy in an adaptive fashion to manage density and power utilization.

The hardware design community employs discrete-event concurrency models (as implemented primarily in Verilog and VHDL) to design highly reliable and understandable concurrent systems. Synchronous models, which originated in the hardware community, are arguably one of the most powerful concurrency abstractions by virtue of their ability to handle complexity in understandable ways. These models have spread to software design, as embodied in such languages as Esterel[7] and Lustre.[8] Even within the culture of the software world, abstractions such as process networks, port-based objects, I/O automata, functional languages, rendezvous-based models (such as CSP or CCS), and data-flow models all provide abstractions for use in their particular problem domain. All of

---

[4]For more information on BSP (the Bulk Synchronous Parallel computing model), see <http://www.bsp worldwide.org/>.

[5]For more information on HPF (High Performance Fortran), see <http://www.crpc.rice.edu/HPFF/>.

[6]Linda is a language for parallel programming in which communication occurs by inserting and retrieving tuples, collections of data referenced by a name, into a shared area. For more information, see the Linda Group at <http://www.cs.yale.edu/Linda/linda.html>.

[7]For more information on Esterel, see <http://www.esterel.org/>.

[8]For more information on Lustre, see <http://www-verimag.imag.fr/SYNCHRONE/lustre-english.html>.

these models, however, are built on top of either the RPC model or the shared object models, and similar limitations with respect to EmNets apply.

NEW MODELS FOR NETWORKED SYSTEMS OF EMBEDDED COMPUTERS

EmNets have many of the characteristics of traditional distributed computing systems, since they are collections of computing elements connected by networks attempting to perform some task in a cooperative fashion. However, EmNets are made up of components that have characteristics very different from those that make up traditional distributed computing systems, components whose limitations make it difficult to implement the standard abstractions of the traditional models. Because of the way EmNets will be used, the design trade-offs made for those systems will often be very different from those made in the design of standard distributed systems, requiring the introduction of new concepts and abstractions to allow thinking about appropriate balance.

A computational model is useful only when the abstractions in the model can be implemented in the technology for which the model is constructed. A useful computational model must also allow the designer to reason about the characteristics of the system that are important. In EmNets a number of characteristics are important that are not present in the standard computational models for distributed systems and that make it difficult to construct the abstractions common in computational models of distributed systems. These characteristics include the following:

- *Reasoning about time and location.* Since EmNets will often interact with the physical world in a way that satisfies real-time constraints, designers will require a model that has reified the notion of time and allows making design trade-offs concerning timely response. The tight coupling of EmNets to the physical world allows those systems to make use of notions of location, colocation, and proximity that are not possible in standard computational models of distributed systems. Because of this coupling, the functioning of EmNets often depends on inputs or requires outputs that are not modeled by an exchange of information between parts of the distributed system. Thus, a computational model in which behavior of the overall networked system is defined by the information exchanged between the computing elements of the system cannot be implemented in EmNets tightly coupled to the physical world.
- *Resource limitations.* The limited resources—in terms of the resources available on the computing elements themselves and of the ability of those elements to communicate—in an EmNet will require a com-

putational model in which the use of those resources becomes part of the model. Notions such as memory limitations, energy conservation, and access to persistent storage cannot be abstracted away but must be an explicit part of the design of EmNets. A computational model that assumes an environment without such constraints will not be implementable in EmNets.

• *Heterogeneity.* EmNets are built out of components that show a high degree of heterogeneity. Some of the components will make use of traditional computing elements with persistent storage and abundant energy supplies and will be connected by wired networks with high reliability and bandwidth. Other components will be built with specialized processors having limited processing power, will have limited or no persistent storage, will be connected using low-bandwidth wireless networking, and will have limited, self-contained power supplies. A computational model that does not allow differentiating the kinds of nodes that will be used to construct these systems will not be able to conserve the limited resources available to the lowest-level members of the network nor will it be able to capitalize on the power of the most competent members of the system.

• *Nonexpert users.* Since EmNets will often be operated by nonexpert or casual users who have only a superficial understanding of the technology, the failure of such systems will need to be communicated to those users in ways that allow the failure to be understood and appropriately responded to. The computational model will need to have a rich failure model, allowing designers to decide which of the failures can be dealt with by the system and which will need to be reflected to the users. Unless the various kinds of failures in such systems are part of the conceptual model, designing a system with such failure models will be difficult or impossible.

• *Many redundant components.* The ability to produce large numbers of similar components cheaply will allow some EmNets to introduce levels of redundancy and scope that are not possible with more conventional computational models for distributed systems.

• *Long lifetimes.* Since EmNets will often be designed for a lifetime that exceeds the lifetime of any one of the components, the need to reason and design around in-process upgrades of the system requires a computational model unlike those used in more conventional distributed systems. In effect, this means that the already high degree of heterogeneity in these systems will also have a time element, with the components changing over time as well as from place to place within the particular system. This will require more than just the kinds of reconfiguration and adaptation talked about in Chapter 3; it will also require a computational model in which the abilities of the various parts of the system can be queried and reacted to within the software of the system.

As has been emphasized throughout this report, no single aspect of EmNets is unique to the emerging field. Other systems have had real-time constraints. Other systems have been built from small, resource-limited components. And other systems have had to interact with the physical world.[9] All of these systems have been based on, or formed the basis of, a computational model that has addressed some of the needs of the computational model for EmNets. What makes developing the computational model for EmNets unique is not any particular aspect of the model, but the combination of large numbers of networked components, resource limitations on those components, duration of deployment, connection to the physical world, and richness of potential connectivity. The mission-critical and, sometimes, life-critical nature of these systems makes a coherent computational model for these systems a high priority for the academic and industrial research communities.

In the next sections, the committee identifies areas in which the computational model can make use of information or needs to allow for reification if it is to account for the unique combination of features and requirements presented by EmNets. The computational models that arise for EmNets may not include all of the areas that are discussed, or they may include features that are not included in the discussion. What follows are the features that appear at this point to be the most promising for enriching a computational model for EmNets.

Models with Resource Constraints

An immediate challenge in creating a computational model adequate for EmNets is to determine the right level of data abstraction. As discussed above, existing distributed system computational models abstract

---

[9]Distributed control systems (discussed in Chapter 3) have operated distributed infrastructures such as the electric grid, pipelines, and railroads that (1) are closely tied to the physical world, (2) must cope with location, and (3) operate under time and resource constraints. However, in each of the above examples, their layout has been predetermined and their interaction with the physical world extremely prescribed. The physical coupling discussed in this report is of a much tighter nature (for example, chips embedded in everyday objects with which the user has experience in interacting directly rather than with the computer system to which it is connected). In addition, the aforementioned systems are generally tethered (that is, connected directly to easily replenishable sources of power and to communications infrastructure) and do not have the power limitations under which many EmNets will have to operate.

away performance issues, both on a node and in the network, and are concerned about the order of events but not their timing. This simplification is often useful but sometimes hides too much information. For example, one way of handling diversity in a system with a long lifetime is to run a virtual machine (VM) on each node. Although this provides an environment in which code can run on any node, it completely prevents the application from determining the available resources of that node. One of the critical problems is to find some new, low-level models that extend the VM notion to allow designers, and even applications, to reason about resources. The difficulty is how to accomplish this while maintaining a general framework that is simple enough to be useful. If applications need to select an algorithm given the current resource constraints, determining which algorithm to run should not consume more resources than are saved by the algorithm selection.

Resource constraints also affect issues such as data abstraction. Data abstraction will continue to be important for EmNets, as will the grouping of abstractions into type hierarchies to allow families of related types of objects and the use of various design patterns to hide implementation details. Such abstractions will be needed to hide the particular types of computing elements used in EmNets (which promise to change radically and rapidly over the foreseeable future) while still allowing reuse of computational models, system designs, and (in some cases) software. It may be necessary to redefine certain data abstractions to give applications in this new domain access to the additional data they need to carry out their functions. The abstractions may need to provide ways for higher levels to negotiate different qualities of service (for example, time to carry out specific methods on this object at this time) or performance trade-offs (for example, speed of communication versus resolution of data provided). Memory constraints can also drive work on finding simpler ways of implementing these data abstractions.

Resource constraints in the network also will stretch current computational models. In the two common distributed system models, communication is abstracted almost completely out of the problem. Although this greatly simplifies reasoning about the system, it seems unlikely that these models will be rich enough to support EmNets. Both models buy simplicity at the cost of considerable complexity in the underlying system; it is not clear that this trade-off will be correct for the small components and subsystems that will constitute EmNets. More troubling than the need for richer high-level models is the possibility that the low-level models for the different communication layers will need to change, too, to reflect the resource constraints and poor link reliability of wireless nodes. The ways that networks are formed, messages routed, and participants described have evolved for networks of stable, stationary computational elements. Researchers need to explore whether the networking layers on which these abstractions are built are correct for EmNets. If not, researchers need to explore how these models can be extended to allow additional information to be available for the communication layers, or available in a simpler form for the application, without making the model so complex that it is no longer useful.

Models Dealing with Failures

To design a reliable system, the designer needs a model that includes the types of failure that the system can experience, so that the design can respond to those failures. Some failures can be handled by the system itself; other failures can only be dealt with by the application, and still others will need to be reflected to the user. Failures may compromise security, safety, and/or reliability. Standard formal models of distributed computing identify failures of the components (such as crash or fail-stop failures); failures in the communication infrastructure; and Byzantine failures, in which a component can act in random fashion (including acting like a nonfailed component that sends incorrect information). Actual systems rarely deal with all of these failure models but vary by which failures they try to handle and which are exposed to the application. Examples of such failure models are provided in Box 5.1. However, these models were developed based on the assumption that a component that fails cannot be replaced, and that failure is generally rare or limited in scope. In the case of EmNets, in which the components are low cost and limited in their resources and functionality, different forms of failure may need to be accounted for within the system. A component may fail for a finite period of time, for example, shutting itself down to conserve energy. A network may fail because of limits on bandwidth, allowing some information to be passed from component to component but not allowing the throughput needed for the propagation of all relevant information. These types of failures may require a richer failure model than has typically been provided up to now.

Responses to such failures may also follow an unusual path in EmNets. Whereas a component failure in a standard distributed system might require failover to some replicated component or the election of a new leader in a master/slave replication, such a failure in an EmNet might require only that information be obtained from a different component of the system. In an EmNet that has large numbers of nodes gathering information, the failure of some nodes might be handled by estimation techniques using the information gathered from the remaining nodes. (This has obvious implications for the reliability and survivability of these systems.) Similarly, a network failure may require finding a different

BOX 5.1
Failure Models

Failure models can have a significant effect on the overall computational model for a system. The introduction of a failure type into a failure model may make the building of an application more complex than it would be with a less complete model, but the resulting application may be more reliable because it can survive failures that are not part of the simpler model. These differences can be illustrated by comparing systems with different types of failure models.

As an example of the simpler model, the Object Management Group's Common Object Request Broker Architecture (CORBA) includes a remote procedure call (RPC) system in which communication failure was not originally part of the computational model. Calls could be made from objects on one machine to objects on a different machine, and it was assumed that the communication infrastructure would ensure that the call would be made and, if expected, a value returned. In later versions of the system, the failure model was enhanced by introducing the notion of an exception that would be thrown when the communication failed. The programmer using the system was not required to handle this exception; if an exception was thrown and no part of the program receiving the exception was explicitly designed to deal with the communication failure, then the client program would simply fail.

CORBA can be contrasted with the model found in the Java Remote Method Invocation (Java RMI) system. The RMI is also an RPC-style system, allowing an object on one machine to make calls to objects on a different machine. However, the RMI system requires that any method that can be implemented as a remote call be declared as possibly throwing a special exception that indicates a communication failure. Further, this exception must be handled by the calling code; if there is no exception handler, then the calling program will not compile. How the exception is handled will be application specific. In some cases, the client may simply shut itself down. In other cases, the client may try to find an equivalent service provider or roll back some internal state or contact some administrator to determine the cause of the communication failure. Thus, the notion of communication failure is part of the RMI computational model in a way it is not in the CORBA model.

As a result, programs written using RMI are somewhat more complex than those using CORBA in the sense that RMI programs must contain code to deal with communication failures, whereas programs with similar functionality written using the CORBA system need not. The RMI programs containing this extra code are also more robust, in the sense that they will survive failures in a network that would cause termination in the equivalent CORBA-based program.

neighbor to use as a pathway for the information (consider, for example, communications routing in the Internet.) The capability of the overall system to adapt to failure rather than to simply replace the failed component with an equivalent offers a new route to failure recovery that cannot be taken in more traditional systems but can be exploited in the circumstances offered in EmNets. This possibility opens up a number of interesting data modeling questions for EmNets, as discussed in the next section.

New Data Models

The kinds of systems that will be built with EmNets present a number of programming model problems. While these problems are not entirely new, they arise in a unique environment that makes traditional solutions to the problems difficult or impossible to use.

A key question is how to model the information gathered by an EmNet. Because many of the components are assumed to be unreliable, some will inevitably fail, and when they do, other parts of the system must be able to take over critical functions or compensate for the failure in some other fashion. In addition, if the components recover or are replaced, they need to continue doing what they were doing before, which may well include knowing some of the information gathered over time. All of these requirements imply a need for persistent data. Furthermore, the ability to have one component take over for another argues for a persistent state that is not stored at the component. One promising approach would be to model the system as if components were largely stateless, with a robust storage device in the network. Although a direct implementation of this approach would lead to a single point of failure and high cost, it is possible to distribute this store among the elements that maintain this abstraction and can tolerate failures in the nodes and networks. The computational model presented in such a system has at least two levels of memory. The first, which is not persistent but which is common at the leaves of the network, requires programming techniques that guard against the loss of information. The second, found in the interior of the network, stores the information in a persistent fashion. One of the interesting programming questions in such a system is how much processing should take place at the leaf nodes of the system. The components will be able to do some computation, and the more the amount of raw data available to the sensors can be reduced before sending it to the rest of the network, the more bandwidth is conserved. However, such computation means that power is being used at the edges of the network and that failures may result in the loss of the data. These sorts of trade-offs can only be made in a computational model that reflects the two levels of memory and allows reasoning about the costs and benefits of the design choices in such a system. Whether these methods are appropriate for EmNets is an open research question. Research is also needed to determine if this information must be handled by explicit programming or if it can be made automatic, and to learn what requirements and costs are associated with automated backup replication and archiving.

Explicit programming to generate a consistent, persistent memory is made more difficult because of issues having to do with concurrency and failures. When information is spread over a set of machines that can fail independently and are connected by a network that also can fail, it is difficult to coordinate changes in that information to ensure global consistency. Further, as different parts of the system manipulate the same information, it is possible that changes are made at inopportune times, giving inconsistent views of the system. A computational model traditionally used to deal with these issues involves the notion of a transaction. In a transactional model, a coordination convention is introduced to ensure that in all but the most extreme of failure conditions, either all the operations in the transaction are completed or none of them is. It is not possible for some to be completed while others fail. Further, the transactional model introduces concurrency controls that ensure that each view of the system is consistent and that all parts of the system will view changes as happening in the same sequence. In systems supporting this model, one need not worry about what happens if a failure occurs halfway through the operation; in addition, transactions ensure that the intermediate state of the atomic collection cannot be seen by other operations in the system.

The transactional model is an example of a computational abstraction that makes the job of the application programmer much easier, at the price of increasing the complexity of the underlying system. The transactional model of memory is very powerful because it simplifies reasoning about many types of interactions; however, implementing a transactional model of memory is quite complex and may not be possible on all of the various kinds of nodes found in EmNets. These implementation issues may make a pure transactional memory model too expensive to be used in the design of EmNets, and it might be possible to create a compromise model for these systems. Some weaker notion, with fewer guarantees but also without some of the implementation problems that accompany the transactions mentioned above, might be developed both to maintain consistency in the persistent state and to accomplish some of the application tasks.

The transactional model is also an example of how a single abstraction can be introduced into a computational model to greatly facilitate the design of reliable systems. Currently, there is no such unifying and simplifying abstraction in the computational model for EmNets, and one is sorely needed. It might be some variation of the transaction abstraction, or it might be a completely different computational construction. The only way to develop it is to encourage research in a number of different directions to find one that bears fruit.

The two-level model of memory leads naturally to a shared memory model of communication, described earlier. But to make a big, persistent store work flexibly, methods of naming the contained objects are needed. One particularly interesting research question deals with the intentional naming of objects—providing a name for an object that is related to its function or other attributes. This naming structure might have significant advantages in systems with high redundancy levels, in which similar data are collected by many different devices. Isolating information so that not all of the information obtained by every component is available to every other component may also require hierarchical or partitioned memory models, in which the placement of information determines which components can access it.

The programming models used by these systems may depart from the familiar in radical ways, or they may take familiar programming notions and apply them in ways that they have not been applied before. Many EmNets are highly event- and datacentric. Especially in sensor networks, users may be more interested in receiving information about a particular event that has been detected (for example, a chemical concentration exceeding a particular threshold) or in receiving a particular set of data (for example, the chemical concentration in a particular geographical region) than in receiving information from a particular node (for example, the chemical concentration reported by sensor number 1234). This may also be true in a smart space in which users wish to send data to the nearest network element, to an element with particular characteristics (for example, high-bandwidth communications capability), or to the nearest element to which they have a direct line of sight. This sort of capability becomes even more important in dynamic systems in which nodes, resources, obstacles, and event triggers themselves move around in unpredictable ways. It implies that many EmNets will need to be designed with a focus on naming and operations on data elements instead of naming and operations on node identities. Event-driven programming is common in areas like user interfaces, where the program is driven by events generated by the user. These techniques, which share the quality of reacting to occurrences in the physical world, are generally not applied in the context of a network, but may provide a fertile area of information exchange between practitioners of different fields of computer science and other disciplines.

Models of Trust

Trust issues enter into the computational model of EmNets for many reasons (see Chapter 4), including the likelihood of changes in the set of entities that make up those systems and the likelihood that such systems will make use of mobile code. Both likelihoods may require adding trust notions to a model for EmNets that are traditionally outside of conventional computational models.

In the case of mobile code, it will often be the case that the environment into which code is moved will need to establish a trust relationship with that code. This cannot be done by some interaction with the code, since by the time such an interaction could happen the imported code will have been loaded into the host environment and will probably have had access to at least one thread of control. Waiting until this point to establish a trust relationship with the imported code is dangerous, since the code could already have damaged the host system. The mechanisms for establishing trust may in fact reside in the underlying system and will only be reflected in the computational model as additional failures that can occur because of security. However, the computational model may need to be enriched beyond that to allow setting various limits on the power of imported code. What will be required for trusting mobile code is not clear; what is clear is that research into the establishment of such trust relationships is needed.

Beyond the trusting of mobile code is the reestablishment of trust when members of the system are replaced, repaired, or upgraded. The discussions of reconfiguration in Chapter 3 only go as far as to allow the establishment of communication and cooperation between such nodes; they are essentially questions of how we can make such nodes work together. The questions surrounding the reestablishment of a trust relationship are fundamentally different in that they involve the set of circumstances under which such working together is not allowed to occur. However, the decision whether or not to trust either new (mobile) code or new elements of the EmNet will need to be part of the computational model.

Models for Concurrency

EmNets are inherently concurrent systems, that is, they are collections of entities that operate independently but attempt to cooperate on a common task. There are no particularly good programming models for concurrent programming; in fact, the general wisdom is to avoid the need for concurrency whenever possible. Concurrency in programs tends to be programmed directly. For example, an active object might begin with a single sequence of instruction execution and as part of that execution, create other, independent sequences of instruction execution. These would occur either in another processor or on another machine, in a logically separate process scheduled by the operating system of a single machine, or in a separate thread of execution in the same process, scheduled by the underlying operating system or by some library. If these so-called threads of execution are cooperating, they must do so by communicating or sharing some information. Access to the communication paths or shared information is generally coordinated explicitly by the programmer, using mechanisms such as locks and semaphores. However, this type of explicit synchronization is a well-known cause of bugs, the most common of which involves a single thread assuming that a piece of shared information cannot be changed over some period of time by any of the other threads of execution, even though no lock is held on the information.

Similar explicit approaches to concurrency control, such as shared job queues that allow coordinating work among the different threads of execution, are also limited in scale or prone to programmer error. Systems that attempt to hide or deal with these issues have automatically been designed around small networks of very large machines, and it is not at all clear that the same principles apply to large networks of very small machines.

Of further concern, almost all existing ways of dealing (programmatically) with concurrency introduce the possibility of very large time delays when there is competition for a resource, a pattern that runs counter to the need of EmNets for predictable, real-time performance. Given that attachment to the real world is a requirement and that it entails known performance parameters, it follows that the usual ways of dealing with concurrency are not applicable to EmNets. An additional constraint in EmNets is the need to support the model on very small system components (for example, 8-bit processors with very limited programming and storage).

There are, however, methods that might be applied to concurrency within EmNets. Optimistic or wait-free algorithms may be applicable in these systems. In addition, some of the techniques of control systems—in which constant approximations are made of future states that are then compared to the actual results—can cut down the requirements for concurrent access to information. This is an open area of research both within the EmNet community and within the larger programming community, and results from both communities should be studied for their applicability to the problems of concurrency in EmNets.

Models of Location

As noted before, a defining characteristic of EmNets is their connection not only to other computing systems but also to the physical world. Because of this connection, there is a mapping from many of the members of such a network to a particular location in three-dimensional space, namely the location at which the system interacts with the world.[10] There are also spatial relationships among the various elements of the EmNets themselves. By adding location information to the basic computational model, it may be possible to invent new algorithms, techniques, or configurations that exploit this additional information to make advances in reliability, trust, or functionality. A number of location-based concepts could be of interest, including absolute location, proximity, relative distance, and relative motion. Whether some or all of these are needed or relevant is an open question that needs to be addressed. In addition, the layers at which location should become part of the model, and the interfaces used to gain access to that information, need to be investigated. Such an approach exploits the impression that many EmNets are event- or datacentric: What matters is not the precise part of the EmNet that is performing some computation but rather the sensing of some occurrence or the computing of some data by any member of the assemblage.

Traditional networked systems have tended to be closed in the sense that interactions take place among members of the system, with little or no connection to the physical world (other than, perhaps, the users of the networked systems and the physical artifacts that are explicitly—and only—part of the system itself). Because of this, such systems were often based on topological principles that abstracted over the physical location of network members and relied only on the connectedness relations between the members. By introducing into the equation the physical location of the elements of EmNets, one can expand the vocabulary for network relationships to include concepts such as proximity, distance, and a host of geometric relationships. This vocabulary (and the information that it allows one to describe) can be used to produce new algorithms that can minimize energy use or maximize computing power in a particular area. It also allows the naming of areas where information is to be gath-

---

[10]In this discussion, EmNets should be distinguished from factory automation systems (for example, systems used to fabricate parts and convey work in progress from one piece of automated equipment to another or those used to automatically retrieve inventory). In a factory, the physical world is a highly constrained, well-understood environment in which the interaction is very prescribed (for example, retrieve item Y from prespecified location X.) In EmNets, components will be physically coupled to elements of their environment that are not as highly prescribed in their function and/or location (for example, a button on a piece of clothing or a free-floating sensor in an urban sewer system.)

ered rather than the nodes in the network that gather that information, and ultimately the naming of the information itself rather than the sensors that receive that information.[11]

Similarly, nodes often use information about their location in three-dimensional space to determine their action (for example, which sensor should be tasked to monitor a particular geographical region or which is the nearest switch that should operate a particular piece of networked audiovisual equipment). Traditional computing systems have not needed such information, so support for geolocation information is relatively weak. Robotics is the best example of a computer science discipline that has faced this problem, and work in this field demonstrates the difficulty of the task (see Chapter 3 for a discussion of distributed robotics). Particular technological approaches for supporting geolocation are discussed in Chapter 2; however, even given the existence of geolocation systems, additional effort is needed to define and refine the abstractions used by application and system developers as they work with geolocation.

CONDUCTING RESEARCH ON MODELS AND ABSTRACTIONS

Computational models are not developed in a vacuum. The computational model for EmNets will evolve as applications of the technology are developed. Full applications need not be completed before this activity can move forward, although enough of a prototype needs to be developed that new models can be tried, measured, and evaluated for their relevance and completeness in the new set of environments and with the new set of assumptions that EmNets present. As experience in building these applications is gained, designers will discover which abstractions are useful, which ones hide information that needs to be visible, and what types of connections between the abstractions will allow people to model and reason about the types of EmNets that they want to build.

Research in this area will require a delicate balance between, on the one hand, application development and underlying system construction and, on the other, the building of the computational model. Although some driving applications will be needed to test the work, the goal needs

---

[11]This calls into question the general naming or description schemes used in distributed systems, in which the base naming identifies members of the network and, relative to that, other names or descriptions can be used to identify events that occur on that machine or data stored at that machine. Research into identification schemes that are based on directly identifying the events or information may insulate EmNets from changes in the particular members of the network that happen to be sensing the event or gathering the information.

to be the construction of underlying systems that can be used with multiple applications. The underlying system should be the instantiation of a computational model that presents the right set of abstractions for reasoning about the overall system infrastructure as well as the particular application. Thus, the building of the application should not be viewed as the end goal of the research but rather as a means for identifying those parts of the model and infrastructure that can be applied more broadly than the application at hand.

As these models are built, run-time environments based on them can also be developed, and this, in turn, will make it easier to develop applications using the models. The development of environments based on the models will allow the application programmers to develop systems based on the models more quickly and researchers to evaluate and modify both the models and the environments more quickly. This scenario forms a positive feedback loop in which run-time environments built to reflect models allow more rapid application development, which in turn allows more complete evaluation of the models. Such a cycle can lead to rapid evolution of the model and the run-time environment in response to the rapid development of applications; however, the initial stages of building this loop will be lengthy relative to the later stages and seemingly chaotic as well, as basic assumptions are tested and computational models are in significant flux.

This is not to say that the initial inquiries into computational models and their associated run-time environments will be completely unstructured. There are a number of areas in which it seems clear even at this early stage that fruitful investigation can be undertaken. One such area of investigation is the network model itself. During the past 20 years, both industry and academic researchers have worked with a computational model exemplified by the Open Systems Interconnection (OSI) seven-layer reference model. This model describes a set of abstractions defined by the interface presented by each of the layers, giving a modular structure to the model of the network. In addition, the model requires that each layer obtain information only from the layer immediately below it and provide information only to the layer immediately above it. The end result is a set of models of a network, each providing more functionality (but at a higher cost) than the layer below. Changes in any layer are isolated in that layer, because each layer is defined by an interface, which by remaining the same, insulates the layer above from changes. (See Box 5.2 for more details on the OSI model.) Clearly, the OSI seven-layer model will be unsatisfactory for EmNets, which seem to require something more lightweight. Such networks may need different abstractions at various layers, requiring that different interfaces be defined for the modular constructs. The strict layering of the OSI model may hide infor-

BOX 5.2
The Open Systems Interconnection Model

The Open Systems Interconnection (OSI) seven-layer model is a standard taxonomic description of networks and a universal reference model for communication protocols. The model is promoted by the International Organization for Standardization, a worldwide federation of national standards bodies from some 100 countries. The seven layers, together with some examples of the types of network entities that occupy each layer, are as follows (top to bottom):

7. Application (network file system (NFS), file transfer protocol (FTP), hypertext transfer protocol (HTTP));
6. Presentation (extensible markup language (XML), ASCII, Java serialization, COM);
5. Session (Sun remote procedure call (RPC), DCE RPC, Internet Inter-ORB protocol (IIOP), remote method invocation (RMI));
4. Transport (transmission control protocol (TCP), user datagram protocol (UDP));
3. Network (Internet protocol (IP));
2. Data link (wire formats for messages); and
1. Physical (wires, signaling).

The standard world of computers on a network is largely homogeneous at levels 3 and 4, permitting great (and largely transparent) diversity at layers 1 and 2 and great diversity at the higher levels. This is effectively a computational model of the network, specifying (at each layer) the interface to the information at that layer, the information that has to be provided to the next layer up, and what guarantees are made by an entity at a particular layer. Each layer acts as an abstraction over the actual workings of the network, with each piece of functionality built on more basic layers. Those underlying layers can change without affecting the upper layers because they are defined by strong interfaces, which do not change from implementation to implementation.

It seems unlikely that this set of abstractions will suffice for EmNets. For example, an EmNet application might need access to the physical layer for information about power in order to save energy or to the network layer in order to do some creative routing. As the chapter points out, new models and abstractions are needed to handle the unique constraints and challenges that EmNets present.

mation needed by EmNets (for example, information about specific nodes or components); accordingly, some relaxation of the layering may be a fruitful area for research.

It should be noted that once models of computation are defined and prototypes have been implemented, significant work will be needed in the design and analysis of algorithms that work within the new models for EmNets. Algorithms that optimize for certain resources, for example, and give near-optimal trade-offs between the various relevant resources will be very important. Designing and implementing algorithms that can both solve the problems EmNets will pose and be implementable within the constrained environment that EmNets will be operating in are likely to be a significant challenge. In addition, the question of how the quality of service might degrade in the presence of partial information (a likely scenario since it may not always be possible, owing to bandwidth or resource constraints, to have all the information) may well need to be answered. Current work on this sort of question deals with time-space trade-offs for computation and trade-offs between the quality of the solution and the precision of the input data, for example. EmNets present yet more kinds of trade-offs that will need to be addressed.

Finally, the examples discussed in this chapter share a characteristic—each identifies an assumption of the current computing model for networks that will not hold in the coming world of EmNets and proposes an alternative to that computing model based on a more reasonable assumption. As people attempt to build applications of EmNets, it will be important for them to identify suspicious assumptions or counterproductive abstractions in the current computing model, and to think of alternatives that can be built into the infrastructure for the application. Many more assumptions and abstractions will be identified than have been listed here. Funding agencies should watch for patterns in which researchers identify a doubtful assumption or abstraction, replace it with another that seems more useful in the context of the application, and determine if the new assumption or abstraction can be used in other applications.

REFERENCES

Birrell, Andrew, G. Nelson, S. Owicki, and E. Wobber. 1994. *Network Objects.* Digital Equipment Corporation Systems Research Center Technical Report 115.

Computer Science and Telecommunications Board (CSTB), National Research Council. 1999. *Trust in Cyberspace.* Washington, D.C.: National Academy Press.

Freeman, Eric , Susanne Hupfer, and Ken Arnold. 1999. *JavaSpaces Principles, Patterns, and Practice.* Reading, Mass.: Addison-Wesley.

Object Management Group. 1991. *Common Object Request Broker: Architecture and Specification.* OMG Document No. 91.12.1.

Schneider, F.B. 1993. "What good are models and what models are good?" *Distributed Systems,* 2nd ed., S.J. Mullender, ed. Reading, Mass.: Addison-Wesley.

Wollrath, A., R. Riggs, and J. Waldo. 1996. "A distributed object model for the Java(tm) system." *Computing Systems* 9(4):265-290.

Zahn, L., T. Dineen, P. Leach, E. Martin, N. Mishkin, J. Pato, and G. Wyant. 1990. *Network Computing Architecture.* Englewood Cliffs, N.J.: Prentice-Hall.

6

Conclusions and Recommendations: An Agenda for Research

EmNets will be embedded everywhere, from automotive instrumentation to precision agriculture to battlefield surveillance. They raise fundamental research challenges in part because they will be performing critical functions and also because they are inherently distributed and tightly coupled to the physical world through sensors and actuators. Moreover, while they are rich in the numbers of elements, they are at the same time highly resource constrained in the capability of the individual elements. This chapter builds on the findings and discussions in Chapters 2 to 5 to specify particular research projects and processes that will be necessary to realize the vision articulated throughout this report.

As outlined in this report, EmNets present a number of research challenges that need to be addressed. An important message for the research enterprise is that new approaches to the study of systems rather than components must be developed as a deeper understanding of the emergent properties of many interconnected elements is gained. To attain this goal, research will need to become more interdisciplinary than ever before as practitioners learn to design, deploy, and—hopefully—trust these large-scale information systems. The need to approach the challenges presented by EmNets from a systems-oriented, interdisciplinary perspective stands out among the many technological problems delineated elsewhere in this report. Failure to meet this need would be the most serious impediment to realizing the full potential of EmNets in society.[1,2]

---

[1] A thorough discussion of the systems imperative, of the growing argument for interdisciplinary research, and of related issues for the broader IT community can be found in *Making IT Better* (CSTB, 2000).

The growing complexity of information technology systems will be accentuated by the evolution of EmNets. This complexity arises not only from the large number of components involved but also from the lack of determinism and the continual evolution such systems will undergo. Effort on the part of the whole community (industry and academia, as well as funding agencies) is necessary. While there are specific EmNet applications emerging from industry, they do not encompass the kinds of scalable, robust, physically coupled EmNets that are discussed throughout this report. In the absence of appropriate funding, issues such as adaptive self-configuration, predictability, and computational models will not be addressed in ways that will enable comprehensive understanding. This lack of understanding will result in a technology that is both prohibitively expensive and prohibitively brittle and will preclude the widespread adoption of EmNets as envisioned here.

The Internet has provided one of the first real examples of a large-scale, heterogeneous networked system. It serves as an excellent model for observation and provides some early indicators of the issues arising from the widespread deployment of EmNets that will need to be addressed.[3] The Internet consists of millions of loosely interconnected components that generate communications traffic independently of one another. There has been standardization in the middle levels of communication protocols, but a wide variety of physical interconnections, from optical broadband to wireless, is supported. However, from the casual user's perspective, the degree of interoperability has essentially been limited to what can be done through a Web browser. For the most part, the currency of the Internet has been in the realm of information. The connections between today's various information services are only now starting to evolve into multilayered and richly connected ensembles.[4] Connections to the physical world have been limited to basic sensors (for example, cameras and weather sensors) and very few actuators (for example, camera motors and home remote control).

As noted throughout this report, EmNets will build on the Internet

---

[2]EmNets provide an excellent illustration of how computer science can benefit from interactions with sister engineering fields, which have long addressed conventional embedded systems.

[3]For a discussion of Internet-specific issues, see the CSTB report *The Internet's Coming of Age* (CSTB, 2001).

[4]The automated shopping agents that query multiple vendors for the best price on a requested item exemplify this. They integrate information in different formats to yield an easy to understand comparison. Automatic purchasing systems are now being built on top of these basic services to trigger automatic purchases that will keep inventory at the specified levels.

experience (itself a product of significant federal research investment) but will also extend it in new directions. The physical world will be coupled to the information space. Sensors and actuators will be spread throughout the everyday environment. People's activities will be recorded and affected by computing systems in virtually all spheres of life. The heterogeneity of the devices that will be interconnected will increase dramatically. From a world of PCs and servers, IT will move to smart dust,[5] swallowable health monitors, and automated buildings. This move will require a much deeper understanding of how to build into EmNets the challenging properties of scalability and robustness.

In this chapter, several overarching research themes are described that draw on the discussions developed throughout the report. Following the description of these themes is a discussion of what will be required of the industrial and academic research enterprises in order to make progress on the substantive research recommendations made in this chapter and throughout the report. In addition, specific recommendations are made to federal funding agencies that, if followed, would facilitate progress in this area.

AN EMNET-SPECIFIC RESEARCH AGENDA

The committee has found eight key areas in which concerted research efforts are needed: predictability and manageability; adaptive self-configuration; monitoring and system health; computational models; network geometry; interoperability; the integration of technical, social, ethical, and public policy issues; and enabling technologies. This research will need to be very broad and very deep and so is unlikely to be achieved through industry efforts alone. Key to developing the research in these areas is the parallel pursuit of the major thrusts described in this report (see Chapters 2 to 5) and the integration of research across the various topics as necessary. Achieving progress in such a research agenda will require forward-thinking, visionary leadership and the willingness to invest in long-term research programs without requiring premature checkpoints or demonstrations and without a priori agreements on specific architecture, so as to allow room for reasonable exploration of the design space.

This section draws on the analysis contained in earlier chapters of the report to identify eight areas that should be part of such a research agenda.

---

[5]The goal of the DARPA-funded smart dust project at the University of California at Berkeley is to integrate sensor and communication systems into a package that is roughly the size of a cubic millimeter.

These areas fall into three categories: (1) research that is needed to build robust and scalable EmNets, (2) research on social, ethical, and policy issues that result from the deployment of EmNets; and (3) research on component technologies that is unlikely to be addressed by the general IT research community.

It should be noted that *networking* is an implicit theme pervading most of these areas and so does not stand apart as a separate research issue. The success of networked systems of embedded computers will depend heavily on the networking research community and work going on there, including the work highlighted in Chapters 2 and 3. Progress in EmNets is not possible without progress in networking. The research issues raised by EmNets constitute a theme around which new networking research programs can be structured. Similarly, issues of *usability* and *manageability* arise throughout this discussion. The human element in complex, not-well-understood systems is critical at all levels, including design, programming, deployment, control, manipulation, and interaction. Human-centered approaches must therefore be incorporated into all of the research areas discussed below.

Predictability and Manageability: Methodologies and Mechanisms for Designing Predictable, Safe, Reliable, Manageable EmNets

Designing for predictability in EmNets requires new methodologies and design strategies that will support characterizable, understandable, and manageable systems. These systems need to allow for isolation of systems components and analysis of the interactions that take place within an EmNet that is exploiting massive amounts of interconnection. At the same time, methodologies are needed for presenting system behavior (including behavior that emerges throughout the lifetime of the system) to end users and system managers; these methodologies must transmit the correct information at the correct abstraction level. Users of EmNets may be experts at the task their computing system is helping them accomplish, but they should not need to know a lot about *how* the computing system is doing it. They need to be able to make certain basic inferences about what they can expect of their EmNet in order to make good, safe use of it.

It is likely that EmNets will radically alter the definition of a system. Instead of simply designing all the individual components of a system and their interactions specifically for a particular system function, people will be fielding components that provide basic capabilities. A "system" will mean exploiting the capabilities of those basic components in a new way by marshalling the capabilities of what is already deployed, altering their function, or adding new elements. Pieces of a system deployed for one purpose may be utilized for other purposes not originally planned.

Moreover, continually changing or adding new elements to the mix will cause new, unintended behaviors to emerge. The Internet is providing some early examples of this: When new services are deployed, their increasing use may cause congestion and a decline in service quality at some points in the network. Once the network is embedded everywhere, every new deployment will probably trigger adjustments and possible detrimental effects on service only because it causes some contention for common scarce resources. Such behavior should occur in an understandable and reasonably predictable fashion. If something has broken, or even worse, is about to break,[6] how should the EmNet inform its users?

EmNets must have interfaces that let users who are not professional system administrators wield them effectively, through normal as well as abnormal conditions such as partial system failures. Sets of abstractions should be developed that have meaning within the computing system itself yet still conform to users' conceptions of the tasks they need to accomplish. EmNets have the same human computer interface problems as existing systems, exacerbated by the other, nontraditional aspects of EmNets, including users who are inexperienced with the intricacies of EmNets, real-time interactions with the physical world, long-lived systems that build user trust at the same time as their internal safety margins may be decreasing, and enormous overall system complexity.

Adaptive Self-configuration: Techniques to Allow Adaptive Self-configuration of EmNets to Respond to Volatile Environmental Conditions and System Resources in an Ongoing Dynamic Balance

EmNets will need to exhibit adaptive self-configuration in order to be viable. The massive numbers of elements, along with the resource constraints on individual elements and the environmental dynamics in which they will need to operate, combine to create a new and likely pervasive requirement for adaptive systemwide behavior that is unparalleled except perhaps in natural systems. The number of elements, resource constraints, and dynamics imply that systems cannot rely on a priori system design or manual adjustment. The system elements cannot simply be

---

[6]If the system is obviously broken, users will know not to rely on it and will go about trying to get it repaired. If users do not know that all redundancy has been used up and the system is on the edge of disaster, they may believe that the system is as trustworthy as it ever was and unwittingly take unwarranted risks.

configured to operate under worst case assumptions, because doing so would make them orders of magnitude less efficient and, in many cases, unable to meet system lifetime requirements. Moreover, EmNets cannot be dynamically configured centrally using global information because acquiring the global information consumes significant amounts of energy and is not scalable. Further, some of the adaptation will need to be done in a very short time frame, one that requires that processing of input and action be completed as quickly as possible to meet the real-time requirements of the application.

The current state of the art with respect to adaptation and configuration is exemplified in Internet protocols. These protocols are somewhat self-configuring and adaptive. However, they have not had to cope with intense input/output, environmental dynamics, and tight energy constraints as a primary design issue. EmNets will require the development of new distributed algorithms and techniques for provable distributed control. They will also require system models and characterizable behavior in order to support embedded systems with strict time constraints (latency, in particular). EmNets will need to provide rich interfaces to the application designers as well. For example, a truly scalable sensor network must self-configure so that the correct collection of nodes (those that have collected good signals from stimuli) collaborates in signal processing to detect and identify phenomena of interest inside the network. The particular sets of nodes that should participate cannot be determined a priori. Such a determination clearly depends not only on the nature of the application but also—and even more so—on the nature of the object(s) being monitored and the signals received by the nodes. EmNets will require nodes and their system interactions to be designed so that applications can influence the parameters and rules according to which nodes adaptively self-configure.

Monitoring and System Health: A Complete Conceptual Framework to Help Achieve Robust Operation Through Self-monitoring, Continuous Self-testing, and Reporting of System Health in the Face of Extreme Constraints on Nodes and Elements of the System

The mission-readiness requirements of EmNets will vary from one EmNet to another, but all will require a minimal amount of overall computational horsepower, a certain amount of interconnection bandwidth and latency, and some minimum amount of sensing and perhaps actuation. With current technology, this mission readiness will be evaluated by having the system perform periodic self-checks on all of those dimensions, with some kind of overall health indicated to the system user or administrator.

EmNets will change over time both in the numbers and kinds of their components and in the applications they are designed to perform. Current notions of system health, which tend to be based on the health of the individual components, do not extend to such systems, where no single component may be critical for the system to perform its intended function as long as the system can adapt to the current conditions. How such health, which is tied to the overall mission of the system rather than the function of the parts, can be defined and monitored by the system itself will be an important area of investigation. A critical challenge is that this system monitoring must be done in the face of resource constraints. For example, pulling system health information out of the system may consume valuable, unreplenishable energy. Just as the system may need to aggregate information about its function inside the network, it may need to aggregate information about its health.

Designing and constructing large systems of many heterogeneous components is already an extremely complex task. The added constraints of EmNets make it even more so. It may be possible to turn to fields such as economics, biology, and statistics for new tools to tackle this growing complexity.[7] New approaches need to be developed for self-monitoring, self-testing, reconfiguration, and adaptation, as discussed in Chapters 3 and 4. Systems will have to be built with self-monitoring and self-regulating devices. Statistical approaches will be needed to properly detect situations requiring attention. Immune systems will need to be developed to counteract the unintended (or intended) effects of new deployments.

Because of the interactions with other requirements of the system, the conceptual framework for robust operation, adaptation, and self-testing cannot stand on its own. It must be part of a large conceptual model that takes into account the other features, requirements, and restrictions of the system, as discussed in Chapter 5. Research needs to be done not only on how to monitor and express this notion of system health, but also on the trade-offs that are possible between these requirements and the other requirements of the system.

Computational Models: New Abstractions and Computational Models for Designing, Analyzing, and Describing the Collective Behavior and Information Organization of Massive EmNets

Systems as complicated as EmNets will present enormous challenges for the analysis of behavior and performance. Existing tools and concepts

---

[7]Various efforts to study complexity already reach out to a wide variety of disciplines. See, for example, the work of the Santa Fe Institute at <http://www.santafe.edu/>.

are barely adequate for understanding simple multiprocessor systems with four CPUs. They are clearly inadequate for systems with many thousands of physically coupled, long-lived, adaptable, self-configuring, interacting nodes. Moreover, defining the right model to handle these many components is not sufficient; the model needs to ensure that it is possible to reason about and understand the interactions of the various parts of the model so that appropriate trade-offs can be made, when necessary, in the design of the entire system.

In particular, in order to take better advantage of the many potential uses and impacts of EmNets, abstractions are needed for designing interactions with the physical world. Sensors and actuators will often play a key role in such systems. Moreover, new abstractions are needed for designing systems that make use of massive redundancy in order to deal with the extraneous data and uncertainty of the physical world. Unknown at this point is what building blocks will be used in EmNet environments that will play the seminal role that transactions and remote procedure call (RPC) played in more traditional systems. Defining appropriate data structures, process interactions, and APIs will require a substantial research effort, one that iterates between experimentation, concept development, and theory building.

The development of new abstractions for reasoning about collective behavior will be one of the biggest contributions of EmNets research (see Chapter 5). Both humans and the artifacts they design will require these abstractions to reason about and adapt to the new situations that will emerge when interesting new mixes of devices and services are created. Abstraction is one of the most powerful tools that mathematics and engineering have brought to the scientific enterprise. Each technological era has associated key abstractions. New eras bring new abstractions and vice versa. It is now time, as the era of EmNets commences, to begin the development of its principal abstractions.

Network Geometry: Ways to Support and Incorporate Network Geometry (As Opposed to Just Network Topology) into EmNets

In many traditional systems, the geographic location of a particular node is not important; instead, what matters is the abstract network topology. The fact that EmNets are coupled to the physical world requires understanding how to generate and use other forms of location information, such as three-space coordinates or logical coordinates associated with a building structure, for example. Such information can be both an important attribute of application-level data and a significant organizational principle for the system itself. When organizing information at the application level, knowing which nodes are in close physical proximity to other nodes can be very helpful. For example, location information could be useful in determining coverage of a particular physical area. At the system level, such information can be used when trying to achieve efficient system behavior. For example, a node might be interested in determining the closest repository for storing long-term data. In such a case, close physical proximity is desirable in order to reduce resource expenditures. Location information is useful in another way as well: Using three-space information in combination with static environmental information allows the creation of logical location information that takes into account the surrounding environment.

As discussed in Chapters 2 and 5, global positioning system (GPS) technology is not sufficient for all of the network geometry needs of EmNets. GPS is a good model for the services needed in many outdoor, three-space-oriented systems but not necessarily for EmNets that are indoors, on the battlefield, or in other remote locations. Moreover, GPS is not ideal for networks whose nodes are small. New kinds of systems are needed that are not constrained in the way GPS systems are. Research into systems that can take into account the logical structure of the geographical environment—for example, walls separating offices, the location of doors, or the inside of a vehicle—is also essential.

Interoperability: Techniques and Design Methods for Constructing Long-lived, Heterogeneous Systems That Evolve over Time and Space While Remaining Interoperable

EmNets will often be embedded in long-lived physical structures (homes, office buildings, hospitals, wells, aqueducts, airplanes, roads, and so on) and thus must be long-lived themselves in order to be effective. To be long-lived, EmNets must be able to evolve, as it is very likely that the functionality required of them will change in some way, perhaps to something for which they were not originally designed. Further, heterogeneous EmNet components will have to interoperate with each other, as well as with various external devices to which they will connect. Achieving such interoperability over the lifetime of the EmNet and over the changing space in which the EmNet will be operating is an open research challenge. As discussed throughout the report, existing techniques and strategies for interoperability are not yet up to the many challenges posed by EmNets.

EmNets will typically operate in an unattended mode, wherein many actions must be taken without human intervention. Aspects of the environment may change, and elements may be moving into and out of the system in unanticipated ways without user assistance. Moreover, while day-to-day operations will need to occur autonomously, the system itself may also have to evolve without human direction. Thus, both the normal operation as well as the system evolution of the EmNet need to be self-configuring. In addition, the operational details of EmNets are often hidden from casual users, and thus the evolution of the system needs to occur as transparently as possible so as not to be obtrusive.

The field of EmNets is developing rapidly but in an uncoordinated fashion. Because they were so badly needed, a number of EmNets have already been designed, built, and deployed, and many of them have come to us from fields other than computer science, such as aeronautics and systems engineering. If EmNets are not to risk becoming obsolete before they are deployed, system evolution and integration standards cannot really start from scratch but must allow the integration and evolution of existing legacy systems.

Accordingly, a research program is needed that will actively challenge EmNet research projects by requiring the integration of unanticipated elements into the research. These unanticipated elements might take the form of new devices, either tethered or mobile, or even legacy systems that could be of use to the overall system. The real aim of this requirement is to ensure that the framework developed for the EmNet is flexible enough to deal with new elements and new requirements. Left to their own schedules, researchers will design for what they foresee the future to be; it is important that this research describe ways to deal with a future that cannot be foreseen.

Integration of Technical, Social, Ethical, and Public Policy Issues: Fundamental Research into the Nontechnical Issues of EmNets, Especially Those Having to Do with the Ethical and Public Policy Issues Surrounding Privacy, Security, Reliability, Usability, and Safety

EmNets are capable of collecting, processing, and aggregating huge amounts of data. With the advent of large numbers of EmNets, the technological stage is set for unprecedented levels of real-time human monitoring. The sensors are cheap and unobtrusive, the computing and communications costs are very low, and there will be organizations with the resources and the motivation to deploy these systems. Thus, EmNets present a difficult challenge in terms of passive information disclosure. In the case of the Internet, privacy issues arise because as users browse for particular kinds of information they are often asked to divulge explicitly other kinds of information, or their clickstreams through and among sites produce information that sites may be storing without the user's informed consent. In the case of EmNets, inadvertent, even unintentional revelations are much more likely. The monitoring these systems do will be almost completely undetectable. The temptation to use such systems for law enforcement, productivity monitoring, consumer profiling, or in the name of safeguarding children from harm will be enormous. At the same time, we have already seen effects of information moving quickly around the Internet (for example, false rumors have had dramatic effects on the stock markets (Walsh, 2000)). EmNets as they have been described here have the potential for even greater and more far-reaching effects.

With respect to security, history has shown that computer systems will be attacked. Data will be stolen or compromised, system functionality and/or availability will be impaired, and the attacks will be incessant. EmNets will be very much at risk for such attacks, since they are deployed specifically to collect important information about the real world and may be capable of acting on it. The security facilities of, say, the Internet, are obviously inadequate. EmNets require much better resistance to malicious intrusions and much better means for detecting and reporting such attempts. These issues are not merely technical, however, and will need to be addressed at a procedural and public policy level as well. The committee believes that purely technical approaches will be insufficient and that policy and technical aspects should be coordinated in order to address these problems. Privacy, security, and ethical considerations need to be considered and incorporated early, during the design and development phases of these systems. These are areas in which inter- and multidisciplinary research efforts could pay large dividends.

The committee believes that the ethical concerns related to security and privacy—which drive legal and policy activity—require a fundamental research agenda. Some of that research will relate to technical mechanisms that can help to ensure authenticated use and proper accountability while safeguarding privacy. But, perhaps more importantly, it may be necessary to develop a new calculus of privacy to be able to evaluate how interactions between new elements will impinge on security and privacy. Users will need ways of comprehending how the aggregation of the information they are divulging to disparate sources can compromise their privacy (e.g., connecting automobile sensor logs to location sensing), and they will need to move beyond concerning themselves only with the security of a Web site's credit card files.

While this report's primary focus has been on a technological research agenda, the committee strongly recommends also examining the policy and social implications of EmNets and other kinds of information systems. How can the development of policy and technical mechanisms be coordinated to encourage realizing potential benefits from EmNets without paying avoidable societal costs? Research that relates technical, social, and policy issues is consistent with the Social, Economic, and Workforce (SEW) component of the federal Information Technology

Research and Development program. This recommendation echoes an earlier CSTB recommendation that networking research should have a component that looks at ethical, legal, and social implications, drawing inspiration from the ELSI component of the human genome initiative.[8]

Enabling Technologies: Ongoing Research into the Various Component and Enabling Technologies of EmNets

In Chapter 2 several fundamental enabling technologies for EmNets were discussed. As described there, research in these areas is still needed in order for the full potential of EmNets to be realized. Several specific issues are mentioned here, although it should be noted that each of these technologies could generate an entire research agenda on its own.

First, continuing research into building low-power processors is essential for ubiquitous, efficient EmNets. Exploring the conflict between power efficiency and flexible functionality raises a number of interesting research questions, and determining the best way to approach this problem is an open question. Continuing research is also needed into wireless communications and network architectures for short-range, low-power systems. Open questions remain about where to place communications in relation to computation and where storage should take place, as well as what appropriate media access control (MAC) or MAC-level protocols should be. Alternative power sources are needed that will satisfy the form factor, communications, and computational requirements of EmNets and their individual components. The use of techniques such as ultra-wideband (UWB) communications for EmNet applications should also be explored.[9]

EmNets will require changes in software functionality and development as well. Upgradability, high availability, and the ability to work with new hardware are just a few of the issues that will need to be taken into consideration when developing software for EmNets. Morever, new and better tools for software development will be needed to effectively and efficiently build software for these systems. Geolocation will also need to be further explored. Determining whether assisted GPS is an optimal location technology for EmNets is an open research question. At the same time, alternative techniques such as acoustic signaling should be explored. Finally, further work in MEMS sensors is needed to develop

---

[8]See *Realizing the Information Future: The Internet and Beyond*, p. 165 (CSTB, 1994b).

[9]The committee recognizes that the potential for UWB may be constrained by regulatory decisions.

sensors that can be realized on the same chips as the electronics needed for control and communication.

STRUCTURING THE RESEARCH ENTERPRISE FOR EMNETS

Ensuring that the right kinds of research are conducted to advance the state of the art in EmNets will require changes in the way the nation's research enterprise is organized. Academia and industry will both have important roles to play. Effective collaboration will be needed not only among industry, universities, and government, but also between IT researchers and researchers in other areas that will make use of EmNets (e.g., the health sciences, manufacturing, and defense). Explicit efforts will need to be made to put mechanisms in place for ensuring such collaboration.[10] While past attempts to achieve similar goals met with mixed results, the pressing needs of EmNets demand redoubled efforts, drawing upon the lessons of history.

Research directions, such as those described in the preceding section, are important to articulate, but it is also *how* that research is conducted that will determine whether the necessary advances are made. In the case of EmNets, researchers will have to gain experience in building and deploying systems. Many of the properties that will need to be studied will emerge only when elements are deployed and begin to be combined and coordinated in ways not foreseen by their designers.

Research funding agencies must be ready to promote a long-term, comprehensive vision and ensure that the appropriate communication occurs between the members of all relevant communities. Building sharing inter- and multidisciplinary communities is essential in a critical research area like EmNets. Once established, these communities fuel research in both universities and industry and further development in industry. Experimental research (not necessarily separate from fundamental research) is key to advancing the EmNet agenda.[11] This means building new systems, deploying them, evaluating them, and then redesigning or retuning the elements as well as the system as a whole. This is an iterative process, and many systems and elements will be thrown away along each cycle as new and better ideas and artifacts are developed.

---

[10]CSTB's report *Making IT Better* elaborates on these themes as related to the broader IT community (CSTB, 2000).

[11]See *Academic Careers for Experimental Computer Scientists and Engineers* for an exploration of experimental computer science within university environments (CSTB, 1994a).

Stimulating Interdisciplinary Research

Mechanisms will be needed to promote interdisciplinary approaches to research on EmNets, which tie computer science to other sciences and other disciplines in general. (See Box 6.1 for a discussion of what may be required when there is an increased emphasis on interdisciplinary and system-level approaches in educational environments.) Domain expertise found in disciplines such as biology, geophysics, chemistry, and medicine will allow the application of EmNets in a variety of areas. These disciplines and others can provide models that couple the world of the networked computer and the physical world and can help in investigations of the wider implications of EmNet society. A wide variety of application domains can serve as testbeds for EmNet ideas and concepts as well as bring richly interdisciplinary teams of researchers and scientists together. However, it is not simply a matter of bringing EmNet expertise to solve problems in the various sciences.

Interdisciplinary benefits will also flow in the other direction. It is clear that if EmNets are going to interface to the physical world, the engineers and computer scientists who will be developing EmNets will need to connect with those who understand the physical phenomena and all their manifestations and variations. These will include bioengineers, environmental engineers, mechanical engineers, nanotechnologists, earth scientists, and chemical engineers. Concepts from control theory and signal processing will need to be in the repertoire of every researcher.

Nor does the challenge end here, for the interdisciplinary net will need to be cast wider still, to bring concepts and techniques from even more distant disciplines, such as systems engineering, biological sciences, economics, and even sociology and political science. Each has a long tradition of trying to understand the aggregate behavior of systems that self-organize or that show coordination without centralized control. EmNets will be systems that are not open to centralized control in the same way that traditional computers or networks of IT machines have been. They will have to be self-regulating, self-configuring, and self-monitoring and will have a much higher degree of autonomy than previous systems, necessitated by the sheer number of devices that will be interconnected in many applications. Moreover, devices will be fielded that, because they will be deeply embedded in the environment or in larger artifacts such as vehicles or buildings, will have much longer lifetimes and will be upgraded by the addition of new elements rather than simple replacement. It is likely that much can be gained from looking at other disciplines to see what kinds of self-organization and decentralized controls have worked in other fields and whether any of the knowledge is applicable to EmNets. Such investigations could add many new pieces to the toolbox of EmNet research and development.

BOX 6.1
Education and EmNets

Increased emphasis on interdisciplinary and system-level approaches is crucial to moving forward in EmNet research. These two approaches are also the ones that require the most attention in the nation's educational system. Related to them are four areas that are largely absent from engineering curricula today:

- Design methodologies,
- Broad interdisciplinary education,
- Design with reusable components and creating components for reuse, and
- System integration, evolution, and maintenance.

Most computer science and electrical engineering departments today are highly compartmentalized. Students are specializing in their studies at an earlier age and often come to higher education along a predetermined path that permits no forays into other disciplines. This tendency to be narrowly focused is often too limiting. Courses that look at the trade-offs between all the levels in the design of a complete system are rare. Furthermore, few institutions are able to couple traditional education with exposure to system prototyping because the technology is constantly evolving and the faculty have limited experience. System prototyping is an area ripe for collaboration with industry.

Interdisciplinary Educational Approaches

Interdisciplinary education is too often interpreted as inter*sub*disciplinary, since it is usually more expedient to think in terms of a single academic department. Students rarely work with students from other departments. Some successful examples come from closely related subdisciplines in engineering departments, but much more needs to be done in preparing for a world of EmNets.

Student design teams need to become broader. For example, the design of a new patient-monitoring and information system should involve students not only from medicine but also from public policy, law, and business, along with the computer science students who will actually write the code. The code they write—its organization as well as its function—may be deeply affected by their collaboration with students from these other disciplines. Electrical engineers developing new environmental sensor technologies, for example, would be well served by working not only with chemists but also with computer scientists, biologists, and other life scientists. This interaction will undoubtedly uncover new uses for the technologies as well as different, possibly much more efficient and/or effective approaches to solving the original problem.

Unfortunately, today's highly specific courses must be taught by faculty from a single department and do not expose students to the rich fabric that interconnects all university disciplines. Graduate education does not correct this deficiency. In fact, it exacerbates the problem by demanding a deeper dive into one subdiscipline. Generalists are generally discouraged in most graduate programs. The emphasis is on depth in a narrowly defined area. Few students are lucky enough to be involved with truly interdisciplinary research projects.

The challenges that lie ahead involve devising models for cross-department faculty collaboration, which is hampered today by antiquated models of teaching. Interdisciplinary teaching is rare, because academic institutions have yet to figure out a way to do accounting except at a departmental level. Finally, industry has a role to play in creating the kinds of educational programs needed for EmNets. By the very nature of the academic establishment, most faculty stop being practitioners for a large part of their careers. This is even more so in engineering than in other fields such as law or medicine. Involving leading industry practitioners in EmNet education is critically important to producing graduate students who think along multiple dimensions and view systems in the large, as integrated wholes rather than individually optimized elements.

Systems-oriented Methodologies

The fact that components rather than systems are taught is an often-heard self-criticism of engineering faculty. But one person's system is another's component. So what is really meant by this? The fundamental difference is one of approach to a problem. Should the emphasis be on abstraction or analysis? Should reuse of modules be encouraged or everything be constructed from scratch? Are system integration issues of interoperability and testing given first-class status or are they afterthoughts?

The nation's current educational system is ill equipped to teach design methodologies. Many perceive the topic as not difficult enough. Furthermore, it is a topic with which faculty have little or no direct experience. Yet, it is clearly a topic that will need much attention as we start to design EmNets, for they present a new framework distinct from that of more traditional systems. Without appropriate methodologies, formalizations, and abstractions it will not be possible to meet the challenge of graduating students at all levels who can function well in this new space. Most engineering disciplines could use courses in aspects of system design from evolution to manufacturing to safety. The focus today is too much on cost or size or power. Rarely are these issues considered in combination, and they are only a few of the many dimensions EmNet designers will need to face.

Reuse

Current teaching methods are based on understanding components, or "design in the small." There is a bias toward teaching students how to design from scratch rather than to reuse what is available. Many faculty members find it difficult to understand how students can complete a degree without knowing how to do every component on their own. However, this style of thinking has led to an overemphasis on design in the small and a lack of exposure to design for reuse and the reuse of designs.

Instead, students should be encouraged to learn not only how to comprehend and build mental models of how others' components work but also how to design so that others can share their design artifacts. Currently, abstractions permit this

BOX 6.1 Continued

at lower levels (for example, logic gates and protocol stacks), but higher levels need to be used (for example, self-updating code and composable network services) if systems of the scale and complexity of EmNets are to be built. Fostering the development of formal models that support higher levels of abstraction and provide students with a curriculum that lets them build on others' work while also providing building blocks for those coming after them is key to this endeavor.

Systems Integration

Finally, one of the most important educational experiences is to work through the process of bringing together a system of many components. This step is crucial to understanding the value of design methodologies and abstractions. System design without the experience of integration is similar to writing code that is never debugged. The art of stepwise integration and debugging needs to be imparted to students as early as possible in their curriculum, and they should be repeatedly exposed to these issues throughout their education.

It is important to understand that the term "integration" is meant in the broadest possible sense. That is, it comprehends not only integration of the components but also the deployment (or integration) of the system into its intended operating environment. Any system will alter that environment and thus affect the assumptions that underlie its own design and development. The closure of that feedback loop is a fundamental lesson in the process of design that few students gain from today's engineering education.

Because of their scope, EmNets offer a new opportunity for cooperation between academia and industry, both in the traditional channels of the computing industry and academic computer science departments and in new channels of interaction between a wider set of academic departments and computing and noncomputing industries, such as medical equipment manufacturers, environmental monitoring consultants, and resource management industries. The committee recognizes that fostering successful interdisciplinary and interinstitutional research is not easy. Encouraging such interdisciplinary and nontraditional collaborations will require the creation of new research venues and new incentives for industrial and academic partnerships. Educational institutions will need to be encouraged to create new centers for research that cross traditional departmental boundaries and ensure that research opportunities within these centers are funded and rewarded. Funding agencies will need to think "outside the box" about the kinds of collaborations they accept and promote. New industrial partners will need to be approached, educated, and enlisted in the construction of new systems that solve problems not currently thought of as part of networks of computers.

WHAT CAN GOVERNMENT DO? RECOMMENDATIONS TO FEDERAL AGENCIES

The federal government has long been a strong supporter of broad-ranging research in information technology. While there have been numerous notable successes—indeed, whole industries have grown out of this funding[12]—fundamental research in information technology is far from complete. This is clearly seen in the context of EmNets. For the most part, EmNets are currently deployed in application-specific, highly engineered contexts. It is essential to develop mechanisms, algorithms, and models that are broadly applicable and reusable to gain experience and confidence with various approaches over time. Similarly, a base of trained technical personnel is needed who understand how to design, develop, and implement these systems. While it is powerful and compelling to demonstrate the concepts and see the potential in various prototypes, such demonstrations alone will not develop the discipline and the techniques to fulfill the vision outlined in this report. Long-lived research programs are essential so that the deeper, harder issues can be addressed and a set of well-understood, characterizable primitives developed for use across many application instances—this is where university research becomes crucial for complementing the more directed and sometimes narrower scope and shorter-term focus of industry.

Federal funding for research guides the focus of the university research community and influences not only what is accomplished there but also what is accomplished in industry. Such funding can cause industry to take a broader perspective and produce more flexible technology for users in the federal government and elsewhere than it would if left strictly to market forces. Collaboration is necessary between industry and academia as the science of EmNets is developed. Today, many university projects are too close to product development, with the lure of start-ups having done much to push things in this direction. Models for joint investigation, fostered by appropriately targeted federal funding, should be renewed if the research community and society are to reap the benefits

---

[12]See *Evolving the High Performance Computing and Communications Initiative to Support the Nation's Information Infrastructure* (CSTB, 1995), as well as *Funding a Revolution: Government Support for Computing Research* (CSTB, 1999).

of a full collaboration. To that end, the committee next describes several ways in which the Defense Advanced Research Projects Agency (DARPA), the National Institute of Standards and Technology (NIST), and the National Science Foundation (NSF) could facilitate research in these areas. It also makes several recommendations to various federal agencies regarding effective sponsorship and support of EmNet-related research.

Recommendations to the Defense Advanced Research Projects Agency

DARPA has already invested in EmNet-related technologies, but it has only scratched the surface of what will be necessary to advance this critical technology. Both its Information Technology Office (ITO) and its Microelectronics Technology Office (MTO) have developed programs that relate to EmNets. It is now time to build on the past successes and present efforts[13] and to broaden and deepen the work in this area. A multifaceted program or set of programs is needed that will pursue the core computer science and information technology issues that have been raised throughout this report. As described previously, narrowly focused solutions and small-scale programs are a good and even essential start, but they are not up to the gigantic task of developing reusable, generalizable, characterizable, and robust techniques for designing, implementing, deploying, and operating large-scale, robust EmNets. It is time to build on these endeavors and turn to systems work that will require extensive breadth and depth in order to be successful.

Publicly funded research is needed to drive innovation that is of sufficient scope—that is, that covers predictability, adaptability, survivability, system monitoring, and so on—and addresses externalities such as interoperability, safety, and upgradability. The development of robust EmNet technology will require the research community to rethink the fundamentals of information technology and the design of computer and communications systems. First and foremost it calls for a systems approach in which design, programming, and control focus on systems composed of massive numbers of networked components and not on optimization of individual or small numbers of elements. A single, isolated,

---

[13]These efforts include Sensor Information Technology (SensIT), MEMS, distributed robotics, Power Aware Computing/Communication (PAC/C), Networked Embedded Software Technology (NEST), Next Generation Internet (NGI), and so on. The networking goals of the Next Generation Internet project, for example, touch on some of the needs of EmNets—for example, the need for large-scale systems that can accommodate a wide range of uses and applications.

short-lived research program will not suffice to address the scope and depth of the problems that must be addressed to realize scalable, robust, and usable EmNets. DARPA should aggressively pursue multiple programs that build upon and interact with one another and with some of the seed programs that have already begun to explore related areas. These seed programs—SensIT is one—have made important initial contributions. It is in part their successful initial forays that now allow the committee to articulate a full-fledged research agenda. However, as mentioned before, they were not of the scale, duration, or scope needed to address DARPA's critical medium- and long-term needs for robust, scalable EmNet systems technologies, and DARPA should now encourage the development of multiple programs that build upon and interact with one another. To truly harness the power of EmNet systems, DARPA should manage these programs in a way that fosters their interaction and creates and builds on conceptual overlaps. The committee emphasizes the need for intellectual collaboration and communication as opposed to requiring prototypes or deliverables from each project for use by one or more of the other projects. There is much to be gained by understanding and exploiting the conceptual commonalities across networked embedded control systems, ad hoc sensor networks, low power design, and smart fabric. And there is much to be lost if such collaborations fail to materialize.

Making progress in an area as large as and, in many ways, as radical as EmNets requires sustained support for research along with a careful rethinking of how best to organize, communicate, and develop the work over the long term. EmNets present an opportunity to continue progress in critical areas of information technology research as well as to discover and advance new capabilities. A long-term research agenda that begins to address these challenges in parallel, while promoting cross-collaboration and interdisciplinary, interprogram work where appropriate, will have tremendous impact. It should have sufficient longevity to explore multiple approaches without insisting on preaward or preresearch agreement on the general architecture and infrastructure. To this end, two recommendations are given below, along with a (by no means comprehensive or canonical) list of possible DARPA programs in this area.

Recommendation 1. The Information Technology Office of the Defense Advanced Research Projects Agency should revise both the substance and process of its EmNet-related programs to better address the research needs identified in this report.

DARPA's Information Technology Office (ITO) took the lead in early research on sensor networks. However, there are several ways ITO's programs could more fully address the research needs explicated in this report. Field demonstrations are clearly critical to DARPA, and such demonstrations should continue. However, the committee suggests that early in a technology's development, research dollars are better spent on exploration of the design space and experimental exploration than on field demonstrations of particular point solutions. Such demonstrations can crowd out more systematic investigations and higher-risk investigations and tend to place too much emphasis on early system integration and convergence to single approaches. Carefully crafted experimental work, on the other hand, can promote real system development and use in a context that provides invaluable feedback to researchers and developers. While it is important for universities to build prototypes, it is crucial to remember that these prototypes are built not for future product development, as are those built by industry, but to understand better the problems of the application. That deeper and more focused understanding is what brings about innovative solutions to problems by deepening scientific understanding (determining, for example, formal models and appropriate abstraction layers). Experimental projects might even involve the definition of interfaces and integration over time without, however, being limited by the constraints of time-sensitive demonstrations. After some period of time, contractors (i.e., industry) should be involved in developing demonstration prototypes and should share their experiences with researchers.

The committee recommends that DARPA focus its efforts on four technical areas in order to realize EmNet technology that is robust, scalable, and widely applicable across Department of Defense needs, both on the battlefield and off (e.g., logistics). These areas are described in Box 6.2. Some of these topics are being addressed by individual principal investigators who are or have been funded under one of DARPA's existing EmNet-related programs, such as Ubiquitous Computing[14] (part of this program focuses on the notion that users do not interact with the computing devices themselves but with the services they provide) and SensIT[15] (the emphasis in this program is creating connections between the physical world and computers by developing the software for networked sensors). Box 6.3 describes more of ITO's current and recent programs in this area. However, the topics addressed by each of these programs deserve and require more exploratory, broader-based investigation. The programs suggested in Box 6.2 are far from exhaustive, but they could serve as the beginning pieces of a much larger systematic effort to address the issues raised in the box.

---

[14]For more information, see <http://www.darpa.mil/ito/research/uc/index.html>.

[15]For more information, see <http://www.darpa.mil/ito/research/sensit/index.html>.

BOX 6.2
Suggested EmNet-Related Programs at DARPA

Designing for Predictability, Reliability, and Safety

As more and more technology is employed in support of mission-critical operations, the inadequacy of system predictability and diagnosability is posing tremendous risks. EmNets intensify these inadequacies, because users will typically interface with the object in which the EmNets is embedded rather than with the system itself. A program is needed to develop abstractions and models that allow users to understand and reason about variable system conditions and failures. Rather than developing models for safety, reliability, and predictability separately, it is critically important to develop models that encompass all three and that address the trade-offs that will be necessary among them. Further, it is increasingly important to build systems with quantifiable (in some cases, provable) properties such as scoping or isolation of system behaviors.

Collaborative Signal Processing

While DARPA has initiated some programs in the area of EmNets that apply to sensor networks, there is a particular need to engage the signal processing community in the development of distributed collaborative signal processing across multiple sensory modalities. Existing programs in these areas require renewed emphasis and support.

Multi-scale Location-aware Systems

Technology has been and is being developed to support particular geolocation techniques. However, many forms of geolocation that are related to proximity and logical location must be integrated into EmNets. There should be a program promoting system technology that exploits multiscale location and involves approaches that will work through a variety of media, including RF, acoustics, and imaging. The program should also explore the difference between infrastructural and noninfrastructural (more ad hoc) approaches.

Interoperability over Time and Space

EmNets will be embedded in our infrastructure and therefore will have lifetimes as long as that of the infrastructure. At the same time, new devices will continually be introduced into the overall system. A program that addresses the challenges of integration and interoperability with new devices over long system lifetimes and changing expectations is needed. It should emphasize research in how to handle legacy devices (for example, how to decommission them while they are deeply embedded). Further, such a program should incorporate the notion that units of interoperability vary: A single device may need to interoperate with other devices, or a cluster of devices may need to interoperate as a unit with other clusters of devices.

BOX 6.3
A Sampling of Current and Recent EmNet-related Projects of
DARPA's Information Technology Office

Networked Embedded Software Technology (NEST)

In this project, DARPA is seeking novel approaches to the design and implementation of software for networked embedded systems. The coordinated operation of distributed embedded systems makes embedding, distribution, and coordination the fundamental technical challenge for embedded software. The goal of the NEST program is to enable fine-grained fusion of physical and information processes.

Sensor Information Technology (SensIT)

The goal of the SensIT program is to create the binding between the physical world and cyberspace. SensIT is founded on the concept of a networked system of cheap, pervasive devices that combine multiple sensor types, reprogrammable processors, and wireless communication.

Ubiquitous Computing

The goal of the Ubiquitous Computing program is to create a post-PC era of computing in which a scarce resource—human attention—is conserved in an environment where computing functionality is embedded in physical devices that are widely distributed. In this environment, users do not interact with any particular computing device but rather with the functionality and services offered by the set of devices at hand.

Recommendation 2. The Defense Advanced Research Projects Agency should encourage greater collaboration between its Information Technology Office (ITO) and its Microelectronics Technology Office (MTO) to enable greater experimentation.

There is an opportunity to take advantage of collaborations between ITO and MTO by enabling experimental EmNet projects with real state-of-the-art sensors and even actuators. MTO-funded research has brought significant advances in MEMS technology, but that research has not yet emphasized the system-level aspects of MEMS. (See Box 6.4 for recent work in EmNet-related areas in DARPA's MTO and its Advanced Tech-

Model-based Integration of Embedded Software

The goal of this project is to create a new generation of system software that is highly customizable and responsive to the needs of various application domains and to the constraints of embedded systems.

Power-aware Computing/Communication

The goal of the Power-aware Computing/Communication project is to enable the intelligent management of energy and energy distribution, providing the minimum power necessary to complete a given task.

Adaptive Computing Systems

The Adaptive Computing Systems program was designed to create unprecedented capabilities for the dynamic adaptation of information systems to a changing environment. It explores redefining the traditional hardware/software boundary to enable the rapid realization of algorithm-specific hardware architectures on a low-cost COTS technology base.

Embeddable Systems

The Embeddable Systems program focuses on leveraging and extending the commercial scalable computing technology base to support defense embedded-computing applications.

Software for Distributed Robotics

The goal of this project is to develop software for the employment and control of large numbers of small, distributed, mobile robots in order to achieve large-scale results from many small-scale robots.

nology Office (ATO).) The idea is to apply well-understood MEMS techniques to produce several types of sensor/actuators that can be integrated into EmNet prototypes by the research community and allow for more realistic experimentation with a range of physically coupled systems. These might take several forms. Examples include a chemical sensor that could be used in experimental monitoring systems, a computational fabric that has a mixture of pressure and temperature sensors, and tension-varying actuators that would enable experimenting with how to control EmNets of this type.

The research community could define standard interfaces to these

BOX 6.4
A Sampling of Current and Recent EmNet-related Projects of DARPA's Microelectronics Technology Office and Its Advanced Technology Office

Distributed Robotics

The DARPA Distributed Robotics program seeks to develop revolutionary approaches to extremely small robots, reconfigurable robots, systems of robots, biologically inspired designs, and innovative methods of robot control. The program focuses on individual robots that are less than 5 cm in any dimension.

Microelectromechanical Systems (MEMS)

The primary goal of the DARPA MEMS program is to develop the technology to merge sensing, actuating, and computing in order to realize new systems that bring enhanced levels of perception, control, and performance to weapons systems and battlefield environments.

Microoptoelectromechanical Systems (MOEMS)

The primary goal of the MOEMS program is to develop the technology to merge sensing, actuation, and computing in order to realize new systems that bring enhanced levels of perception, control, and performance to military and commercial systems.

Smart Modules

The Smart Modules program is developing and demonstrating novel ways of combining sensors, microprocessors, and communications in lightweight, low-power, modular packages that offer warfighters and small fighting units new methods to enhance their situational awareness and effectively control their resources on the battlefield.

Future Combat Systems Communications

The goal of this program is to produce communications technology for ad hoc networks that can operate under severe operational constraints, such as a hostile electromagnetic environment. These mobile networks will have both airborne and terrestrial platforms deployed in an autonomous fashion to provide needed coverage on an ad hoc basis.

Global Mobile Information Systems (GloMo)

The goal of the GloMo project was to make the environment a high priority in the defense information infrastructure, providing user-friendly connectivity and access to services for wireless mobile users.

devices and enable relatively inexpensive prototyping in a widespread manner. Such technologies would provide the academic research community, in particular, with the kinds of artifacts it will need to better explore applications of MEMS technology to EmNets and the system-level issues that result.

Recommendations to the
National Institute of Standards and Technology

NIST, and in particular its Information Technology Lab, has worked in a variety of areas to help make information technology more secure, more reliable, more usable, and more interoperable. All of these characteristics are, as has been described, crucial to current and future EmNet-related technologies. NIST has played a valuable role in promoting standardization and acting as a verification agent (see Box 6.5 for information on EmNet-related NIST programs). In this role, NIST establishes trust in techniques and mechanisms by establishing testing and evaluation standards. Many applications and components of EmNets will require verification, and NIST is in an excellent position to act as arbiter between developer and user.

NIST has already begun to play a role in wireless interference and associated power and frequency standardization. This effort will become even more critical as more wireless devices are deployed at greater densities.[16] New applications of EmNets will call for entirely new metrics for evaluation (such as system lifetime and system manageability or instrumentation). A wide range of standardization efforts will be launched as an offshoot of EmNet activities, including sensor, actuator, wireless, and cross-system interactions.

NIST is in an excellent position to foster interaction by devising the appropriate metrics for measuring the effectiveness of EmNet elements as well as the requirements for performance and quality of service for the more abstract services that will be built upon those elements. In addition to metrics, NIST can also act as a collector of and repository for experimental data. There is a growing gap in access to critical evaluation data. This is already evidenced in the case of the Internet. Unlike in the early days of computing, when most researchers could manage to measure the performance of their own computing equipment, today a national- or even a global-scale infrastructure is required for collecting data-traffic information. Such an infrastructure is accessible to only a very few large

---

[16]It should be noted that the Federal Communications Commission also plays an important role in this area.

BOX 6.5
A Sampling of NIST's EmNet-related Programs

The NIST Smart Space Laboratory

Smart spaces are work or home environments containing embedded computers, information appliances, and multimodal sensors. NIST's goal is to address the measurement, standards, and interoperability challenges that must be met as tools for these environments evolve in industrial R&D laboratories worldwide. NIST is also working to develop industrial partnerships and is sponsoring workshops with DARPA and NSF in this area.

Networking for Smart Spaces

This project explores the use of Java, Jini, and multicast technology in conjunction with wireless systems such as Bluetooth and HomeRF as a networking foundation for pervasive computing or smart spaces.

The Aroma Project

The goals of the Aroma project are to help research, test, measure, and standardize pervasive computing technology by, among other things, measuring the resource requirements and performance of emerging pervasive computing software and networking technologies; developing software tools for testing, measuring, and diagnosing pervasive software and networks; and creating standard abstractions and models for developers.

---

companies. Expanding access to this data by more researchers is an important role for a government agency.

The committee believes that NIST also has a particularly critical role to play in this realm as the agency that establishes confidence in information systems. NIST is seen as an outside observer that can provide objective services and analysis. It has an important role in the standards-development process, allowing the work done in industry to be illuminated in a fair and open fashion. As this report has emphasized, interoperability for EmNets will be very important, and standards will be needed for such interoperability. Given that many of the standards in this arena are likely to arrive as de facto rather than de jure standards, NIST can provide an objective analysis of them and reduce barriers to entry with reference implementations of the technology itself and/or reference implementations of conformance testing tools. More specifically, NIST, through activities such as its Aroma Project,[17] which focuses on testing,

---

[17]For more information, see <http://www.nist.gov/aroma/>.

measuring, and standardizing pervasive computing technology, should play a significant role in the two areas as EmNets become ever more widespread.

Recommendation 3. The National Institute of Standards and Technology should develop and provide reference implementations in order to promote open standards for interconnectivity architectures. It will be important to promote open standards in the area and promote system development using commercial components by making public domain device drivers available.

Recommendation 4. The National Institute of Standards and Technology should develop methodologies for testing and simulating EmNets in light of the diverse and dynamic conditions of deployment. Comprehensive simulation models and testing methodologies for EmNets will be necessary to ensure interoperable, reliable, and predictable systems. In particular, the development of methodologies for testing specification and interoperability conformance will be useful.

In the process of these endeavors, NIST can play a key role in data collection and dissemination of EmNet-related information for use by the larger research and development community.

Recommendations to the National Science Foundation

The National Science Foundation (NSF) has a strong track record in promoting multidisciplinary research and integrated research and education programs. More recently, it has been increasing its support for integrated systems projects—for example, the Information Technology Research (ITR) program. All three areas—multidisciplinary research, integration of research and education, and integrated systems approaches—will be of great importance in the support of EmNet-related research projects, and all of them—in particular, systems-oriented work—should be aggressively pursued and include cross-divisional efforts where necessary. Specific recommendations for NSF are below.

Recommendation 5. The National Science Foundation should continue to expand mechanisms for encouraging systems-oriented, multi-investigator, collaborative, multidisciplinary research on EmNets.

NSF is funding work in several areas related to EmNets (see Box 6.6). Much of this work continues to be done by a single principal investigator (and graduate students) operating on a small budget. As noted in this

---

BOX 6.6
**A Sampling of the National Science Foundation's
EmNet-related programs**

Scalable Information Infrastructure and Pervasive Computing

NSF is supporting work in scalability, security, privacy, sensors and sensor networks, and tetherfree networking and communications in this program. Its goal is to advance the technical infrastructure to support human-to-human, human-to-computer, and computer-to-computer remote communication.

Wireless Information Technology and Networks

This program funds research to provide a foundation for designing high-information-capacity wireless communication systems for full mobility. Such design will require synergistic, multidisciplinary research efforts encompassing a breadth of communications functions from the physical through application layers.

Electronics, Photonics, and Device Technologies

This program funds research in the areas of micro- and nanoscale devices, components, and materials, advanced methods of design, modeling, and simulation of such devices and components, and improved techniques for processing, fabrication, and manufacturing.

---

report, research on EmNets will require that such single investigator research be complemented by collaborative experimental research that brings together researchers from different disciplines to focus on a common problem. Had this report been written several years ago, it would have recommended that NSF move toward larger-scale, experimentally driven, risk-taking research. NSF's ITR program appears to be doing just that. ITR also reinforces attention to the social and economic dimensions of information systems. This program, or others like it, could serve as a useful vehicle for pursuing some of the topics pinpointed in this report. The key to achieving successful multidisciplinary research is not just a matter of funding levels. A flexible process is required that can incorporate perspectives from a broad range of relevant disciplines.

Recommendation 6. The National Science Foundation should develop programs that support graduate and undergraduate multidisciplinary educational programs.

With respect to education (see Box 6.1), NSF could take the lead in tackling institutional barriers to interdisciplinary and broad systems-based work. NSF has a history of encouraging interdisciplinary programs and could provide venues for such work to be explored (as is being done in the ITR programs) as well as foster and fund joint graduate programs or joint curriculum endeavors. One way to do this would be to provide incentives to programs that successfully cross disciplinary boundaries. For example, faculty working on interdisciplinary research often have difficulty securing institutional support for work deemed outside the scope of their home department. A program that removed this drawback by providing funding for such work could stimulate interdisciplinary research and course material in colleges and universities. Another way would be to expand the Graduate Fellowship Program to support more interdisciplinary proposals. Suitable evaluations of proposals would be needed to implement this recommendation.

Recommendations to Other Federal Agencies

The National Aeronautics and Space Administration (NASA) and the Department of Energy (DOE) were two of the earliest innovators and adopters of EmNets. While NASA and DOE application domains can be quite specialized, two things are clear: The computer science community would benefit from hearing of and seeing this earlier (and contemporary) work, and NASA and DOE themselves would benefit from the more general pursuit of this technology by the broader computer science community. Both agencies have long histories in systems engineering as well as in computer science and so could serve as a useful bridge between various communities, especially regarding the development of EmNets. NASA, for example, has a strong interest in safety and reliability, and DOE has long been involved in reliability issues. Their expertise, when applicable, could be shared with others in related research areas; in addition, the two agencies would benefit from the generalizations that the broader research community could provide. More explicit cooperation and communication would be beneficial to everyone and would greatly advance the field.

The agencies with needs for EmNets should together promote expanded experimental research with a shared, experimental systems infrastructure. The committee expects that coordination needs could be supported by the various organizations and groups associated with federal information technology research and development.[18] Open-platform sys-

---

[18]The National Coordination Office for Information Technology Research and Development and related groups can facilitate cross-agency coordination, for example.

tems of various scales, low-power components and the software drivers for these components, debugging techniques and software, traffic generators—all can be shared across research programs when applicable, avoiding inefficient redundancy in those parts of the system where there is more certainty. The research communities should combine their efforts in creating enabling components, such as a range of MEMS-based sensors and actuators that are packaged in such a way as to be easily integrated into experimental EmNet systems. This would enable experimentation with EmNets in environmental and biological monitoring applications, for example, that are relevant to a variety of agencies, such as the Environmental Protection Agency, the Federal Aviation Administration, the National Institutes of Health, the National Oceanic and Atmospheric Administration, DOE, and NASA, as well as research groups working in these areas. Cross-collaboration and communication and the development of general enabling components will be essential for broad-ranging experimental work with EmNet systems.

SUMMARY

EmNets present exciting new challenges in information technology, posing fundamental research questions while being applicable to a broad range of problem domains and research disciplines. Unfortunately, progress in this area will probably be confined to domain- and application-specific systems unless a concerted, comprehensive effort is made to broaden and deepen the research endeavor. It is unlikely that such a broad-based, widely applicable research agenda will be undertaken by industry alone. While systems can be built individually, the accumulated understanding will be insufficient without fundamental work promoted and supported by federal funding agencies. The technology would also be much more expensive, only narrowly applicable, and far less extensible and robust. Long-term, forward-thinking, and broad-ranging research programs are crucial to achieve a deep understanding of EmNet impacts on society and of how to design and develop these systems.

REFERENCES

Computer Science and Telecommunications Board (CSTB), National Research Council. 1994a. *Academic Careers for Experimental Computer Scientists and Engineers.* Washington, D.C.: National Academy Press.

CSTB, National Research Council. 1994b. *Realizing the Information Future; The Internet and Beyond.* Washington, D.C.: National Academy Press.

CSTB, National Research Council. 1995. *Evolving the High Performance Computing and Communications Initiative to Support the Nation's Information Infrastructure.* Washington, D.C.: National Academy Press

CSTB, National Research Council. 1999. *Funding a Revolution: Government Support for Computing Research*. Washington, D.C.: National Academy Press.

CSTB, National Research Council. 2000. *Making IT Better: Expanding Information Technology Research to Meet Society's Needs*. Washington, D.C.: National Academy Press.

CSTB, National Research Council. 2001. *The Internet's Coming of Age*. Washington, D.C.: National Academy Press.

Walsh, Sharon. 2000. "Feds make arrest in Internet hoax case." *The Standard*, August 31. Available online at <http://www.thestandard.com/article/display/0,1151,18153,00.html>.

Appendixes

A

Biographies of Committee Members

DEBORAH L. ESTRIN, *Chair*, is a professor of computer science at the University of California at Los Angeles and a visiting scholar at the University of Southern California's Information Sciences Institute. She is recognized for her research in computer networks and internetworking, protocol design, scalability, and multicast routing. Her current research focuses on the design of protocols for large-scale wireless sensor networks. Dr. Estrin served as chair of the 1998 DARPA Information Science and Technology study on simple systems, whose focus was networked embedded computers. She has participated in a number of CSTB studies, including those that produced the reports *Evolving the High-Performance Computing and Communications Initiative to Support the Nation's Information Infrastructure*, *The Changing Nature of Telecommunications Infrastructure*, *Academic Careers for Experimental Computer Scientists and Engineers*, and *The Internet's Coming of Age*. Dr. Estrin holds a B.S. in electrical engineering from the University of California at Berkeley and an M.S. in technology and policy and a Ph.D. in electrical engineering and computer science from the Massachusetts Institute of Technology. She was selected as a Presidential Young Investigator (1987) and is a fellow of the Association for Computing Machinery (2000) and the American Association for the Advancement of Science (2001).

GAETANO BORRIELLO is a professor in the Department of Computer Science and Engineering at the University of Washington. He received his Ph.D. from the University of California at Berkeley in 1988 and was employed at the Xerox Palo Alto Research Center in the early 1980s. His current research interests focus on the design, development, and deployment of embedded systems, with particular emphasis on mobile and ubiquitous devices and the applications they will support. He is also interested in system development environments, user interfaces, and networking. These interests are unified by their goal of making new computing and communication devices that simplify life by being as invisible as possible to their owners; being highly specialized and thus highly efficient for the task at hand; and being able to exploit their connections to each other and to the greater worldwide networks. Dr. Borriello is currently director of Intel's Seattle Research Laboratory and is active on the program committees of several conferences and workshops on system-level design topics. In addition, he recently served as program chair and general chair of the Institute of Electrical and Electronics Engineers (IEEE)/Association of Computing Machinery (ACM)/ International Federation for Information Processing (IFIP) International Workshop of Hardware/Software Codesign (1998) and the UW/Microsoft Research Summer Institute on the Technologies of Invisible Computing (1999). He is a member of the IEEE Computer Society and the ACM Special Interest Group on Design Automation.

ROBERT PAUL COLWELL led Intel's architecture development effort for the P6 microarchitecture (the core of Intel's Pentium II and Pentium III processors) and managed the Pentium 4 microarchitecture development. Dr. Colwell joined Intel in 1990 as a senior architect on the Pentium Pro project and became manager of the Architecture Group 2 years later. In 1996 he was elected an Intel fellow, the highest rung on Intel's technical career ladder. From 1985 through 1990, Dr. Colwell was a CPU architect at VLIW pioneer Multiflow Computer. From 1980 to 1985 he worked part-time as a hardware design engineer at workstation vendor Perq Systems while attending graduate school at Carnegie Mellon University's Electrical and Computer Engineering Department. He was a member of the technical staff at the Bell Telephone Labs from 1977 to 1980, working on the BellMac series of microprocessors. Dr. Colwell received his BSEE from the University of Pittsburgh in 1977, his MSEE from Carnegie Mellon University in 1978, and his Ph.D. from Carnegie Mellon University in 1985. He holds 44 patents.

JERRY FIDDLER is founder and chairman of Wind River Systems, the world leader in embedded software and operating systems. Wind River's software is widely used in applications from the very high tech (the operating system for the Mars Pathfinder) to the very high volume (Hewlett-Packard printers, General Motors engine controllers, Kodak digital cameras, and Nortel telephones). As chairman, Mr. Fiddler provides technical oversight and guidance, travels and communicates widely within the embedded community, and is a prominent industry expert and spokesperson. He is on the board of Crossbow Technology, a private company making MEMS-based sensors, and serves on other corporate boards as well. He is a fellow of the Lester Center for Entrepreneurship at the University of California at Berkeley. Mr. Fiddler holds an M.S. degree in computer science and a B.A. in music and photography from the University of Illinois, Champaign-Urbana. He served as a senior computer scientist at the Lawrence Berkeley National Laboratory from 1978 to 1981, when he founded Wind River Systems.

MARK HOROWITZ is director of the Computer Systems Laboratory at Stanford University and is the Yahoo Founder's Professor of Electrical Engineering and Computer Science. Dr. Horowitz received his B.S. and M.S. in electrical engineering from the Massachusetts Institute of Technology in 1978 and his Ph.D. from Stanford University in 1984. Since 1984, he has been a professor at Stanford in the area of digital system design. His work in this area is quite broad, ranging from circuit design to multiprocessor architecture. While at Stanford he has led a number of processor designs, including MIPS-X, one of the first processors to include an on-chip instruction cache; Torch, a statically scheduled, superscalar processor that supported speculation; and Flash, a flexible, distributed shared memory multiprocessor. He has also worked in a number of other chip design areas, including high-speed memory design, high-bandwidth interfaces, and fast floating point. In 1990 he took leave from Stanford to help start Rambus, Inc., a company designing high-bandwidth memory interface technology. His current research projects include work in high-speed IO, low-power VLSI design, VLSI computer architecture, and new graphics IO devices.

WILLIAM J. KAISER is chief technology officer and vice president of research and development at Sensoria Corporation and professor in the Electrical Engineering Department of the University of California, Los Angeles. He and his team developed Wireless Integrated Network Sensors (WINS), the first distributed embedded computing technology for "Internetworking and the Physical World." Sensoria, founded in 1998, is a rapidly growing company that provides end-to-end WINS solutions for wireless network access to distributed vehicles and embedded systems, sensors, and controls. His background includes distributed wireless sensing and computing, low-power analog and digital electronics, and low-power RF communication systems. Dr. Kaiser received a Ph.D. in solid-state physics from Wayne State University in 1984. His graduate research at Ford Motor Company included the development of automotive sensor technology ranging from the development of measurement methods, through circuits, structures, and materials, to large-volume commercial sensor production. In 1986, Dr. Kaiser joined the staff of the Jet Propulsion Laboratory (JPL), where he initiated the NASA Microinstrument Program. In 1994, he joined the faculty of the University of California at Los Angeles Electrical Engineering Department, where he served as chairman of the department from 1996 through 2000. His awards include the Allied Signal Faculty Research Award, the Peter Mark Award of the American Vacuum Society, the NASA Medal for Exceptional Scientific Achievement, and the Arch Colwell Best Paper Award of the Society of Automotive Engineers. Dr. Kaiser has over 100 publications, 100 invited presentations, and 21 patents.

NANCY G. LEVESON is professor of aerospace software engineering in the Aeronautics and Astronautics Department and also professor of engineering systems at the Massachusetts Institute of Technology. Previously she was Boeing Professor of Computer Science and Engineering at the University of Washington. She has served as editor in chief of *IEEE Transactions on Software Engineering* and on the board of directors of the International Council on Systems Engineering. Dr. Leveson is a fellow of the ACM and is currently an elected member of the Board of Directors of the Computing Research Association, a member of the ACM Committee on Computers and Public Policy, and a member of the National Research Council's Advisory Committee for the Division on Engineering and Physical Sciences. She received the 1995 AIAA Information Systems Award for "developing the field of software safety and for promoting responsible software and system engineering practices where life and property are at stake." She is author of a book, *Safeware: System Safety and Computers*, published by Addison-Wesley. Dr. Leveson is a member of the National Academy of Engineering and was awarded the 1999 ACM Alan Newell Award.

BARBARA H. LISKOV is the Ford Professor of Engineering at the Massachusetts Institute of Technology. Her research interests lie in the areas of programming methodology, programming languages, and programming systems, and she has done research on data abstraction, program specifications, object-oriented programming, concurrency control, fault tolerance, parallel and distributed programs, and algorithms for distributed systems. Her projects include the design and implementation of CLU, the first programming language to support data abstraction; the design and implementation of Argus, the first high-level language to support implementation of distributed programs; and the Thor object-oriented database system, which provides transactional access to highly available objects in a wide-scale, distributed environment. Professor Liskov is a member of the National Academy of Engineering and a fellow of the American Academy of Arts and Sciences and of the Association for Computing Machinery. She received the 1996 Achievement Award from the Society of Women Engineers. Professor Liskov has published more than 100 technical papers and is the author of several books, including *Program Development in Java*, which was recently published by Addison-Wesley.

PETER LUCAS is chief executive officer of MAYA Design, which he cofounded in 1989. He has guided the growth of MAYA as a premier venue for interdisciplinary product design and research, serving both the private and public sectors. Dr. Lucas received his Ph.D. in 1981 from Cornell University, where he studied educational and cognitive psychology and psycholinguistics. He did postdoctoral research at the University of Wisconsin and was a Sloan postdoctoral fellow in cognitive science at Carnegie Mellon University. His research interests lie at the intersection of computer architecture and product design. He is currently focused on developing a distributed architecture for ubiquitous computing that is designed to scale to nearly unlimited size, depending primarily on market forces to maintain tractability and global coherence. He holds 13 patents and has coauthored a book on letter and word perception. He was founding chair of Three Rivers Connect, an initiative of business and civic leaders that promotes the development of "civic computing" in the Pittsburgh region. He sits on a number of boards in both the public and private sectors. He is adjunct associate professor in the Human-Computer Interaction Institute of Carnegie Mellon University.

DAVID P. MAHER is chief technology officer of InterTrust. He previously served as head of the secure systems research department at AT&T Labs. He has a Ph.D. in mathematics from Lehigh University, and he has taught electrical engineering, mathematics, and computer science at several institutions. He joined Bell Labs in 1981, where he developed secure wide-band transmission systems, cryptographic key management systems, and secure voice, fax, and data devices. He was chief architect for AT&T's STU-III secure voice, data, and video products, used by the President and DOD officials for top secret communications. Dr. Maher was made an AT&T fellow for his work in communications security. He has published papers in the fields of combinatorics, cryptography, number theory, signal processing, and electronic commerce. He has been a consultant for the National Science Foundation, the National Security Agency, the National Institute of Standards and Technology, and the congressional Office of Technology Assessment. Recently, Dr. Maher has been doing research on electronic payment systems and the protection of intellectual property distributed over the Internet.

PAUL M. MANKIEWICH is presently head of the Wireless Technology Research Department at Lucent Technologies. He is also Wireless Research Hardware and Architecture Director in the Wireless Network Group business unit and in that role is responsible for shepherding research technology into wireless products. His research department has responsibility for novel wireless system and radio architectures, adaptive antenna technologies, and radio and modem technologies for next-generation wireless data and voice networks. His group has been responsible for a diverse set of programs such as a steered-beam, next-generation, fixed wireless system, various issues regarding system improvements through baseband signal processing, algorithms for cellular network optimization, 3G wireless system architectures, and system-level issues regarding home networking and BlueTooth. He joined Bell Labs in 1981. He received his Ph.D. from Boston University in applied physics. He began working in wireless in 1988. Since then he has been involved in and responsible for all aspects of wireless system and radio design.

RICHARD TAYLOR is a principal scientist at Hewlett-Packard Laboratories, where he leads research programs in the areas of embedded systems analysis and design, distributed media processing, systems architecture, and hardware-software codesign. Dr. Taylor graduated with a B.Sc. (honors) in computing and cybernetics from the University of Kent at Canterbury, England, and a Ph.D. in computer systems engineering from the University of Manchester. Following his Ph.D., he worked for the Christian Michelsen Institute (Bergen, Norway) as a computer scientist, combining research and consultancy in the area of high-performance distributed and parallel computing. He joined the electronic systems department of the University of York in 1989, founded and then led the computer systems engineering group, concentrating on the design and development of novel embedded and real-time systems. In 1993 he joined the departments of computer science and electrical engineering at the University of Western Michigan, again leading a team researching the design and application of high-performance embedded computing systems. He joined Hewlett-Packard in 1995. Dr. Taylor has published more than 50 papers and patents in the areas of embedded, parallel, and distributed computing.

JIM WALDO is a Distinguished Engineer with Sun Microsystems, where he is the lead architect for Jini, a distributed programming system based on Java. Before that, he worked in JavaSoft and Sun Microsystems Laboratories, where he did research in the areas of object-oriented programming and systems, distributed computing, and user environments. Before joining Sun, Dr. Waldo spent 8 years at Apollo Computer and Hewlett Packard working in distributed object systems, user interfaces, class libraries, text, and internationalization. While at HP, he led the design and development of the first Object Request Broker and was instrumental in getting that technology incorporated into the first OMG CORBA specification. He edited the book *The Evolution of C++: Language Design in the Marketplace of Ideas* (MIT Press) and was the author of the Java Advisor column in Unix Review's *Performance Computing* magazine. Dr. Waldo is an adjunct faculty member of Harvard University, where he teaches distributed computing in the department of computer science. He received his Ph.D. in philosophy from the University of Massachusetts (Amherst). He also holds M.A. degrees in both linguistics and philosophy from the University of Utah. He is a member of the IEEE and ACM.

B

Briefers at Plenary Meetings

DECEMBER 1-2, 1999

Jerry Linn, National Institute of Standards and Technology (NIST)
Srikanta Kumar, Defense Advanced Research Projects Agency (DARPA)
Karen Sollins, National Science Foundation (NSF)
Janos Sztipanovits, DARPA
David L. Tennenhouse, Intel Corporation
Ellison C. Urban, DARPA

FEBRUARY 28-29, 2000

Andrew Berlin, Xerox Palo Alto Research Center (PARC)
Janusz Bryzek, Maxim Integrated Products, Inc.
Robert Dolin, Echelon Corporation
John Hines, National Aeronautics and Space Administration (NASA)
Rodger Lea, Sony Distributed Systems Laboratory
K. Venkatesh Prasad, Ford Research Laboratory

APRIL 17-18, 2000

David D. Clark, Massachusetts Institute of Technology
Alan Davidson, Center for Democracy and Technology
Shankar Sastry, DARPA
Jonathan Smith, University of Pennsylvania